A SAVAGE DREAMLAND

Also by David Eimer

The Emperor Far Away: Travels at the Edge of China (2014)

A SAVAGE DREAMLAND

Journeys in Burma

DAVID EIMER

BLOOMSBURY PUBLISHING
LONDON • OXFORD • NEW YORK • NEW DELHI • SYDNEY

BLOOMSBURY PUBLISHING
Bloomsbury Publishing Plc
50 Bedford Square, London, WC1B 3DP, UK

BLOOMSBURY, BLOOMSBURY PUBLISHING and the Diana logo are trademarks of
Bloomsbury Publishing Plc

First published in Great Britain 2019

A catalogue record for this book is available from the British Library

Library of Congress Cataloguing-in-Publication data has been applied for

ISBN: HB: 978-1-4088-8387-7; TPB: 978-1-4088-8388-4; EBOOK: 978-1-4088-8386-0

2 4 6 8 10 9 7 5 3 1

Typeset by Newgen KnowledgeWorks Pvt. Ltd., Chennai, India
Printed and bound in Great Britain by CPI Group (UK) Ltd, Croydon CR0 4YY

MIX
Paper from
responsible sources
FSC® C020471

To find out more about our authors and books visit www.bloomsbury.com
and sign up for our newsletters

Contents

CONTENTS

vi

Burma as represented on a modern political map is not a geographical or historical entity; it is a creation of the armed diplomacy and administrative convenience of late nineteenth-century British Imperialism.

Edmund R. Leach,
'The Political Future of Burma' (1963)

Modern Burma is only dead Burma reincarnate.

C. M. Enriquez,
A Burmese Enchantment (1916)

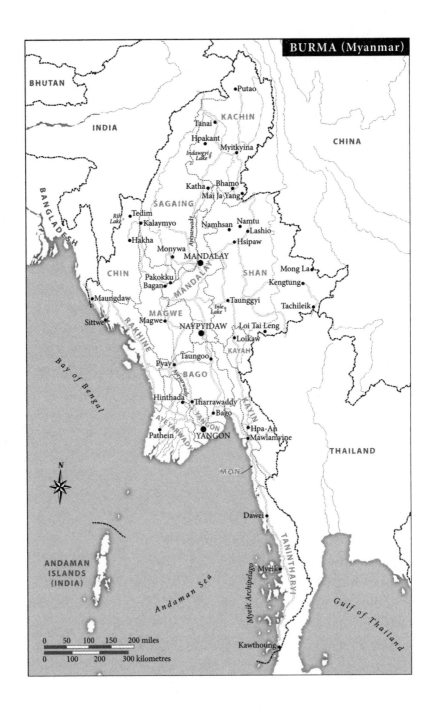

BURMA (Myanmar)

BHUTAN

INDIA

CHINA

BANGLADESH

KACHIN

Putao

Tanai
Hpakant
Indawgyi
Lake
Myitkyina

Katha Bhamo
Mai Ja Yang
SAGAING

Tedim
Rih
Lake
Kalaymyo
Namhsan Namtu
Lashio
Hakha
Hsipaw
Monywa
MANDALAY

CHIN
Pakokku
Bagan
MANDALAY
SHAN
Mong La
Kengtung

Maungdaw
MAGWE
Inle
Lake
Taunggyi
Tachileik

Sittwe
Magwe
NAYPYIDAW
Loi Tai Leng
Loikaw
KAYAH

RAKHINE

Bay of Bengal

Taungoo
Pyay
BAGO

Hinthada Tharrawaddy
Bago

Pathein YANGON
Hpa-An
Mawlamyine

THAILAND

MON

N

Dawei

ANDAMAN
ISLANDS
(INDIA)

Andaman Sea

Myeik Archipelago
Myeik
TANINTHARYI

Gulf of Thailand

0   50   100   150   200 miles
0   100   200   300 kilometres

Kawthoung

Introduction

BURMA 2010

I came to Burma in search of the road less travelled. In early 2010, this was a mysterious nation: little-visited, barely mentioned, hardly known. A paranoid military dictatorship had ruled for almost fifty years and Burma had become the monster in the Southeast Asian attic, the unhinged relative locked in a top-floor room. While its neighbours hosted an ever-increasing number of tourists, the generals sought to isolate the country from outside influences and regarded foreigners with intense suspicion.

Three years before, in 2007, I had attempted to reach Yangon, Burma's largest city and the former capital, to cover the so-called Saffron Revolution, the latest popular uprising against army rule. Along with many other reporters, my visa application was refused. The closest I came to Burma was standing on the banks of the Moei River in the Thai border town of Mae Sot, waiting for the expected flood of refugees to wade across from the other side. But the exodus never happened.

When I applied again for a visa in Bangkok in January 2010, with a new passport untainted by any evidence that I was a journalist, it was still more in hope than expectation. Returning to the Burmese embassy the next day, my surprise on finding I had been granted twenty-eight days to visit was rather too visible. I boarded a plane for Yangon the next morning, just in case the officials changed their minds.

After the hustle of Bangkok's Suvarnabhumi Airport – a giant, crowded shopping mall with runways – Yangon's international terminal could have been a provincial bus station on a slow day. There were no queues at passport control. A sole luggage belt revolved. Stepping outside, there was a sudden blast of heat, a cloud-free, azure sky and a bright sun that made me squint. I climbed into a taxi, its windows open in lieu of air conditioning, and asked the driver to take me to downtown.

We set off along a half-empty road overseen by palm and pipal trees, shaded in different hues of green. Their spreading leaves and branches partially masked the wooden houses topped with corrugated iron roofs and undistinguished concrete buildings behind them. Chinese-made trucks wheezed by belching black smoke, their exhausts mimicking the chimneys of the factories they had emerged from. There were few privately owned cars. Most, like my taxi, were falling apart in slow motion, their drivers unable to afford or find spare parts.

Walking along the broken-down pavements, or waiting for overloaded buses and pickup trucks, whose teenage conductors hung out of the doors and off the backs of their vehicles shouting out their destinations, were the locals. Almost everyone wore the sarong-like, traditional Burmese dress: sober-coloured *longyi* for men, brightly patterned *htamein* for the women. Only the Buddhist monks in their crimson robes stood out from the uniformity of the crowd.

What I was seeing could have been a street scene from the Yangon of twenty or thirty years before. Burma was in stasis; a country marooned under the junta that had snatched power in 1962. There were other reminders of the lack of progress, too. My mobile phone was in my pocket, its screen dark. There was no international network coverage in Burma. I discovered soon that the internet was a barely available, mostly non-functioning new invention as well.

But the shock of the old was alleviated by the faces I saw as we drove south. When my taxi stopped at the few traffic lights, people looked across at me from their crowded buses and some offered a shy smile, one that widened into a beguiling beam when I reciprocated. They made me feel like I was being welcomed to Burma, and that is the greeting every traveller hopes for.

A Chinese-owned hotel on the western edge of downtown was my first base. Yangon slopes gently downhill towards its eponymous river from its highest point, the hill where the Shwedagon Pagoda, Burma's most holy religious monument, sits. By leaning out of the window of my room and twisting my neck to the left, I could see down Wadan Street as it ran for three blocks to the Strand, the riverfront road, and the city's docks.

Yangon's port was the second busiest in the world throughout the 1920s and 1930s, after London, and the city – then known as Rangoon – was riding high as one of Asia's pioneer world cities. The docks were much quieter in 2010, but there were still enough ships to keep the port lively. The sound of their mournful horns rose easily above the noise of the traffic eleven storeys beneath me, as the ships slipped their moorings and floated downstream on the mud-brown waters towards the Ayeyarwady Delta and the Andaman Sea.

The river gave birth to Yangon. By the fifth or sixth century CE, Indian traders were already tacking east across the Bay of Bengal from the Coromandel Coast in search of new markets. Some penetrated the tangle of rivers and tributaries that make up the Ayeyarwady Delta, the region west of Yangon, and eventually landed at the small fishing village that would grow into Burma's biggest city. Those same adventurers founded the Shwedagon, probably as a Hindu shrine initially, at the village's highest point.

There is no record of the settlement's original name, and not until the fifteenth century do written accounts of the place begin to emerge. By then, 'Dagon', and sometimes 'Lagun', was the name being used to describe the scruffy collection of wooden shacks that had grown up around the golden stupa of the Shwedagon, which had long since abandoned its Hindu origins and was already a revered Buddhist pilgrimage site.

Only in 1755 did the town become known as Yangon. The name, meaning 'end of strife', was chosen by the then king, Alaungpaya, after he had vanquished a rival southern kingdom. Almost a century later, though, the British seized lower Burma and Yangon's name changed again. The invading armies employed translators from Arakan in the west of Burma, the region closest to what was then British India. The Arakanese pronounce 'ya' as 'ra', so Yangon became Rangoon.

In June 1989, the junta ordered that the name revert to Yangon once more. Burma became Myanmar at the same time, although many locals objected as of course they were not consulted over the abrupt change of their nation's name. Some countries, like the UK and US, use Burma officially still, rather than Myanmar. I do, too, not being willing to abide by a unilateral decision made by a group of generals eager to rewrite history for their own purposes.

Other names associated with British rule disappeared in 1989 as well. Arakan, for example, became Rakhine State. But some have survived, like the Strand, Yangon's riverfront road. As I walked it that first day, passing crumbling colonial-era edifices whose cupolas, towers and white stone pillars could have been transplanted from London, I understood why the name was once considered appropriate. The great travel writer Norman Lewis described Yangon as a city 'built by people who refused to compromise with the East'. Not much appeared to have changed since his visit in 1951.

It was a British trope to impose themselves architecturally on the cities of their colonies. In Yangon the crowning incongruity is the Secretariat, the now abandoned seat of power in colonial times and afterwards. A collection of red and yellow brick buildings set around a neat quadrangle and surrounded by high walls, the Secretariat was an Oxford college planted in the commercial heart of an Asian city to remind its residents of who was in charge.

Downtown Yangon's collection of colonial-era buildings is the largest in Southeast Asia. But even without their presence, I felt I had slipped back through time and arrived in a city that looked, smelled and sounded as it must have done decades before. The sweet aroma of food-stall curries and the disconcerting odour of *ngapi* – the pungent fish paste used in Burmese cooking – mingled with the more straightforward stink of open drains. Street vendors shrilled their wares while balancing them on their heads as they walked.

Trishaw drivers glistened with sweat as they stood on the pedals of their contraptions, hauling old ladies home from the markets. A few taxis competed with them for customers and space, as they edged down the narrow streets running back from the Strand that had not been designed for motorised vehicles. The buildings rising above them, whether the grand structures of the colonial past, or the tenements and apartment blocks built after the Second World War, were all neglected and in need of repair.

Pedestrians wielding umbrellas against the sun pushed past each other as they negotiated an ankle-twisting assault course of desperately uneven, cracked and potholed pavements. With the junta unable to supply electricity on a regular basis, and the Yangon Council too cash starved to install adequate street lighting, walking the streets at night could have disastrous consequences. After a fall that left me with ripped trousers and cut hands and knees, I learned not to stroll back to my hotel after a few drinks.

Avoiding the streams of maroon-coloured spit ejected from the mouths of Burma's legions of betel addicts was also necessary. Chewing betel, a nut with nicotine-like qualities that is flavoured with lime and wrapped in a betel leaf, stains the teeth of its adherents an unattractive red and requires them to expectorate frequently. It was easy to get splashed, especially when walking by street-side teahouses and beer stations – Burma's version of the pub – or when a bus was passing and the passengers gobbed out of the windows.

Everyone was shadowed by seamy-eyed, mange-ridden street dogs, limping and creeping in their perpetual search for sustenance. The Buddha's ban on killing animals, except for food, is taken seriously in Burma and Yangon's canine population is huge. When the British attempted culls, people hid the hounds in their homes. Unchecked and unneutered, the animals roamed everywhere. At night they curled up on pavements and in doorways and Yangon became a vast, open-air dog dormitory.

Most of the locals I met were friendly, courteous and curious about me and my life. I was wary of discussing politics, but many people brought up the junta unprompted. There was both rage and resignation about life under the generals, the latter often expressed with a vertical wave of the hand from side to side; the Burmese way of saying that something is unavailable, not possible or that nothing can be done about a situation.

Opposition to military rule was ruthlessly and violently suppressed. The dissidents in prison were proof of that. But no one appeared obviously cowed in their daily demeanour, and the Burmese have the knack of making the most of simple pleasures. Girls linked arms under their umbrellas and sang as they walked. Teenage boys played guitars at the side of the street. Families made excursions to their favourite pagodas. And the teahouses were always full of amateur philosophers deep in conversation, making a cup of tea and a samosa last hours.

Travelling is like watching a never-ending movie, either framed by a car, bus or train window, or an outdoor, panoramic experience. In Yangon, though, I was confused not only by the plot but by which film era I was in. In close-up, every scene appeared in vivid Technicolor. Step back and the people in their traditional clothes, the lack of the trappings of modern life, the cloak of colonial architecture, all conspired to present the city as a sepia image and Burma as a flickering black and white newsreel of a nation.

George Orwell's *Burmese Days* is a near-obligatory text for foreigners who come to Burma. I was no exception. But I thought it telling that a novel published in 1934, and inspired by Orwell's experiences as a police officer in 1920s Burma, should still be the most widely read book in English about the country. It was like coming to London having read only Charles Dickens, and the popularity of Orwell's novel seemed to perpetuate the idea of Burma as a place frozen in time.

Leaving Yangon to take the road to Mandalay, from where I travelled east into the hills of Shan State, helped bring contemporary Burma in all its complexity into focus. About the size of Germany and Poland combined, Burma feels bigger than its appearance on a map suggests. The majority ethnic group are the Bamar, the people commonly called 'Burmese'. They cluster in the lowlands close to the Ayeyarwady River, which winds through the country from the north to the south, in the regions between and around Yangon and Mandalay.

One third of Burma's fifty-five million-odd people are not Bamar, though, and they mostly occupy the borderlands, an area that covers over 40 per cent of the country. In the early 1990s the generals assigned this segment of the population to 134 different ethnic minorities, although that was probably an attempt at divide and rule rather than an accurate anthropological exercise. Most of those 134 minorities are in fact sub-groups of the estimated twenty to thirty ethnicities found here.

That is still more than enough to make Burma the true melting pot of Southeast Asia, a place where over a hundred different languages have been identified. The minorities are transnational peoples, inhabiting Shan and Kachin states in the east and north, where Burma is caught between the Asian giants India and China, and Rakhine and Chin states in the west, next to Bangladesh and India again. To the south are Mon, Kayin and Kayah states and Tanintharyi, all bordering Thailand and home to their own ethnic groups.

Many of the minorities have been fighting for autonomy over their regions almost since the moment Burma gained its independence from Britain in January 1948. There are over thirty ethnic armies and militias in Burma and their battles with the *Tatmadaw*, the collective name for the Burmese military, are the longest running civil wars in modern history. Nor is everyone in Burma a Buddhist. Christians and Muslims make up around 10 per cent of the population, and there are smaller numbers of Hindus and animists, too.

Christianity is disproportionately popular among the minorities, but there are churches in all the major cities and towns. Islam's followers include the descendants of Arab, Indian and Chinese immigrants, some of whom have intermarried with the Bamar, and the Rohingya, the most reviled and persecuted ethnic group in the country, whose roots are in present-day Bangladesh, as well as the Middle East.

Burma is rich in resources, too, even if the people and everything around me in 2010 suggested the opposite. One of the first Burmese traits I noticed was how many locals stare downwards when they meet a foreigner, towards their feet. A pair of shoes or trainers is both a novelty and a luxury in a country where flip-flops – called 'slippers' in Burma – are the standard footwear and plenty of people still go barefoot.

Out in the hills of Kachin and Shan states, though, are vast deposits of jade, precious gems, gold, copper, tin and other minerals. There is oil and teak, too, while in the south along the land and maritime frontiers with Thailand are rubber and palm oil plantations and natural gas fields. It was the urge to exploit those natural assets that prompted Britain to colonise Burma in the nineteenth century. British Petroleum, for instance, can trace its origins back to the Rangoon Oil Company, founded in 1886.

Under the junta, only the generals and their business associates – referred to always as the 'cronies' – were benefiting from Burma's riches. Their houses behind high gates in the exclusive Yangon neighbourhood of Golden Valley were built in the Chinese nouveau riche style: mock Doric columned facades, terraces and balconies, a multitude of cars outside and teak furniture everywhere inside. But out in Yangon's far suburbs people were living on £1 a day in shanty towns that lacked electricity and running water.

Injustice and inequality walked hand in hand in Burma, so much so that it seemed as if the country embodied all the difficulties facing Southeast Asia. Like Thailand, the military had been in charge for most of Burma's recent history. The country was as corrupt as Cambodia and Malaysia. A creaking bureaucracy that did everything in triplicate mirrored Vietnam, while the languor induced by totalitarian regimes, which allow advancement only to a chosen few who embrace the system, reminded me of Laos.

My twenty-eight days in Burma were soon up. But already the gentleness of the individuals I encountered and the exhilarating, untamed landscapes that I passed through was fusing uncomfortably in my mind with the country's combustible mix of peoples, religions and resources. I realised, too, how incomplete the outsiders' map of the country is, because Burma is home to places that few foreigners have heard of, let alone been to.

Also obvious was the yearning for change. Yet even in 2010 I wondered what the removal of the junta-imposed restrictions which had governed society for so long would mean for such an elusive nation, a land that is home to so many different agendas and underlying tensions. But I knew that it would be fascinating to witness this unruly country stir itself after being becalmed for fifty years. As I returned to Bangkok, I was already planning my next visit.

YANGON 2015

Late October and the last days of the monsoon season seemed interminable. The rain had been falling since May, drumming off the metal roofs of houses and apartment blocks and flooding streets whose drains dated back to 1888. Mould had taken hold on walls and pavements, making the latter even more hazardous than usual. Now, when the rain stopped, the mercury rose quickly, resulting in a sticky, unpleasant heat. It was the final twist of the knife before November ushered in a few rain-free months of lower temperatures, the most pleasant time to be in Burma.

Tim and I were in a beer station in Dagon Township, a mile north of downtown and south of the Shwedagon. We sat facing each other across a low wooden table, pockmarked with cigarette burns. Around us, the other customers – all men – sat with their legs crossed on plastic chairs, their *longyi* tucked up underneath them, sinking glasses of Myanmar Lager – the national beer – or sharing small bottles of Grand Royal, a local brand of whisky, and the spicy tea-leaf salads that often accompany alcohol in Burma.

Outside, only the headlights of passing cars and a few dim street lamps penetrated the deep black of the night. But the semi-open-air, wood-framed building we were in was illuminated by strip lighting: dust-wreathed tubes that emitted a harsh white glare. Unlike a traditional English pub, with their separate bars and nooks shielded from view, there is no hiding place in a beer station. The television was showing a football match and a few ancient fans turned slowly on the ceiling, circulating gentle currents of smoky air around those sitting under them.

No one moves to Yangon for the nightlife. Western-style bars are a new phenomenon and far too expensive for most locals. There are still only a small number of them in the city. Even the karaoke parlours, where you imbibe between songs, cost too much for the average person. Instead, ordinary people do their drinking at beer stations, like the one Tim and I were in. It is a predominantly male environment, as many Burmese women consider it disreputable to be seen in such surroundings.

Pursing his lips, Tim made a kissing sound to attract one of the teenage waiters. It's a uniquely Burmese way of getting service, although considered impolite in smarter restaurants. Two more beers arrived, we clinked glasses and Tim carried on telling me about how challenging it was returning to Yangon after more than a quarter of a century away.

'It's like moving back to a different country. So much has changed. It's taken me a year just to find my bearings again,' he said, sounding half exasperated and half excited. 'Yangon was so quiet, so peaceful, when I was growing up here in the 1970s. We used to play on all the vacant land they are building on now. There was no television in Burma then, so my brother and I would sit out on the street and count the cars going by. We'd see maybe one or two an hour.'

Life had moved on since both Tim's childhood and my first visit five years before. The half-empty roads I had driven down from the airport in 2010 were a distant memory. Now they heaved with new cars, trucks and a fleet of buses with the name of the city of Busan written on their sides, part of an aid package from South Korea. Traffic jams had arrived in Yangon, just another consequence of modern life that Burma had previously avoided, and even the stray dogs had learned to look left and right when crossing the road.

Accompanying the influx of vehicles were people like Tim: the Burmese who had gone into exile after the 1988 pro-democracy protests. The demonstrations had gone on for months, starting on university campuses in Yangon and then spreading across the country. But like every other attempt at ousting the junta, they ended in failure. Thousands died at the hands of the army, and many more were imprisoned or fled overseas.

Now those émigrés were returning, along with others who had managed to leave Burma legally in search of a better life than the one offered by the military. Looking and speaking Burmese, but with different passports after having spent so long in Australia, Europe or the United States, the exiles weren't locals anymore but nor were they foreigners like me. Instead, they were known in Yangon as 'repats', an amalgam of the words 'returnee' and 'expatriate'.

They were back because of the political and economic changes that had come in a rapid, dizzying procession since June 2010, when the generals swapped their jungle-green uniforms for *longyi* and announced the creation of a new political organisation, the Union Solidarity and Development Party (USDP). Almost overnight, they transformed themselves into a nominally civilian government.

Five months later, the former junta sprang an even bigger surprise by freeing Aung San Suu Kyi from fifteen years of on and off house arrest. She had emerged as the leader of the democracy movement and the principal opponent of the generals during the 1988 protests, when she co-founded the National League for Democracy (NLD) party. Since then, she had become the symbol of Burma's suffering under military rule and her release was an unexpected shock both at home and around the world.

By March 2012 I was in Yangon again, following Aung San Suu Kyi as she campaigned to become an MP at by-elections that saw the NLD win forty-three of the forty-five parliamentary seats contested. The locals in her future constituency had yet to adapt to the change in her status. Many still referred to her as 'The Lady': the pseudonym used for her before her release, when the mere mention of her name in public could result in arrest. Now, though, she was 'Daw Suu', or Auntie Suu, Daw being an honorific given to older Burmese women.

With the generals seemingly gone, foreign aid, investment and loans started sloshing into Burma, unleashing a new, febrile energy. It was most obvious in Yangon and Mandalay, where those who could afford it scrambled to acquire previously unobtainable material possessions. But even in the countryside the slumber of the junta era was over, as people began moving to the cities in search of better-paid jobs, or headed to Thailand as migrant workers.

More than anything else, Burma had embraced the mobile phone. In 2010, when my Blackberry went dark on arrival in Yangon, only North Korea had fewer mobile phones than Burma. Five years on and you could buy a Chinese-made handset for £20 and farmers who rode to their fields in ox carts were shouting into them. In the beer station Tim and I were surrounded by people sending, scrolling and swiping.

Mobile phones presented men in particular with a problem, because the *longyi* most still wear doesn't have pockets. They get round that by tucking them into the back of the garment. In the rainy season street vendors sell plastic wallets worn around the neck to keep the phones – the most treasured and expensive item for many people – dry.

For Tim the lack of storage space in a *longyi* wasn't an issue. He was in his usual jeans and short-sleeved shirt, his unkempt hair covered by one of the trilbies favoured by teens and twenty-somethings over the last few years. Tim is my age, fifty, so not especially young, but we both dress as if we have only just left college. 'I didn't wear a *longyi* for twenty-five years while I was in America. It feels weird putting one on now,' said Tim.

He had been back in Yangon for over a year, but Tim was still an exile, only now in the country of his birth. 'Yangon doesn't feel like home. Sometimes, I think I'll leave again,' he told me. 'But you get to a point where your own needs are unimportant. Issues and causes are more important to me than where I feel comfortable. I feel satisfied with my life here, maybe not happy. But I don't miss my job in the States.'

Like many Burmese I had met, there was a quixotic streak in Tim. It was why he had swapped his Manhattan apartment and life as a financial analyst on Wall Street for a room in his sister's house in Yangon, where he worked for almost nothing running a small NGO. That same idealism was perhaps what prompted him to turn his back on his privileged youth alongside the children of senior junta figures in the smart Yangon suburb of Golden Valley, and throw in his lot with the pro-democracy protestors back in 1988.

His decision had come at a cost. Tim's mother died in 2006, when any returning exile faced arrest, and so he had missed her funeral. His role as a cheerleader for his fellow students in 1988, encouraging them to join the demonstrations, had meant that he had been forced to flee his homeland. 'When

I left in 1989 it was because I had no other options. They had already tried to arrest me a few times,' recalled Tim.

Not even the fact that his uncle had been a spokesman for Ne Win, the general who led the 1962 coup and who was still running Burma in 1988, could save him. Tim spent months in hiding around the country, before making an unlikely escape to the States by posing as a monk, one of a group travelling to Los Angeles for a meditation retreat. He picked up two degrees in California, before moving to New York for the last eight years of his quarter of a century away.

Despite the political reforms that had allowed him to return to Yangon, he was still wary enough of the generals not to use his real name. Instead, Tim had taken the first name and surname of his grandfather, an English barrister. 'He came to Burma as an official and had a relationship with a local woman, my grandmother. I still have my Burmese name, but it's not on my passport. An Anglo name is a good disguise,' he said with a wry smile.

Names in Burma are nebulous anyway. Traditional surnames are unknown and most people employ composites of names previously used in their families, or choose symbolic, auspicious titles. It is considered perfectly normal to change them to mark different periods in one's life. I thought Tim's odyssey from Burma to Southern California, New York and back had given him the right to a new moniker.

Compared to Tim, my journey to Yangon was far more mundane. I had made repeated visits to Burma since 2010, until I decided that I needed to be living here full time. This was a unique opportunity: both to chronicle the awakening of a country as it returned to the global fold after so long as a pariah state and to explore a fractured nation, much of which was closed to foreigners for decades. I have been roaming the backroads of Asia for as long as Tim was in exile, and Burma's are some of the least-known of all.

Moving to another country is always a leap of faith. But I found Burma to be a tougher prospect even than China, where I lived for seven years. The authorities were still getting used to the idea of westerners staying here, as opposed to visiting as tourists. My first hurdle was obtaining a long-stay visa, without which it is not possible to rent an apartment, and that can only be done before you arrive.

Contacts in Yangon advised me to apply for a business visa. But writing is hardly a business in the conventional sense, and I lacked both a local company to employ me and the invitation letter required from them. Then I was given the name of Frankie, a travel agent in Bangkok who had a reputation for getting things done at Burma's embassy in Thailand.

Frankie was mournful and middle-aged, with a pageboy fringe and a soft drawl of a voice. On the wall behind his desk was a sign stating, 'Don't worry, ask Frankie'. I took the advice and explained my situation. He winced when I told him I wanted to live in Yangon to write a book. 'You'll never get a visa by saying that,' he said.

How would I get a visa then? 'Everyone can be a businessman in Burma now,' Frankie explained slowly, like a teacher for whom the summer holidays can't come quickly enough. 'There are a lot of opportunities opening up there. You could be trading, or going into partnership with a local company. And tourism is a big sector now. Lots of new tour companies are starting. How about working in the travel industry like me?'

So it was decided. I was to be a tourism consultant: the potential business partner for a Yangon-based travel operator arranging tours for foreigners. For a financial consideration, plus two passport photos, Frankie would provide the necessary letters and deal with the embassy. By handing over the cash, not only would I get a visa but a new career as well.

Of course, there was a catch: the visa system itself. As explained by Frankie, it was akin to the never-ending Buddhist pursuit of merit. My first visa would be a single-entry one for seventy days. Assuming I didn't do anything to offend the authorities, the subsequent visa would be a double-entry one. The third would be multiple entry and valid for six months. Only after that would I reach the Nirvana of a year-long permit.

Making merit is the goal of all devout Buddhists, for whom this is just one life of many. Doing good works is a way of ensuring that your next existence doesn't see you reincarnated as a snake or a rat. Accumulating merit is taken especially seriously in Burma, one of the most religious countries in the world. Some of the former leaders of the junta have paid for giant gilded pagodas, in the hope that that will erase the litany of sins they committed during their time in power.

Ordinary people set out jugs of water for any passer-by to refresh themselves, or are assiduous in handing food to the monks and nuns who make their daily rounds of neighbourhoods and villages collecting alms. Others give money to monasteries – the Shwedagon has ATMs for people to withdraw cash for donations.

Our drinks finished, Tim headed back to his sister's house and I set off up Shwedagon Pagoda Road towards Burma's most sacred Buddhist site. Ahead, the gold *zedi*, or stupa, of the Shwedagon gleamed brilliant and bright, its colour accentuated by the darkness surrounding it, as it soared almost one hundred metres above the platforms and terraces that surround it.

Much of Yangon is now a building site, as new apartment and office blocks zoom up, but the Shwedagon still stands in splendid isolation atop a small hill and remains visible from many of the city's thirty-three townships, or neighbourhoods. It has always been Yangon's focal point. In 1852 Charles Austen, brother of novelist Jane, used the Shwedagon to guide the invading fleet he was commanding into Yangon's river at the beginning of the Second Anglo-Burmese War.

Even now the Shwedagon is the true centre of Yangon, just as it was in 1583 when a Venetian merchant named Gasparo Balbi, the first European visitor to record his impressions of Dagon, as it was then known, observed the pagoda's hold over the Burmese. Balbi wrote of how the Shwedagon, 'is a place of great devotion amongst them and yearly multitudes of people come by sea and by land'.

Day or night the complex is always busy. People stop by before or after work to pray, to promenade around the base of the vast *zedi*, or to sit and talk in its shadow. I preferred it in the early morning, arriving just as a pink dawn was breaking and the stupa began to glow until it appeared to be radiating rays of golden light. With everyone required to go barefoot, as at every Burmese pagoda, you could walk the marble-tiled floor in comfort, too, unlike later in the day when the sun heated the tiles up so much that you had to hop along.

Almost every Burma journey starts at the Shwedagon, whether you are a tourist, expatriate or VIP, although not everyone goes to the lengths of putting on a *longyi* to visit, as Richard Nixon did in 1953. Somerset Maugham, who landed in Yangon in 1922, thought the sight of the towering *zedi* represented 'sudden hope in the dark night of the soul'; a glimpse of heaven amidst the commercial cut and thrust of colonial Rangoon.

To me, though, the pagoda captures all Yangon's contradictions, corralling them in one single spot; a holy metaphor that you can walk around. Its likely origins as a Hindu shrine reveal how Yangon has always been a cosmopolitan settlement. The gold- and jewel-laden stupa acts as a reminder of how the city's riches are nearly always out of reach for the vast majority of people who walk or travel for hours on overcrowded buses to pray beneath it.

Above all, the shrine's sheer longevity is a riposte to those who have sought to impose their own reality on Yangon, whether it was the Burmese kings of old, British colonists or the generals of the junta. The Shwedagon has survived wars, earthquakes and fires that burned the city below it to the ground. It predates the written Burmese language and is far older than the nation of Burma itself. No wonder all our journeys start here.

I

Down the Rabbit Hole

15th Street was chaos. Cars were parked on both sides of the road, leaving just enough space in the middle of the street for vehicles to inch past the pedestrians and stray dogs avoiding the loose concrete slabs that passed for the pavements. Ladies selling vegetables out of baskets occupied the top end of the road, along with a betel-nut vendor and a roadside food stand, a few plastic stools grouped around the proprietor, her noodles and condiments ranged on a table in front of her.

Ahead of me, Nilar padded along in her velvet-cushioned, platform flip-flops, dressed demurely in a black *htamein* and white top, her face daubed with *thanaka*, a cream-coloured natural sunscreen made out of wood bark. Applying it with a generous smear across both cheeks and forehead, or sometimes in intricate patterns, is the first thing most Burmese women, and some men, do after waking up. Unique to Burma, *thanaka* is a guaranteed way of spotting natives of the country, whether they are working on a Thai island or in a Malaysian factory.

Deftly sidestepping a man who was squatting on the pavement, Nilar came to a halt outside a dark doorway and turned to me as I joined her. 'Everyone is trying to do their business. But there is no mutual understanding,' she said with a sigh. Downtown's congested streets, though, can be blamed on the British, like many of the problems Yangon grapples with.

After taking full control of Burma in 1886 at the end of the Third Anglo-Burmese War and exiling its last king, Thibaw, to India, the British set about remaking Yangon in their own image. Or at least in the image of their other colonial possessions in Southeast Asia. Yangon was to mimic Penang and Singapore with its architecture, the role it would play as a port and trading hub and in how its indigenous population would be first swelled and then supplanted by Indian and Chinese immigrants.

New streets were laid out on a symmetrical chessboard pattern, the standard design for freshly colonised cities. Major roads were named and minor ones numbered. But the lieutenant in the Bengal Engineers overseeing the planning decided that the smaller streets needed to be only thirty feet wide. By the 1920s, people were already complaining that they were too narrow. Now, even after individual streets have been designated as one-way traffic, travelling in downtown during the day is often a tediously slow process.

Along with its neighbouring lanes 15th Street runs back from the Strand and the river, travelling south to north and intersecting with the main roads that cut west to east across downtown. It is lined with post-Second World War tenements that loomed as high as eight storeys above Nilar and I, and a smaller number of decrepit colonial-era houses that have been chopped into apartments, a mix of housing common throughout downtown.

Washing hung from small, barred windows, or was draped over fretwork balconies. Long cords with rusty bulldog clips tied to the ends descended from the upper storeys, dangling head high above the pavement. Groceries and newspapers were attached to them, so that the residents of the top floors could haul them up and drop them down again with their payment. The cords saved the elderly especially from walking the steep stairs to and from the street. Only the newest and most expensive Yangon apartment blocks have lifts.

Nilar and I were flat-hunting. Her fluent English meant she had been designated by the letting agency to show me their apartments for rent. Stick-thin – she told me her friends had nicknamed her 'toothpick' – with long lank hair, Nilar was in her late twenties but looked ten years younger. She ushered me through the doorway and we ascended two tight flights of concrete steps to a wooden door guarded, like most Yangon apartments, by a metal grille.

Inside, the flat consisted of a long room. A window looked out onto the street, while a cupboard made up the furniture. At the back of the apartment, divided from the living space by a thin partition wall, was a kitchen that consisted of a sink and a tightly shut window. When I opened it the smell of garbage wafted in. The bathroom was a cubicle off the kitchen. There was just enough room between the toilet and the wall to stand under the hose that was the shower. I told Nilar the flat wasn't for me.

Foreigners had only recently been allowed to live in downtown. During the junta era they were technically confined to condominium compounds north of the Shwedagon, mainly located in Bahan Township. Bahan is home to Golden Valley and the southern shoreline of Inya Lake, Yangon's two most desirable neighbourhoods, whose residents include Aung San Suu Kyi, ambassadors, cronies and generals.

Making foreigners keep to an expensive ghetto where they could be monitored more easily was another manifestation of the military's deep distrust of westerners. But even now, when the restrictions on where expatriates can reside have been lifted, those foreigners who can afford it – diplomats, senior United Nations and NGO staff, the representatives of big overseas companies – still mostly choose to remain in Bahan alongside the local rich.

There they are insulated to some extent from the noise and crowds of a city whose century-old, creaking infrastructure cannot cope with the official population of 5.2 million people, let alone the seven million who actually live here. It is a figure that is expected to double in the next twenty years, assuming Burma follows the same path as its Southeast Asian neighbours and becomes a predominantly urban economy.

Many of Golden Valley's foreign residents live in a neo-colonial style, their contact with the locals restricted to employees and servants: the maids who clean their homes, the drivers who chauffeur them to work and the nannies who pick up their kids from the nearby international schools. That was a world away from the Yangon I wanted to experience. But I was beginning to doubt if I could cope with the depressingly dark apartments from a different age that Nilar was showing me in downtown. I knew I needed more amenable surroundings than an unfurnished room two floors above a car- and pedestrian-snarled street.

The solution was to compromise between living like a local in downtown and hiding away as an expat in Bahan. I did just that by locating an apartment in a small enclave known as Min Ma Naing. Strategically sandwiched south of the

Shwedagon and north of downtown, this meant that I could walk to either in twenty minutes. If I strolled east for ten minutes I arrived at two semi-fashionable streets, known as York and Lancaster Roads in the colonial era, where there were cafés and restaurants, as well as the high school Aung San Suu Kyi had attended in the late 1950s.

I felt a little guilty for not embracing the mayhem of downtown. But I justified my retreat to Min Ma Naing with the knowledge that I was staying in Yangon's historic heart, in the township that still bore the city's original name of Dagon. Yangon's first street, Shwedagon Pagoda Road, was just a five-minute walk away. Originally, it had run uphill to the Shwedagon from the jetty on the river where pilgrims had landed, before roads connected Yangon to the rest of Burma.

Yangon's centre of gravity was shifted south from the Shwedagon to downtown by the British, who built what was essentially a foreign city on Burmese soil. Prior to that, the then Dagon consisted only of a few streets running from the river to Sule Pagoda, which sits now in the middle of downtown and is said to be the oldest Buddhist shrine in Yangon. Two further neighbourhoods of wooden houses and monasteries stretched east and west of the Shwedagon.

That was the town King Alaungpaya renamed Yangon in 1755. Many villages in Burma are reminiscent of how Yangon must have looked in the middle of the eighteenth century: bamboo and wooden huts with thatched roofs, raised off the ground on stilts, livestock living beneath and crop fields nearby. The only difference from old Yangon is that Alaungpaya's town was fenced in by a teak stockade, which kept out the tigers which roamed the tangle of jungle beyond.

My apartment in Min Ma Naing was sited west of Shwedagon Pagoda Road in an area that would have once been covered by the ramshackle homes of Yangon's first residents. It was on the fourth and final floor of one of a series of red-brick buildings, all topped by corrugated iron roofs, originally constructed in the 1960s as accommodation for army families.

Unlike the downtown apartments I'd seen, which ran straight back from the street, my flat ran parallel to the side of the building, allowing for more windows and plenty of natural light. It faced away from the street, too, onto an enclosed communal area in the middle of which rose a giant saman tree, known locally as a *kokko* tree. Thick-trunked, it stood higher than the apartment block, its green-leaved branches splaying out in all directions. By leaning out of the window by my desk, I could almost touch them.

Nature seems a distant ideal in downtown, and the car-clogged roads ensure that pollution levels there rival those of Beijing, but parts of Yangon are a green delight, thanks to the array of trees and bushes that line the streets. Alongside the different varieties of palms and ferns are banana, banyan, mahogany, mango, pipal, tamarind and teak trees. And while tigers and other dangerous animals are no longer a threat, apart from a few snakes lurking in the outlying suburbs, there was plenty of wildlife in Dagon Township.

Crows congregated in the *kokko* tree, squawking non-stop, along with many squirrels. Closer to the Shwedagon, fruit bats squeaked in the upper branches of the palm trees, before emerging when the sky shone red at dusk to shoot off in arrow formation on a sortie to an unknown destination. At ground level turquoise-striped lizards, tongues flicking, scurried in and out of the undergrowth that lined Min Ma Naing's roads.

Chubby black rats moved around, too, unfazed by the feral cats which lived alongside them. Male frogs croaked through the night during the rainy season, calling to their potential partners.

All sorts of airborne insects flew in and out of the windows during the day, until I shut them in the early evening to keep the mosquitos away. Ants found the four-storey climb from the street easy, and marched across the small kitchen's work surfaces. Geckos clung to the ceilings and walls, occasionally losing their grip and free-falling onto the wooden floor. Spiders of varying sizes spun their webs across the building's concrete stairwell and on the metal gate outside my front door.

Apartments in Yangon have their own idiosyncrasies. Washing facilities in the older ones consist of a tank in the bathroom, from which you ladle water over yourself. I did have a shower, but getting the water for it required using an inconsistent pump stationed four flights below, which sent the liquid upwards to a tank through an elaborate network of plastic pipes. The pump could only be turned on twice a day at specific times. Failure to switch it on for a couple of days meant I ran out of water. If I left it on for too long, the kitchen flooded.

Power cuts occurred on a regular basis, especially in April and May as the heat peaked before the start of the monsoon season and fans and air-conditioning units ran full blast, overloading the grid. Invariably the electricity went when I had just put on the washing machine, was about to watch a DVD, or it was so hot that it was impossible to do anything except sit, sweat and wait for the power to return. I was fortunate to be in Yangon. In provincial towns, electricity is normally only available for a few hours in the evening.

Most of the flats housed different generations of one family. I was the lone foreigner and my arrival was swiftly noted. Early one morning, soon after I moved in, my neighbour knocked on the door and offered me a bowl of *mohinga*, noodles in a fish sauce that are typical breakfast fare in Burma. Other residents asked if I had eaten yet, the standard Burmese greeting, when we passed on the stairs. Some stopped to comment on how it was either extremely hot or very wet, the only two meteorological possibilities in Yangon. A small minority ignored me.

Opposite the entrance to the building was a grassless five-a-side football pitch, flanked by a tumbledown tea shop run by two cheery old ladies and a decaying stand that was missing so many slats that only two levels could be sat upon with any sense of security. Boys, teenagers and men turned up to kick a ball around in the early evening and all through the day on weekends. Their matches were the loudest activity, bar the crows, in the immediate vicinity.

Some played barefoot, others wore the latest model of fluorescent orange, pink or green boots, but all sported replica football shirts of the usual suspects: Manchester United, Real Madrid, Chelsea, Barcelona, Liverpool, Bayern Munich and Arsenal. It is an Asian trait to support only the best-known and most successful football clubs. No one I met in Yangon wanted to talk about the local teams.

When the pitch wasn't in use it was the domain of the local street-dog gang. The start of a game saw the hounds loping to the stand, slumping on its remaining rungs and acting as apathetic spectators. There were separate crews of stray dogs throughout the area, all surviving on scavenging and charity: people laid out rice on newspapers, or occasionally in bowls, once a day for them to devour.

From eight in the evening the street grew quiet. The vendors who passed through during the day singing out their stocks of food, flowers and brushes were gone. So, too, were the mobile music men, who pushed wheeled carts with an on-board CD player and speaker around the neighbourhood, selling and playing pirate versions of the latest Burmese love songs and pop videos. Televisions were on and only a few people were outside, talking and walking, enjoying the cooler evening air and the chance to escape crowded homes.

Going to bed early is a habit for most Yangonites. People wandered around in their pyjamas from the late afternoon. And many parents frown on the idea of their daughters being out and about at night, no matter their age. By 10 p.m., the lights in the apartments were going off. But not for long. Within seven hours, people were stirring. When I opened my windows at around seven in the morning, the smell of cooking was already powerful and unwelcome, children were leaving for school and barefooted monks were collecting alms.

Min Ma Naing was unusually tranquil for somewhere so central and I came to regard it as an oasis, albeit one whose boundaries were jammed main roads, in a city trying to catch up with the twenty-first century after having missed fifty-odd years of development. It didn't take much of an imaginative leap to picture how rural Min Ma Naing must have been in Alaungpaya's time, with only the steady stream of monks and pilgrims passing through on their way to the Shwedagon to disturb the serenity.

Just as the Yangon River had brought Indian adventurers to wake up a sleepy fishing village thirteen centuries before, however, so Alaungpaya's new city was given a geographical fillip as waterways in the surrounding region shifted their courses. From being known solely as the site of the Shwedagon, Yangon became the principal port of call for ships entering the Ayeyarwady Delta from the Bay of Bengal. And by the late eighteenth century increasing numbers of foreigners were landing in Burma.

Those arrivals were relative latecomers. Indians were the first visitors, and were soon followed by the Chinese and Arab and Persian traders. Marco Polo mentions Burma in the account of his travels, although there is no evidence that he came to the country. But it is likely that the first Europeans to arrive in Burma were merchants from Venice like Niccolò de' Conti, who stopped by in the early fifteenth century while on an epic journey through the Middle East and Asia. Portuguese traders and mercenaries were also present by the sixteenth century, and Armenians from the early seventeenth century.

Only after Alaungpaya had renamed Yangon did the British show up. In 1795 the rapacious East India Company, which had been busy conquering and asset-stripping India, turning it into one vast monopoly for themselves and the British government, sent a delegation to Burma. It was led by an Irishman named Michael Symes. He asked permission from King Bodawpaya for a British agent to be allowed to reside in Yangon to look after the interests of King George III's subjects there.

Symes's request was granted, but it was spurious at best. There were only a handful of Britons living in Yangon then, and none were the sort of people whose welfare King George would normally be concerned with. In an account of his Burmese expedition published in 1800, Symes noted how 'Rangoon, having long been the asylum of insolvent debtors from the different settlements of India, is crowded with foreigners of desperate fortunes'. Almost all the British in Yangon were hiding from their creditors in India.

Instead, the stationing of an agent in Yangon was a reconnaissance mission so that the East India Company could later establish itself in Burma. Since the seventeenth century, there had been sporadic contact and trade with different parts of the country, including Arakan, which bordered India, and regions in the south which at that time were ruled by Thailand. But commerce between India and Burma was largely an informal affair in the hands of individuals who traded cotton, sugar, tobacco, opium, wool and cheap metal goods for prized Burmese teak.

By 1795 there was enough demand for teak from shipbuilders in Calcutta and Madras for the Company to send Symes to negotiate with King Bodawpaya. Britain was at war with France, too, so there was a need to counter French attempts to win favour with the Burmese king. But money was always the main affair for the East India Company, something exemplified by the fact that 'loot', the Hindi slang for 'plunder', was one of the first of the many Indian words to enter the English language during the eighteenth century.

Despite the presence of an official representative the British population of Yangon hardly increased. They were far outnumbered by the Chinese and Armenian communities. Teak aside, trade remained negligible, too. But the Yangon of the early nineteenth century wasn't a tempting town for Europeans. Contemporary accounts describe a dirty, damp and unsanitary place that stank. Cholera, dysentery and smallpox were rife, snakes swarmed in the untouched undergrowth and every visitor commentated on the sheer number of stray dogs.

Yangon is a challenge for foreigners even now. Unlike Thailand, it offers little in the way of the luxuries that make life more comfortable for those who arrive from the West.

Food poisoning is an occupational hazard, and few first-time visitors leave without suffering a dose of diarrhoea or a spell of fever. Eating at a street stall is unwise, unless it is something that can be barbecued in front of you. And Burmese curries are generally made in the morning, before being left to float in oil for the rest of the day.

Lack of development, though, is the principal reason why Yangon feels more alien to foreigners than other cities in Southeast Asia. Withdrawn for so long from the world under the junta and starved of investment, Burma sticks out noticeably from its more homogenous neighbours with their ubiquitous shopping malls, western fast-food outlets and, above all, the abandonment long ago of their traditional dress.

Yet I had arrived at the time when foreign companies and aid organisations were supposedly rushing to help escort the country into a brighter, more westernised age. In November 2015, Aung San Suu Kyi and the NLD won the first free and fair general election held in Burma since 1960. A new wave of assistance was expected to follow, as people, both inside and outside the country, hailed her victory as a rebirth for the nation.

Certainly, it was a resounding win for Daw Suu, with the NLD receiving over double the number of votes garnered by the military-backed USDP. The celebrations began days before the official result was announced, with crowds converging on the NLD's tiny headquarters in Bahan. For a month after the election people showed off the red ink-stained tips of their left little fingers as evidence they had voted.

Daw Suu couldn't become president, though. The junta had redrafted the constitution in 2008, inserting a clause barring people with foreign spouses or children from Burma's top office. It was designed with Aung San Suu Kyi in mind, because her late husband was British, as are her two sons. But Daw Suu didn't regard that as a problem. She would rule through a proxy with the title of State Counsellor. In her words, she would be 'Above the president'.

Burma has a strong authoritarian tradition. For centuries, the country was ruled by kings who wielded absolute power over their subjects. Elections were unknown. The arrival of the British resulted in the end of the monarchy, but the colonists ruled in its place with a similar disregard for public opinion. Independence in 1948 ushered in a brief period of flawed democracy, before the army took control in 1962.

Now it was already becoming apparent that Daw Suu would be an uncompromising head of the country as well, only one who had been democratically elected. Such is her dominance of the NLD that few people in Burma can name any other senior politicians from the party. Teahouse cynics like Tim were well aware of Daw Suu's autocratic tendencies. 'That's the problem with our leaders,' he told me soon after the election. 'You're just supposed to obey them.'

She is tied to the *Tatmadaw*, too. When the generals rewrote the constitution in 2008, they made sure to reserve a quarter of the seats in both houses of parliament for their nominees. The NLD's representatives sit alongside unelected army officers. Nor can the constitution be revised without the approval of over three-quarters of all parliamentarians, thus ensuring that the military can veto any attempt to remove it from the political process.

Partial democracy is better than no democracy. Yet the *Tatmadaw*'s continuing involvement in government, even if it is now as a back-seat driver rather than steering the ship of state, taints Burma still and makes it much harder to view the country as being on the brink of a new golden era. But the unlikely sharing of power between Daw Suu and the generals also acts as a salutary introduction to the complexities of life here, a reminder that nothing in Burma is entirely as it appears.

2

Clubland

It was a short walk from my apartment to one of the most evocative remnants of the colonial era. Heading west past the kiosk where I paid my electricity bill, and then along a leafy road lined on one side with grubby government housing and on the other by new-build houses for Yangon's rising middle classes, brought me to the back wall of the Russian embassy. Directly opposite stands a sorry looking two-storey teak building, topped by the inevitable corrugated iron roof.

Partially hidden from view by tall palm and *kokko* trees, its windows are broken, the gutters dangle bent and loose, and washing has been draped over the long balcony rail outside. Nothing suggests that this was once the Pegu Club, the haunt of the British elite. From the time the club opened here in 1882 until it closed in March 1942, when the Japanese army occupied Rangoon, the Pegu was the most exclusive place in Burma.

Used as a brothel by the Japanese, who also turned the main Anglican church into a sake brewery, the Pegu was taken over by the *Tatmadaw* after the Second World War and became a club for officers. The army prevented Paul Theroux from exploring when he passed through Yangon in 1971, but later left and the Pegu fell into disuse. The *Tatmadaw* own the land still, and families of former soldiers were occupying part of the complex when I made my first visit. A sign at the front gate said permission is needed to enter. I ignored it and walked in.

Along with the other top clubs in Rangoon, the Pegu barred the Burmese from membership. Only European men could join. The army families staying there still abided by that rule, inhabiting the back buildings surrounded by banana trees, rather than the former clubhouse and the sturdier and newer concrete structure in fading yellow next to it that once housed the club's bedrooms. 'It's not safe to go in there,' a women told me, only to be contradicted by a bare-chested man perching on the balcony rail, who motioned towards the clubhouse door.

Inside, dogs were curled up in the corners where the parquet floors were giving way. Mouse droppings were everywhere and I could hear the rodents scuttling behind the skirting boards. Wide wooden stairs with still-firm bannisters swept upstairs to huge rooms with elaborate ceiling cornices. Ancient fans looked down on me. I could almost see the ghosts of the members, sunk in their leather armchairs, ordering another round of Pegu cocktails, the club's signature concoction of gin, lime, orange curaçao and bitters.

Yet the comforts on offer at the Pegu belied the fact that Britain had struggled to impose itself on Burma. It took no less than three wars to colonise the country. The first was prompted partly by the prospect of opening up a new market for the East India Company, but more by fears over the threat posed to India by Burma. King Bagyidaw's armies, under his top general Maha Bandula, had pushed into Arakan in the west of Burma and what is now Bangladesh, right next door to British India.

Much to the surprise of the Burmese, the East India Company responded by invading Yangon in May 1824. The city's residents fled ahead of the mixed force of British and Indian soldiers, who took up positions at the foot of the Shwedagon. Subsequently, another British army moved into Arakan. By the time a truce was signed in February 1826, Maha Bandula was dead and King Bagyidaw was forced to cede control of Arakan and a chunk of the far south of Burma to the Company.

Tens of thousands of Burmese were killed in the battles, while 15,000 British and Indian soldiers died, most from disease, in what was a mismanaged campaign. Those who lived succeeded in burning down much of Yangon by accident, after looting every bottle of alcohol in town. The war was also expensive. Anger in London over the bill for the invasion – around £1 billion in today's money – led to the East India Company being stripped of its lucrative monopoly to sell opium in China. The decision marked the beginning of the end of the Company's avaricious reign in the Orient.

Twenty-six years later the British returned to Burma for the sequel. The Second Anglo-Burmese War proved to be shorter, lasting less than a year, and not as costly in terms of lives and finances. It resulted in Britain acquiring Yangon – which was renamed Rangoon – and lower Burma, thus cutting off the then capital of Mandalay from the sea.

That wasn't enough for the British trading houses who quickly established themselves in Rangoon. They were already eyeing central Burma's deposits of oil, copper, lead and tungsten, as well as its seemingly endless teak forests. Oil has been bubbling to the surface at Yenangyaung near the town of Magwe for centuries, something noted by Michael Symes on his 1795 scouting mission to Burma, and a deal had already been signed for some of it to be sold to the UK.

Why pay for oil, though, when you can just take it? This was the jingoistic late Victorian era in Britain, when belief in the might and right of the empire was at its zenith. As the business community in Rangoon pressured London to finish the job and take over all Burma, there was also concern over the unpredictable behaviour of King Thibaw. Burma's last king had a taste for brandy and a willingness to listen to French overtures for an alliance.

In November 1885 the final act took place. The Third Anglo-Burmese War lasted just twenty-two days. Burma was officially annexed by the British on New Year's Day 1886. Thibaw was exiled to India. But for the next ten years a conflict of varying intensity took place in the hills of upper Burma, as bands of guerrillas fought the British army, the first of a series of rural rebellions against colonial rule that continued into the 1930s.

Britain reacted by pioneering the tactics it would use a few years later in the Boer War: exiling the relatives of rebels from their villages, or simply burning their homes to the ground, and conducting mass executions. Among the dead was Aung San Suu Kyi's great-grandfather: beheaded for leading a local resistance group. Today, the *Tatmadaw* employs similarly repressive strategies in its efforts to subdue the ethnic minority armies who are fighting for autonomy in the borderlands.

Insurgents in upper Burma were so distant as to be little more than a rumour for new British arrivals to late nineteenth-century Rangoon. They concerned themselves instead with business and recreating upper-middle-class English life in a city where tigers still prowled the edges of the outlying suburbs and elephants were used for transport. The Pegu was part of that elaborate charade, a place for a sundowner after work. On the weekends, there was tennis and golf, horse racing at the Turf Club, sailing on Inya Lake and dances in the evening.

There was a strict hierarchy among the British in Rangoon and the Pegu was for those at the very top: senior officials and army officers and prominent businessmen. Maurice Collis became Rangoon's Chief Magistrate in 1929. Installed in a Golden Valley house and elected to the Pegu, he detailed his experiences in his book *Trials in Burma*. Damning his fellow clubmen as 'aloof and all-powerful', Collis especially noted their complete lack of empathy with the people they ruled.

To be what the Pegu members called 'pro-Burman', which could range from simply being interested in the locals to taking their side in disputes, was the worst sin of all. In George Orwell's *Burmese Days* it leads to the downfall of Flory, the hapless and hopeless central character of the book. Orwell's novel is a devastating portrayal of clubland in the colonial period. It chronicles the turmoil unleashed when the small-minded, deeply racist members of a British club in provincial Burma are forced to elect a non-European member.

Orwell based the club in *Burmese Days* on the real one in Katha, a tiny, tree-lined town on the banks of the Ayeyarwady River, a day's journey north-east of Mandalay. Katha was Orwell's final posting during the five years he served as a police officer in Burma between 1922 and 1927. The town is just as small now as it was when Orwell was stationed there and the clubhouse exists still, although much modified over the years. Almost adjacent to it is the tennis court Orwell and his fellow clubmen played on, its '1924' sign indicating when it was laid out.

Nearby are crumbling mansions from the same period, including Orwell's old home, occupied now by the present-day chief of the local police. It is hard to think of a less sympathetic job than being a colonial policeman: enforcing the law of an alien culture in someone else's country is an unenviable task. Its effect on Orwell was to induce a degree of self-loathing evident in the hyperbolic prose he uses to describe the bigotry, tedium and feuds of Katha club life.

But *Burmese Days* is fiction, and Orwell set out to paint the worst possible portrait of colonial society. Flory, the timber merchant who is knowledgeable about Burmese culture and rails against imperial rule, is pathetic, paralysed by his inability to stand up to the hideously prejudiced other club members. Nor do the locals in the novel come off well, being mainly represented by Flory's money-grabbing mistress and the scheming, venal, monstrously fat local kingpin U Po Kyin.

Daily life for Europeans in colonial-era country Burma was certainly as stultifying as it is portrayed in *Burmese Days*, but it was also rather less segregated than the entitled existence enjoyed by the Pegu's members. In Rangoon, the British could glide daily by car from their homes in Golden Valley to their offices in downtown and then on to the club without encountering any Burmese bar servants.

Foreigners were far scarcer in the provinces and, inevitably, they had much more contact with the locals. Perhaps the most surprising thing about the British Empire is how few British people were actually involved in running it. Even at the height of the Raj there were never more than a thousand or so British officials in the Indian Civil Service, which administered both India and Burma. On the eve of the Second World War, the Burma Frontier Service was employing just forty men to govern well over one-third of the country.

Hardly more numerous were the British based in rural Burma to make money. John Ritchie Gardiner, always known as 'Ritchie', was one of them. He began his career as a real-life Flory: a forestry assistant harvesting teak trees. Adventurous and from a family with a history of working overseas, Gardiner recalled some of his experiences in a private memoir. For eight months each year he lived in the forest and jungle-covered hills surrounding Taungoo, a town around 170 miles north of Yangon, with only his Burmese workers for company.

Four months a year were spent in Taungoo, where the handful of Europeans lived side by side in houses opposite the club with its bar, billiards table and tennis court, the only entertainment apart from a sandy golf course. By the time the 22-year-old Gardiner arrived in early 1926, the Taungoo club was accepting Burmese and Indian members, although Gardiner wrote of how 'colour then was a touchy subject in clubs'. And unlike most members of the Pegu, Gardiner learned to speak fluent Burmese, a requirement of his job, as it was for Orwell.

Life as a forestry assistant was lonely and arduous but lucrative. If living in the jungle for months on end didn't send you mad, drive you to drink or see you succumb to the annual attacks of malaria, you could expect to return to the UK in your mid-forties with enough money to retire. Gardiner was a robust and resilient man, but his memoir records bouts of depression, especially in the rainy season, and details how some of his colleagues died, or had to be sent home after suffering breakdowns.

A Scotsman from Ayrshire, Gardiner came to Burma after answering an advertisement in the *Glasgow Herald* placed by Macgregor & Co. Macgregor's had been in business since the early nineteenth century, soon after it became apparent that

Burmese teak was just as good for building ships as the less plentiful supplies of English oak. Scottish firms dominated the timber trade in Burma, and would later be prominent in oil, rice and rubber, too.

Today, the most lasting legacies of the Scots in Burma are football and golf, both introduced by Scottish expatriates. But from 1886 companies like Macgregor's, the Steel Brothers and Burmah Oil, founded in Glasgow, helped to transform Rangoon into an economic powerhouse, as rice mills, timber yards and oil refineries opened. Soon, ships no longer needed to use the Shwedagon to guide them into Rangoon's harbour: the smoking chimneys lining the waterfront did the job just as well.

Burma was colonised more by capital raised in the City of London than by any significant movement of people from the United Kingdom. Yet cheap labour was still needed to build roads, houses and power stations, to work the docks and railways, man the police force and staff the hospitals, as well as to act as clerks and semi-skilled workers. The British knew just where to look for them: across the Bay of Bengal in overpopulated India. The fact that Burma was ruled as a province of India until 1937, as opposed to being its own colonial state, made it even more logical to import Indian workers.

Immigration from India began to jump dramatically from the mid-nineteenth century. The British believed it was easier to employ Indians in almost any capacity than to train the locals to do the jobs. Indians made up almost half of Rangoon's population by 1881 and they kept on coming over the next few decades. In 1927 so many Indians arrived that their numbers outstripped those of the immigrants disembarking at Ellis Island in New York.

Chinese migration to Burma and especially Rangoon peaked in the late nineteenth and early twentieth centuries, too. A distinct Chinatown emerged, which still exists in the west of downtown Yangon, and Chinese shopkeepers and rice traders flourished. Some Chinese made fortunes out of mining in the north of the country, or rubber plantations in the south, and joined the British in running their racehorses at the Rangoon Turf Club.

Increasingly, the Burmese were pushed to the swampy fringes of Rangoon. A torrent of construction was creating a new, foreign downtown of European-style buildings, while churches, mosques and even a synagogue were appearing to rival the Shwedagon and other Buddhist temples. But the locals were still confined to the same wood and bamboo homes that had characterised King Alaungpaya's Yangon over 150 years before, only now much farther away from the river.

Lacking jobs and exiled to the boundaries of the city, the number of Burmese in Rangoon dropped steadily until, by 1937, they made up less than a third of the estimated population of 400,000. From being a small Burmese town, Rangoon had joined Calcutta, Manila, Shanghai and Singapore as one of Asia's first global metropolises. It was not so much a melting pot as a bear pit where different nationalities and ethnicities competed for a share of the spoils, while the indigenous people could only look on.

Newcomers to Rangoon were quick to remark on the relative lack of locals. One reporter covering a visit to the city by the Prince of Wales in 1906 noted wryly, 'This is Burma without the Burmans, who are the scarcest commodity in Rangoon'. In her 1907 travel memoir *A Bachelor Girl in Burma*, G. E. Mitton wrote, 'The crowd is cosmopolitan, not by any means distinctively Burman, and the general effect is bewildering.' Mitton did not stay single in Rangoon for long: she married James George Scott, the man who introduced football to Burma.

More pertinent were the comments a year later of J. S. Furnivall, a colonial official who would later become an academic. Writing home soon after arriving in 1908, Furnivall categorised Rangoon's foreign residents as 'a crowd of greedy folk recognising no duty to the country where they have been striving to make their fortunes'. Furnivall observed how the different nationalities and races in Rangoon stayed segregated from each other, mixing only for business purposes, and that unofficial apartheid inspired him to come up with the concept of the plural society.

Inevitably, given their numbers, it was Indian immigration that had the biggest impact. Hindustani was the lingua franca of the Rangoon business world and British recruits to the trading houses were required to learn to speak it, rather than the Burmese language. Indeed, until 1930 it was impossible to make a phone call in Burma without speaking English or Hindi, as all the telephone operators were Indian.

Burmese resentment at the Indian presence, and to a lesser extent the Chinese, crystallised quickly. Anti-Indian riots erupted in Rangoon in the 1890s and continued at regular intervals in the colonial era and beyond, the worst occurring in 1930 when hundreds of Indians were killed and British soldiers had to be deployed to restore order. Attacks on the Chinese community took place from 1931, too. In Burma today there is continuing, if not always spoken, animosity towards the descendants of the Indian and Chinese immigrants of a hundred years or more ago.

But it was in the Ayeyarwady Delta, west of Rangoon, that the Indian influx into Burma would have the most catastrophic consequences. A combination of the opening of the Suez Canal in 1869, allowing for much faster journeys to Europe, and the American Civil War, which put an end to rice cultivation in the southern US states, made Asian rice a valuable export to Europe. The British set about turning the Delta into the world's most profitable rice paddy.

Little has changed geographically in the Ayeyarwady Delta since the nineteenth century. It remains a vast, flat patchwork of lime-green fields interspersed with endless tributaries and small rivers that flow into the Andaman Sea. But it was an underpopulated region until rice became a cash crop. At first, the British encouraged Indians to move there to take up farming. Then, after 1885, Burmese from the newly conquered lands of upper Burma began migrating south to the Delta.

Between 1860 and 1930 there was a 600 per cent increase in the amount of land given over to rice farming in the Ayeyarwady Delta. But the cost of opening up fields was higher than most Burmese could pay and rice prices fluctuated. From the 1890s many farmers in the Delta found themselves in debt and reliant on high-interest loans from the Chettiars, Indian bankers and moneylenders from Madras who operated all over Southeast Asia.

Soon, farms started passing into the hands of the Chettiars as they called in their debts. There were also Burmese and Chinese moneylenders, but the Chettiars were dominant and, by 1937, they owned a quarter of all the land in the Delta. Not only were the Burmese being excluded from government and employment in their country, now they no longer owned the land they lived on.

Overseeing this mercenary capitalism were the British. 'The British hold us down, while the Indians pick our pockets,' went the local saying. Rangoon was governed by the Legislative Council, made up mainly of representatives of the most important trading houses, which acted more like the board of directors of a company than a city government. Business interests were always prioritised over the welfare of the Burmese.

Out in the countryside the traditional system of governance by local leaders, whose authority had stemmed from the now discarded monarchy, was abandoned for direct rule by village headmen overseen by British officials. Monks, who played a crucial role as educators and arbiters of society, were largely ignored by the British, who were entirely secular colonists and had no interest in or understanding of Buddhism's role in Burma. And the rural population was subjected to new laws and taxes that were completely foreign to them.

Lounging in the Pegu, cocktails in hand, the members of the Legislative Council must have been happy as they watched Rangoon throw off its frontier-town look and assume its place alongside the other British possessions in Asia as a fully functioning trading hub. Burma was booming, with oil, minerals and teak in demand alongside rice and, by the 1920s, Rangoon had reached its colonial apotheosis, as luxury hotels, department stores, cinemas and nightclubs sprang up.

Ritchie Gardiner took his place at the Pegu bar in the late 1930s. His efficiency had been noted and, after ten years in the Taungoo forests, he was promoted and assigned to Macgregor's Rangoon office. He made a brief trip back to Scotland to get married before returning with his new wife to a position as an assistant director of the company. In 1937 he joined the Rangoon government as Macgregor's representative on the Legislative Council.

Gardiner was in some ways an atypical Pegu clubman. He spoke Burmese and maintained friendships with selected locals, including Ba Maw, a lawyer and politician who was jailed by the British and again by the generals in the junta era. He understood, too, that the metropolitan hothouse that was Rangoon did not reflect the reality of life in wider Burma. But Gardiner was no radical: he had a strong sense of duty and he knew his place within the colonial system. Unlike Orwell, his experiences in provincial Burma had not turned him into a fervent anti-imperialist.

His photograph album from this period reveals how privileged life at the top table in Rangoon was: formal garden parties at the governor's mansion, with guests in morning coats, long dresses, uniforms and extravagant hats, smiling servants clutching Gardiner's young children on the manicured lawn of their house in Golden Valley, the table outside set for afternoon tea. Groups of men with clipped moustaches and in khaki drill shorts hold shotguns on shooting expeditions, or stand by the shore of Inya Lake waiting to board boats.

Even now in Yangon, there are still echoes of the social life Gardiner and his contemporaries enjoyed. The bar at the sailing club on Inya Lake remains a popular spot with expats on Friday nights, the comparatively high prices keeping out most locals. And there is still a British club, part of the large compound that is the residence of the UK's ambassador. Homesick Brits can sip English beer, or sit in the garden and watch a touring company put on an evening performance of *Much Ado about Nothing*, while fireflies dance above the heads of the actors.

The Pegu was deliberately located halfway between the homes of the officials and most prosperous merchants in Golden Valley and the offices in downtown where they spent their days. Then as now, Golden Valley was Rangoon's smartest neighbourhood. Straggling south down winding, tree-shrouded lanes that loop from the southern shoreline of Inya Lake towards the Shwedagon, Golden Valley feels almost rural in comparison to downtown.

Behind high walls are the relics of the colonial era: teak and brick houses with gothic-style turrets, or mock-Tudor facings, and long balconies. Some are still private homes, others are government or United Nations offices, embassies and company headquarters. Almost all are surrounded by sizeable, well-tended gardens which explode in reds and yellows when the flowers bloom and are guarded by palm, mango and rain trees.

Other houses are less aesthetically pleasing. They are painted white or bright pastel colours, with the grandest employing much marble and glass, and are fronted by columns in faux-Palladian fashion. These are the latest additions to Golden Valley, dating from the 1980s onwards, and built in the same unabashedly opulent style that characterises the homes of the newly rich across Southeast Asia and China.

Golden Valley is just as rarefied as it was in colonial times, even if Yangon's current elite no longer congregate in places like the Pegu. Instead, they meet in restaurants, or bars and nightclubs where western dance music is the soundtrack and ordering a bottle of whisky is a prerequisite of entry. But it is a society as clubbish as the one epitomised by the Pegu.

Like almost everywhere in Asia, Burma is a country where connections are everything. A lucky few buck the trend occasionally and succeed without them, but when they do they are quickly absorbed into the circles where senior members of the *Tatmadaw* mix with the cronies – the businessmen who prospered under the junta – and politicians, their relationships cemented by marriages between their families.

One night, Ar Kar explained to me how those personal and professional ties are the most important asset in Burma. 'I grew up in a bubble,' he said. 'My whole family lived in one compound in Golden Valley and that is very different from the other areas of Yangon. It wasn't about how rich you were, it was about how connected you were to the military and the government.'

We were having dinner at the House of Memories, one of Ar Kar's favourite Golden Valley spots. Over a hundred years old, the building is a kitsch blend of British architectural styles: part Scottish shooting lodge, part Surrey suburban mansion. Before it was a restaurant it served as the Second World War headquarters of the Burma Independence Army, the forerunner of the *Tatmadaw*, founded by Aung San, the father of Aung San Suu Kyi.

Ar Kar was a friend of a friend, a broad-faced, solidly built, sentimental character in his mid-thirties, prone to crooning old Burmese love songs with the House of Memories resident pianist after a few drinks. He was honest, too, the only Yangonite I ever met who admitted to voting for the USDP, the party of the former junta, in the 2015 election won so convincingly by Daw Suu and the NLD. 'Our MP is a friend of the family, and I think he did a good job for the constituency,' said Ar Kar apologetically.

During the 1980s his grandfather had been a senior government minister, until he was fired in the fallout from the 1988 pro-democracy protests as the junta remodelled itself in an unconvincing attempt to mollify its opponents. 'I still remember when he lost his job, and the BMW and the driver had to go back to the government because it was their car,' recalled Ar Kar. 'My grandmother told my parents we would have to economise and that she was going to sell the VCR. Man, I hated that. I couldn't watch cartoons anymore.'

At that time the regime was a relatively austere beast, still doggedly pursuing what the junta called 'The Burmese Way to Socialism'. Ar Kar insisted that his grandfather had been 'straight', and had not benefited financially from his ministerial position. But just as the British coveted Burma's abundant mineral deposits, so many members of the junta, with the connivance of the cronies, would prove equally adept at enriching themselves at the expense of the rest of the country.

From the 1950s the *Tatmadaw* began to involve itself in commercial enterprises, starting with the purchase of the Rowe & Co. department store, the then Yangon equivalent of Harrods or Bloomingdale's. But frontmen were still needed for the businesses and the cronies, often the relatives of senior army officers, performed that role. 'People started cashing in on their connections after 1988. Maybe the heads of the junta were planning ahead for their retirement,' said Ar Kar, a resigned smile on his face. Few people in Burma are surprised or shocked by the capacity of the country's elite for corruption.

When Than Shwe, a devious and intensely secretive general, took over as Burma's leader in 1992, the graft reached new heights. 'It was in the 1990s that shopping malls and condominiums started to appear in Yangon and Mandalay. Most of them were financed by illegal money,' said Ar Kar. Than Shwe is still notorious in Burma for staging a supremely lavish wedding for his daughter in 2006. A leaked video of the ceremony revealed a bride bedecked in a diamond-encrusted necklace, while the value of the gifts she and her husband received was said to total £26 million.

Crony and *Tatmadaw*-backed businesses are still involved in everything from airlines and banks to construction and insurance companies, real estate and TV stations. The army owns around two million acres of land, too. But some of the illicit cash surging into Yangon and Mandalay came from the borderlands, where heroin and methamphetamines are produced in the Golden Triangle and Burma's jade deposits, the largest in the world, are mined.

Jade and illegal narcotics are by far Burma's most profitable industries, worth a combined £40-odd billion annually, according to NGOs and the United Nations Office on Drugs and Crime. Keen to benefit from the drug and jade trade, too, the generals laundered the profits in return for a cut. After 1988 private businessmen were offered an amnesty. As long as they paid a 25 per cent 'tax' on their assets, no matter how they were gained, they could invest in legitimate businesses, especially property.

Just as the generals have escaped punishment for their crimes, so none of the cronies have been held to account for helping to prop up the junta financially and joining with it in exploiting Burma's resources for their own gain. Some were subject to international sanctions, but those were swiftly lifted in the euphoria that followed the 2015 election.

Nor is there much appetite in Burma to see them hauled up in court. 'There's a different level of hatred for the cronies than there is for the generals,' explained Ar Kar. 'It's a basic Buddhist tenet that if you're making money, you must have done something good. It's a reward for what you have done in your past lives. So on that level the cronies are not entirely hated, even if they are not exactly role models.'

Members of the Pegu would have been surprised at the entrepreneurial skills of the cronies. It was a British axiom that the Burmese were too lazy to compete for jobs with the Indian immigrants and too easy-going to have a chance in business against the Chinese. That view persisted until the end of the colonial era. In the 1940s Sir Arthur Bruce, an adviser to the then governor, spoke for many officials when he said 'The Burman was a happy-go-lucky sort of chap, the Irishman of the east, free with his smiles.'

Ne Win, the architect of the 1962 coup, would use similar arguments to justify military rule twenty years later. Ne Win claimed that democracy couldn't work in Burma, that people weren't prepared to work hard enough and needed to learn discipline. The generals were already imitating the way the British had squashed rebellions. Later, they would prove just as determined to line their pockets as the colonists had been. Now, they were even endorsing the British stereotype of their own people.

Opposition to Ne Win's coup started almost immediately, just as resistance to the British takeover of Burma began as soon as King Thibaw was bundled onto a boat to India. In a neat twist of history it would begin on the campus of Rangoon University, a few minutes' journey from Golden Valley, where Ne Win himself had studied in the 1930s and the campaign for Burma's independence had taken shape.

As for the Pegu Club, that has become just another money-making scheme for the *Tatmadaw*. On my last visit, there were security guards at the gate and I was turned away. Puzzled, I walked around the corner to find Tun Tun, the son of a retired soldier who I'd first met living in the Pegu with the rest of his family. As usual, he was manning his betel-nut stand, where he wraps the narcotic in leaves and lime from six in the morning to ten at night, seven days a week.

'You can't go in,' Tun Tun told me. 'The club has been leased by a Japanese company. They want to make it into a hotel. All the families had to move out. We're living near the airport now.' I thought there was a certain symmetry to the Pegu being Japanese-run once more, just as it had been in the Second World War. But Tun Tun didn't see it that way. 'I miss living here,' he said. 'It was my home for fourteen years.'

3

Rangoon Revolutionaries

Yangon University was hushed to the point that the birds in the giant Ceylon ironwood trees dotted around the tidy lawns of the campus were making more noise than the few humans visible. Undergraduates had been banned from attending the university in 1996 after a series of demonstrations against the junta. It was yet another display of the university's appetite for protest, a militant tendency which dates back to 1920 when the institution was founded as Rangoon University.

Now only a few hundred postgraduates were allowed to study at Burma's premier university, once regarded as the best in Southeast Asia. Even so, I found it bewildering that such a proudly seditious seat of learning could be so sleepy, especially given what was happening outside the campus. This was March 2012, sixteen months after Aung San Suu Kyi had been released from house arrest. By-elections were due and she and other members of the NLD were being permitted to stand for parliament for the first time since 1990.

I had flown in from a still cold Beijing to cover the story. Yangon was oppressively hot and its residents appeared to be both dazed and on edge. It was as if people couldn't believe what was happening and were wondering if it was just another performance, a *yokhte pwe*, or puppet show, being put on for the benefit of the outside world.

When I told the taxi driver who dropped me at the university that I was here in search of Min Ko Naing, he reached into his wallet and handed me an old banknote for one kyat, pronounced 'chat', the Burmese currency. It was a pre-1988 note, no longer legal tender, issued by the former People's Bank of Burma. Staring out from the centre of it was the face of Aung San: Aung San Suu Kyi's father and a near-deity in Burma for spearheading the drive for independence in the 1930s and 1940s. 'Keep it. It is good luck,' said the driver.

It was an entirely appropriate gift. Min Ko Naing had been one of the leaders of the 1988 pro-democracy uprising, which was inspired by anger over Burma's dire financial situation. He had also facilitated Aung San Suu Kyi's entry into politics, introducing her to a crowd of half a million people gathered at the Shwedagon at the height of the protests. And one of the many consequences of the turmoil of 1988, and the threat it had posed to the generals, was that Burma's banknotes were redesigned and Aung San's image removed from the currency.

Born in Mon State in southern Burma in 1962, the year of the coup that marked the start of the junta era, Min Ko Naing was originally named Paw Oo Tun, after a famed Burmese scholar and royal adviser from the twelfth century CE. But by the time of the 1988 demonstrations he had adopted his much more ominous new name, which means the 'slayer or conqueror of kings'.

He had entered Yangon University in 1985 as a first-year zoology student. At that time it was known as Rangoon Arts and Science University, always abbreviated to 'RASU' by its

alumni and pronounced 'ra-su'. Three years later Min Ko
Naing was the best known of the student protestors, leading
rallies of thousands of people both on the RASU campus and
the streets of Yangon.

His activism was a direct result of decades of economic
illiteracy by the junta as much as it was about the desire for
democracy. In 1988 resources-rich Burma was near-bankrupt
and had just been downgraded by the United Nations to
'Least Developed Nation' status. The kyat had been devalued
twice in three years, wiping out precious savings used, among
other things, to pay university tuition fees. With the kyat
almost useless, rice became a substitute currency and food
and commodity prices soared.

Discontent spread, as underground dissident groups
formed across the country. But the anger over military rule
was most obvious on the campuses of Yangon's universities.
The generals reacted by closing the colleges. Protests
continued, though, until on 8 August 1988, a date chosen
for its auspicious '8888' number sequence, a general strike
paralysed Burma, as schools, factories, farms and government
offices all stopped working.

Just over two weeks later, Min Ko Naing introduced Aung
San Suu Kyi to a huge audience in front of the Shwedagon.
It was her political debut, and it is hard to imagine a more
spectacular or dramatic one. In her speech, she described the
1988 uprising as 'the second struggle for independence'. Daw
Suu didn't explicitly name the *Tatmadaw*, but it was clear to
everyone that she was comparing the generals to the British
colonists of forty years before.

Choosing Aung San Suu Kyi to address such a large crowd
was both an obvious and inspired decision. Her father, Aung
San, is a bigger name in Burma than she is. From the late

1930s he led the campaign to get the British out of Burma, and was de facto prime minister when he was assassinated six months before the country became independent. He founded the *Tatmadaw*, too, and pictures and statues of him are everywhere.

Aung San was a difficult man. One memoir describes him as 'an impenetrably private and taciturn person'. He could be curt and rude. In January 1946 he was addressing his own rally at the Shwedagon when the microphone failed. Aung San turned to the monks sitting behind him and shouted, '*Sauk than ma kya bu*', or 'Fucking useless'. He wasn't shy about berating his fellow Burmese for being complacent and idle, warning them that they needed to work harder than ever to rebuild their country after the ravages of the Second World War.

Khin Kyi, Aung San's wife and the mother of Aung San Suu Kyi, was an equally strong character. She shed no tears at her husband's funeral, determined to deny his killers the chance to revel in their deed. Left alone to raise her three children, Khin Kyi was a strict and demanding parent and passed on her unwavering belief in Buddhism to her only daughter.

At the time of the 1988 protests, though, there was no hint that Aung San Suu Kyi would go on to become as uncompromising and self-contained a character as her father, or turn out to be as stubborn and single-minded as her mother. By the time I moved to Yangon, Daw Suu's unwillingness to brook criticism was already legendary in embassy and NGO circles, as was her disconcerting habit of castigating both local and foreign politicians, diplomats and senior aid organisation figures for their apparent failings.

In 1988, however, Aung San Suu Kyi was still little known in Burma, having only arrived back in the country in March that year to care for her ailing mother after almost three decades away. She had left Yangon in 1960, first for New Delhi when her mother was appointed Burma's ambassador to India, before studying at Oxford and then working for three years at the United Nations in New York. By 1972 she was back in Oxford and married to Michael Aris, an English academic. They had two sons and for the next sixteen years, Daw Suu was a largely anonymous housewife in north Oxford.

Yet there is no doubt that Aung San Suu Kyi was already an icon in waiting as she stepped on stage at the Shwedagon in August 1988. Her status as Aung San's daughter tapped into the Asian tradition of political dynasties, where prominent families assume the roles of long-gone feudal overlords. She appeared also to embody the Buddhist archetype of a benevolent, charismatic and enlightened leader. Aung Sang Suu Kyi became the undisputed star of the pro-democracy movement almost overnight, while the black and white photos of the petite and pretty woman with flowers in her hair commanding vast crowds were seen around the world.

A month after her Shwedagon bow Daw Suu co-founded the NLD. But by then the uprising was over, as the junta reincarnated itself with a new leadership, at least in public, and viciously put down the demonstrations. Within a year Aung San Suu Kyi was confined under house arrest in her mother's home on University Avenue by Inya Lake, with only the odd servant and the superannuated disc jockeys of the BBC World Service for company. She would remain there for much of the next two decades. Two years later, she was awarded the Nobel Peace Prize.

Min Ko Naing was less lucky. He went on the run after the protests ended, moving nightly between the houses of sympathisers, before being arrested a few months later. Incarcerated in the British-built monstrosities that are Burma's jails, often kept in solitary confinement and sometimes suffering torture, he spent most of the next twenty-three years in prison.

Tall and vigorous in a white shirt and green *longyi*, Min Ko Naing proved to be a little grumpy when finally I tracked him down to the run-down hall on the campus where he was attending a reading by 1988 activists turned writers. It was only ten in the morning, but the sky was a high, clear blue and the heat was already taking its toll. By the time I arrived at the meeting my shirt was decorated with sweat stains.

Out of jail for only two months, his release an offering to Washington from the former junta, Min Ko Naing appeared to be in surprisingly good health. But he wasn't in the mood to talk, at least not when I approached him after waiting almost an hour for a break in the readings. Cagey on the subject of Aung San Suu Kyi, he seemed stoical about the way their lives had diverged since 1988.

Nor did he express surprise at the junta's conversion to a quasi-civilian government. He was certainly in no rush to hail their decision to allow the NLD to take part in the upcoming by-elections, or to free him after so long in prison. 'I was arrested for political reasons and I was released for political reasons,' he told me. 'I am not an optimist or a pessimist about the present situation. I look always to the reality.'

Life under the generals had transformed Min Ko Naing from a small-town student into a zealot for democracy. It was a journey similar to the one undergone by Aung San in the 1930s. He arrived at Rangoon University in 1933 as the eighteen-year-old son of a provincial lawyer. By the time he left in 1938, without a degree, he was a vehement critic of British rule, increasingly drawn to Marxist theory, and the firebrand organiser of numerous strikes.

Rangoon University in the 1930s was in the grip of a fervent student nationalism noteworthy even by its own subversive standards. The list of Aung San's contemporaries reads like a *Who's Who* of Burmese politics between the 1930s and 1980s. Future junta leader Ne Win was expelled in 1931 after failing his biology exams. U Nu, who became Burma's prime minister after independence, before being overthrown by Ne Win, was also briefly suspended along with Aung San in 1936 for leading a strike.

Studying alongside them were other men – and they were all male – who would play lesser-known roles in the struggle for independence and in the fierce battles for political power afterwards. Most were from the provinces, and it was only when they reached Rangoon University that they got a first-hand glimpse of how colonial rule had turned the then capital of Burma into an alien city. With the campus sitting on the edge of Golden Valley, the students did not have to look far to see the grand houses that were proof of how the British were benefiting at the expense of the locals.

Those 1930s activists, though, were also following in the footsteps of previous protestors. In December 1920, Rangoon University students organised the first anti-British strike ever held in Burma. It was a shocking event, catalysing political awareness throughout the country. Angered by a new law that all classes be taught in English, the students boycotted lectures. The strike spread to schools across Burma, with pupils ignoring their normal curriculum in favour of self-taught classes on nationalism.

Rebellion at Rangoon University didn't end after independence. The student body fractured into factions, mirroring the fight for political control between various communist groups and the Anti-Fascist People's Freedom League, the coalition led first by Aung San until his death and then by U Nu. Ethnic minority students began to agitate for self-rule, too. Former Rangoon University students from Shan State organised the first armed Shan opposition to the government in 1958.

Around the same time, Kachin students formed the Seven Stars group, regarded as the forerunner of the Kachin Independence Organisation, which is still campaigning for autonomy for Kachin State. And in the days before the Rohingya Muslim minority became Burma's favourite public enemies, first marginalised and then persecuted, Rangoon University's Rohingya students had their own association.

So synonymous was the university with protest that one of Ne Win's first acts after seizing power in 1962 was to order the student union to be dynamited as revenge for protests against the coup, thus setting a repressive, vindictive tone for his regime from the beginning. Around one hundred students died in the ensuing rioting. More were killed in December 1974, when soldiers broke up demonstrations on the campus. Ne Win justified the deaths years later by using the language of the 1930s student rebels, saying it was his duty as a 'revolutionary leader' to crush dissent.

That continuity of resistance, whether against the British or the junta, informed the 1988 generation of student protestors, like my friend Tim. 'At some level, we were trying to connect with the past,' he told me. 'We knew the history: Aung San, the strikes and student movements of the 1920s and 1930s. We talked about the 1962 and 1974 protests in our speeches on campus. I knew about the 1974 protests because my uncle had been involved in them. I learned later that some of the 1988 student leaders were in touch with some of the 1974 people.'

Forced into exile, Tim never graduated from RASU but is still proud of his time there. 'We were the last generation of real RASU students. After 1988, the junta began moving most of the faculties off the main campus to the outskirts of Yangon, so the students couldn't gather in the city proper to cause trouble. They're letting some undergraduates back now, but it's not the same,' he said.

Scattering the students to the four winds of Yangon had a profound effect on the quality of their education, too. Many people were forced to study remotely, rarely meeting their lecturers. And that was when the universities were open. From 1962 onwards, colleges were periodically shut by the generals, sometimes for years at a time, as retribution for protests. Those who can afford it now attend universities overseas, but for everyone else a broken higher education system is just another unwelcome legacy of military rule.

Tim had hardly been a model student even when classes were being held. He chuckled as he recalled his misspent youth at one of our meetings in a coffee shop near People's Park, an expanse of green west of the Shwedagon. 'I was a fourth-year geography student in 1988. I didn't go to many lectures. I thought I was destined for the army anyway, like a lot of my family. Back then, I was a member of the elite. I grew up living next door to senior junta people, I had money and my friends were the same. Nineteen eighty-eight was a real wake-up call for someone like me.'

Sporadic protests had been going on for months, but the death of a Rangoon Institute of Technology (RIT) student in a confrontation with riot police on 12 March 1988 sharply escalated tensions between the students and the government. Four days later, Tim was one of a group milling around the recreation centre on the RASU campus. 'The crowd got bigger and bigger and people got up on the roof of the centre to give speeches, telling people how the police had raided the RIT campus the day before and fought with the students there.'

Spontaneously, as he remembers it, Tim decided to join the speakers on the roof. 'I talked about Ne Win and what he'd done over the years; rumours and stories I'd heard from my family and other people with connections to the government,' he recalled. 'Then everyone started to leave the campus. The idea was that we were going to join up with students from RIT and other universities.'

Under a sweltering sun, close on four thousand students marched along Pyay Road on the western edge of Inya Lake, until they were forced to come to a halt at a spot known as White Bridge. 'We ran into an army roadblock: barbed wire, two armoured cars at each end and soldiers behind the wire pointing guns at us,' said Tim. 'We had no banners or anything, the protest wasn't really planned. We wrote down our demands with a pencil on a piece of paper and handed them over to one of the officers.'

Their terms were simple: an inquiry into the death of the RIT student, an official apology to his family and the right to form a student union. 'We weren't asking for anything political really,' said Tim. 'But I was freaking out by now. There was the army in front and the crowd of students behind and I thought, "If they shoot, there's no cover." We all raised our arms to show that we weren't carrying weapons and we sang the national anthem, to tell the soldiers that we were Burmese too. Then we sat down on the road.'

Whether the students' demands were ever communicated to the generals is unknown. But after thirty minutes of waiting for a response, Tim noticed that people towards the back of the protest were starting to push their way out. 'That chaos got closer and closer, until I saw the police charging the crowd. They were riot police and they were hitting people with batons. Then we started to run away from the police towards Inya Lake. Some people jumped in the water, but the police dragged them out to beat them.'

Escaping in the other direction, Tim and other protestors leapt over the fences guarding the houses on Pyay Road and ran through their gardens. 'We were very angry, screaming, "The police are killing the students." People just looked at us as if we were mad,' said Tim. 'I ended up jumping on a bus and going home.'

Estimates of the number of students who died are as high as two hundred. Many more were arrested. The attack by the riot police and the soldiers on a peaceful crowd who were sitting placidly lasted an hour and left large pools of blood congealing on the road. Some people were simply bludgeoned to death, others drowned in Inya Lake. A few were shot. Women who were caught were gang-raped in police vans.

Even by the junta's brutal standards, the level of violence employed was excessive and unnecessary. An inquiry was launched into the death of the RIT student, but Ne Win never acknowledged what happened at the White Bridge. For Tim and many of his contemporaries it was the end of their university careers, although they didn't know it then.

'We went back to the campus the next morning and that's when I heard about the number of deaths and that female students had been raped,' said Tim. 'The rector asked us to stay on the campus. He said if we didn't leave we would be OK. So we stayed. But over the next couple of days people started to disappear. They had been arrested. And then the campus was shut down. I went back briefly in June when it reopened, but I was kind of lost with so many people I knew gone. But then they shut it down again and I never went back.'

For the next six months people took to the streets in cities and towns across Burma calling for the introduction of multi-party democracy. The protests peaked in August with the general strike and the rally of half a million people at the Shwedagon. An evening curfew was imposed in Yangon and groups of five or more people were banned from gathering. Ten thousand felons were released from jail, an attempt by the junta to smear the demonstrators as mere criminals. And the death toll continued to mount.

By the time what is known in Burma as the '8888 uprising' came to an end in late September, with the army machine-gunning its opponents on Yangon's streets, up to ten thousand people are believed to have been killed. Most perished in clashes with the police and soldiers. But some died at the hands of the protestors. 'It was a crazy time,' said Tim quietly. 'There were so many informers among the students and the professors. At meetings, someone would shout "He's a spy" and then everyone would set on him. People were being beheaded – literally.'

There is no doubt that the six months from March to September 1988 was the most violent period in urban Burma since the Second World War. It was the closest the junta came to being forced from power. The response of the generals was to recruit more soldiers; over the next ten years the *Tatmadaw* would double in size. Only the army could guarantee the nation's security, even if it meant killing its own people to do so.

Protestors were arrested in their thousands. Others fled to the jungle along the border with Thailand, where they found refuge in the camps of ethnic minority militias. Tim was already gone by then. 'They came to arrest me at my parents' house in early July, but they missed me because I was staying in a nearby temple,' he remembered. 'The next day I caught the overnight train to Mandalay and stayed with my aunt. She knew I was in trouble and after one night she took me to a monastery in Bagan.'

Sporting a shaven head, Tim posed as a novice monk while plotting his escape from Burma. 'It was abroad or the jungle. There was no other choice. The monks were planning a meditation retreat in the US. They asked for my help preparing their documents. I went with them to Yangon and the American embassy and spoke to one of the staff there. She said, "Don't you want to come to the States too?" I had a passport, so they gave me a visa and the monks got a disciple in the US to pay for my air ticket.'

Landing in Los Angeles as a counterfeit holy man, Tim stayed with the monks initially, before striking out on his own. 'I got a job pumping gas in Pomona, where there was a Burmese community. My first ever job for $4.25 an hour,' he grinned. 'I ended up going to college in San Diego and staying in the States for twenty-six years.'

Coming back in 2014 offered the chance to reconnect with his RASU classmates. 'I see a few of the 1988 crew. We have to make allowances for each other after so long apart. A few are bitter. They resent me for leaving while they were struggling or in prison. There are some disappointed people and some jealous people. I try not to impose my views on them, try to talk to them in a way they understand.'

Tim's time in exile has left him with his own scars. He is a gregarious man, but also unmarried and solitary, a self-made loner. 'My parents never really knew much about what I did in 1988,' said Tim. 'It was safer that way. Not talking was a way to protect the ones you love. Now, it's kind of second nature not to share stuff. All my girlfriends have complained that I won't talk about things. They think it's a trust issue. But it's not, it's just the way I am now.'

Totalitarian regimes survive on terror, on scaring people into self-censoring their thoughts and actions, forcing them to withdraw into themselves so that they present no external threat. Everyone who experienced the half-century of the junta suffered that repression of feeling at one stage or another. Learning to live again without the fear of knowing you can be arrested at any time is no easy task.

Returning to Yangon and working for an NGO is Tim's way of purging the past. 'It's a very different life to the one I had here before 1988,' he said. 'I'm working at ground level now. It's been liberating, actually. There's a lot to reflect on when you sit in a bamboo hut that is falling apart and home to seven people. You see what life is for them and it affects you. Coming back has been a very profound and emotional experience.'

4

Shanty Town

Thida and I were on our way to Hlaing Tharyar, Yangon's most notorious township. We had been crawling through the rush-hour traffic from Min Ma Naing for over an hour, following the Yangon River as it slides west past downtown and then turns north. Now, we were opposite Yangon's largest fish market and almost at the bridge that would take us across the water, sometimes known in this part of town as the Hlaing River, to the far west of the city.

For Thida, who was coming along to translate, it was a route she knew well. The road to Hlaing Tharyar carries on to the Ayeyarwady Delta, where Thida lived until she was fourteen. Our taxi driver, a native Yangonite, was less impressed at having to haul us out to the city's western extremities. He wasn't shy about offering his jaundiced opinion of our destination. 'It's not just Yangon people who think Hlaing Tharyar is a bad area,' he said. 'People all around the country know it because so many people from different regions have come there to live.'

Finding a ride to the township is difficult at night. Enough taxi drivers have been robbed by their fares on evening trips to Hlaing Tharyar to make them wary about travelling there after dark. Just as Golden Valley is associated with wealth, so Hlaing Tharyar is a byword for crime and deprivation. The most populous township in Burma, and one of the largest, it is also home to the biggest shanty town in the country. Its residents are routinely blamed by the media and other Yangonites for the rise in crime across the city in recent years.

Around half of the 700,000-odd people in Hlaing Tharyar live in the shanties, known as *kwetthis* in Burmese, literally a new lot of land, without electricity or running water. Most are relatively recent arrivals to Yangon – 'squatters' in the parlance of officials. They are drawn to the fringes of the big city by the prospect of jobs in the many garment and light industry factories that have opened in Hlaing Tharyar since the junta ended its rule.

As we crossed the bridge, pickup trucks and buses were heading in the opposite direction with their cargoes of people from Hlaing Tharyar bound for work elsewhere in Yangon. On the other side of the river we bounced along a potholed road lined with scrubby trees, passing a large *Tatmadaw* base – one of a number that strategically encircle Yangon – and FMI City, an incongruous gated compound of smart houses. They are the homes of businessmen from South Korea, Taiwan, Hong Kong and China, the owners and operators of some of Hlaing Tharyar's 650 or so factories.

Only then did the first shanties come into view. A line of flimsy bamboo huts, some roofed with tarpaulins, straggled along the left-hand side of the road, resting on spindly stilts over pools of stagnant water that had collected in the deep ditch that marked the boundary of the highway. Looming above the huts in the near distance were the factories, a cluster of grey and blue box-like buildings running back as far as the eye can see, surrounded by high concrete walls topped with barbed wire.

Hlaing Tharyar's setting seemed almost feudal once we turned off the main road onto the broken-up lanes that intersect the industrial zone. The factories and their walls came together to form a giant commercial castle, while the shanty homes that sat on every available inch of land around them were the equivalent of a village taking root in the lee of a medieval fortress, hoping for protection in times of trouble. The shanty dwellers weren't paying a tithe, or tilling the land of their masters; they manned assembly lines and sewing machines instead.

Abandoning the taxi, we set off on foot. Trishaw drivers touting for customers outside a tented tea shop pointed us in the direction of the lane where the woman we were planning to meet lived. Hlaing Tharyar is hardly on the Yangon tourist trail and sees few foreigners, but as usual it was Thida who drew the most stares as we passed young women walking arm in arm in crocodile formation, their tiffin boxes containing their lunch in one hand, on their way to work.

Short, snub-nosed and dark-skinned, Thida looks like many women from the Ayeyarwady Delta, a region of rice farmers and fishing folk who spend their days working under a harsh sun. But Thida has rejected traditional Burmese female garb in the belief that the tight-fitting *htamein* is a male conspiracy designed to keep women subservient. 'When I wear a *htamein* I feel like I am in hell,' she told me at one of our first meetings. 'You can't even run in them. A boy can tuck up his *longyi* and run, but a girl can't do that.'

Instead, Thida wears western clothes, jeans or dresses that daringly for Burma rise above her knees, which show off her slim figure to its best advantage. She scorns the ponytail favoured by most Burmese women in favour of styled hair that curls around her neck, while a long fringe obscures her forehead. And rather than the *thanaka* that every second woman in Burma smears across their cheeks, Thida caps off her look with frequently applied tabasco-red lipstick.

Thida's rebellious nature extends to her private and spiritual life. She married her first boyfriend secretly at eighteen, and then divorced him after graduating from university, again without telling her parents. Thida is dismissive of some of Buddhism's most treasured tenets, too. 'Reincarnation is bad for people, it makes them selfish,' she insisted. 'They do good works only because they think they have to so that their next life isn't a bad one.' Despite her mother urging her to spend more time at the temple, or risk returning as an insect in her next existence, Thida remains a reluctant Buddhist.

Beginning her day at 5 a.m. by speed-walking for miles through Yangon's darkened streets, Thida spends the daylight hours teaching English to the offspring of Yangon's new middle classes, whose parents are already planning to send them to college overseas. It is a successful business, and I was lucky that she enjoyed the opportunity to escape her spoiled charges every so often and do some translating for me.

I was anticipating also that Thida's roots in Mawlamyinegyun, a town in the far south of the Ayeyarwady Delta, would be an asset in Hlaing Tharyar, because the majority of the shanty residents hail originally from the Delta. Soused by the Ayeyarwady River and its many tributaries and flanked by the Andaman Sea to the south and the Bay of Bengal in the west, the Delta is supremely fertile: the reason why so many people from the more arid lands of upper Burma migrated there in the colonial era to open up rice farms.

Today, the Delta has an official population of over six million, making it the most populated region of Burma, even if Yangon has more residents now. It remains the principal rice-growing area, with around 600,000 hectares given over to the cultivation of the country's staple crop. The Delta is also Burma's main source of fish and marine products. People across lower Burma are addicted to *ngapi*, a fermented fish or shrimp paste that features as a condiment for any meal, or can be used in soups and salads, and the Delta is its spiritual home.

Burma was the world's largest rice exporter before the Second World War, but decades of economic decline and mismanagement since then has made rice farming far less profitable. Now it is Burma's neighbours, India and Thailand, who dominate the global rice trade and even Italy sells more rice overseas than Burma does. Commercial fish farms have swallowed up smallholdings, too, so there is far less land for people to work.

Compounding that fall in fortune was the devastating impact of Cyclone Nargis on the Delta, the worst natural disaster in Burma's recorded history. Nargis is the Urdu word for a daffodil, but there was nothing spring-like about the weather that Nargis brought when it made landfall in the Delta on 2 May 2008. Generating wind speeds of 135 miles an hour as it spiralled across the Bay of Bengal, Nargis sent two-storey-high storm surges rolling thirty miles inland across the rice paddies.

There were no hills to escape to for the millions in Nargis's path; the Delta is the lowest lying region in all Burma. The towns and villages closest to the coast and on the banks of the waterways that cut through the Delta suffered the worst, with vast numbers of people swept away in flash floods. Screaming winds splintered wooden homes and sent rusty metal roofs slicing through the air, causing hideous injuries to anyone in their way. Most of those who survived did so by clinging for hours on end to trees bent almost double in the wind, their clothes ripped from their bodies.

No one knows how many people died as a result of Nargis, one of the deadliest cyclones of all time. The official toll of 138,000 dead and missing is widely believed to be an underestimate, with some sources alleging a figure three times higher. But everyone in Burma remembers the response, or lack of it, from the generals. Nargis caused more destruction to the Delta than it suffered in the Second World War, with almost all buildings in the region damaged or destroyed. Yet film footage recorded clandestinely in the worst-hit areas days after the cyclone shows hardly a soldier or government official in sight.

Worse still, and in a move unprecedented in the history of global disasters, the junta refused all offers of international help at first, whether from individual countries or the United Nations and aid agencies. Planes loaded with relief supplies sat backed up on the runways of Bangkok, Dhaka and Dubai for almost a week waiting for permission to land in Yangon. Ships from navies around the world floated fruitlessly off the coast of the Delta, unable to send in helicopters with desperately needed medical teams.

Those aircraft carriers and destroyers congregating in the Andaman Sea probably played a large part in causing the regime to act as if nothing had happened, despite the generals being warned in advance by the Indian government that Nargis was a nightmare heading their way. Than Shwe, the then leader of the junta, is thought to have believed that the foreign ships were there not to provide assistance to the people of the Delta, but to invade Burma and end the decades of military misrule.

It was just eight months since the 2007 Saffron Revolution protests, so the junta was already on edge. But while the generals closed their eyes to the survivors huddling naked in the open without food, water, shelter or medical help, ordinary people started to organise makeshift convoys to the Delta with whatever supplies they could muster. Accompanying them were a few intrepid film-makers who risked imprisonment for making and distributing samizdat DVDs, which revealed how Nargis's survivors had been abandoned by the authorities.

If leaving the residents of the Delta to starve wasn't bad enough, the regime also refused to let their plight delay a nationwide referendum on its planned amendments to the constitution. Eight days after Nargis hit, the referendum went ahead. Some survivors were turfed out of the schools they were sheltering in so they could be used as polling stations. Others were threatened with being forcibly returned to their devastated villages if they voted against approving the revised constitution.

Widespread voter fraud occurred across the country, with officials paying people to vote yes, or making them endorse already completed ballot forms. Many people were simply too scared, or in such a state of shock post-Nargis, to vote no. But some did refuse to back the new constitution. 'A lot of people who voted in Yangon drew dead people on the ballot papers, or defaced them with swear words,' one of the film-makers who travelled to the Delta after Nargis told me.

That made no difference to the result, which was a foregone conclusion anyway. Twenty days after Nargis, the junta announced that the revised constitution had been approved by over 90 per cent of Burma's voters. The new amendments included a clause barring anyone married to a foreigner or with foreign children from the presidency, and one reserving a quarter of all seats in parliament for *Tatmadaw* officers. The generals had got their way. Aung San Suu Kyi would never be president and the military would hold the balance of political power for the foreseeable future.

Nargis and its aftermath is the single most shameful episode in the junta's inglorious history. It was a stunning display of ruthlessness and incompetence, a governance model that the generals made their own and one which, sadly, Aung San Suu Kyi's administration has yet to disown. Above all, it revealed to everyone in Burma just how little their rulers cared about them, if they didn't know it already.

Not even the Chinese Communist Party, the only real allies of the regime and hardly advocates of liberal democracy, could condone the junta's response to Nargis. Indeed, ten days after the cyclone slammed into the Delta, China demonstrated how a government should respond to a natural disaster, after a powerful earthquake struck a mountainous region of Sichuan Province in western China.

More than 69,000 people died, 370,000-plus were injured and almost five million left homeless. Ninety minutes after the 'quake, China's prime minister was on a plane to the affected area. Four days later I reached Beichuan, a city close to the earthquake's epicentre that had been home to 160,000 people, to report on the relief operation. I was staggered by the sheer scale of the catastrophe. Beichuan looked as if it had been subjected to a vengeful fury straight out of the Old Testament.

Boulders the size of houses had crashed down from the surrounding hillsides, punching giant holes in buildings, roads and bridges and flattening cars. Most of Beichuan had been reduced to a heap of twisted metal and crushed masonry under which lay the bodies of its former residents. The sickly sweet smell of death was so pervasive it had desensitised the noses of the sniffer dogs working with the rescue teams, rendering the animals useless.

Already, though, there were 130,000 troops toiling in the earthquake zone and the Chinese were welcoming help from across the world. There was the deeply strange sight of United States Air Force transport planes parked at Chengdu's airport. And the government had relaxed its usual restrictions on the foreign media, so I found myself standing twenty metres away from China's then president, Hu Jintao, as he toured Beichuan.

At the same time in Burma, two weeks after Nargis's apocalyptic arrival, Than Shwe acknowledged finally the enormity of the cyclone's impact. The generals started allowing aid into the country, but it had to be handed over to the *Tatmadaw* for distribution. They stole some of it for themselves. Those Nargis victims who did receive overseas relief supplies were told they were a gift from the junta. If it hadn't been for China setting such an immediate example of how to react to a natural calamity, it's possible that no foreign aid would ever have reached the Delta.

Precious little was distributed in the end. A month after Nargis, the United Nations estimated that only around half of the almost 2.5 million people affected had received any aid or help, and that assistance was classified as 'basic'. With their homes gone many survivors had nothing left to stay in the Delta for, and they started moving to Yangon and Hlaing Tharyar.

My contact in the township was one of the Nargis refugees. Htay Htay Myint lost her six-year-old son when the cyclone destroyed her village. 'He was taken away in the flood,' she told me as she squatted on her heels, washing up dishes. Like many Nargis victims, his body was never found and was probably swept out to the Andaman Sea, or else he decomposed in some unknown rice paddy or inlet alongside countless others.

His mother had little time or energy to mourn him properly. 'My house collapsed and all my possessions were lost,' she said in a flat, emotionless tone. 'We had to stay in a monastery after that. The government gave us money for rice, but nothing to rebuild my house. We didn't own land anyway, so my husband and I and our eldest son decided to come here.'

Her home, when Thida and I finally found it, is a one-room shack. Almost all the shanty dwellings are a similar size, and some house large families. Htay Htay Myint and her husband sleep on mats on the floor, cook outside on a wood fire and have to pay 100 kyat (5p) for every bucket of water they use. Such living conditions are standard for many people in rural areas across Burma, but this was Yangon, by far the most prosperous place in the country.

Diminutive with an amiable, determined face, Htay Htay Myint is forty and house-proud. Her shack was spotless: its wooden floor overlaid with a dusted plastic covering which we sat on, clothes hanging from nails and cooking utensils stacked neatly in a corner. Halfway up one of the walls was a small altar with flowers, incense and a picture of the Gautama Buddha.

Every day she takes it in turns with her husband to man a roadside stall selling cold drinks. 'We make 3,000–4,000 kyat [£1.50–£2] a day at best. On a bad day it's just 1,500 kyat [75p],' said Htay Htay Myint. It is enough for them to eat, but not to pay the 40,000 kyat (£20) a month rent for their home. The days of squatters being able to put up their own huts in Hlaing Tharyar are long gone. Yangon's council is much more rigorous about banning new shacks from being built, so some of the first arrivals to the area have become landlords, renting out the places they constructed years ago.

Having lived in a number of different shanties during their time in Hlaing Tharyar, Htay Htay Myint and her husband rely now on their surviving son and his wife to remit the rent each month. They left Hlaing Tharyar to work in a fish-canning factory in Thailand. 'I don't think it is fair that we have to pay so much to live here, but we have no choice,' said Htay Htay Myint. Rents have risen everywhere in Yangon since the NLD's 2015 election victory, even in the slums, an unwelcome democracy dividend.

Like every squatter, she and her husband face the prospect of being evicted without notice: 'The government says our houses are all illegal and that this is their land. If they want to evict us, they can do it any time.' U Hla Myint, Htay Htay Myint's neighbour and no relation, can testify to that. 'Our first house here was demolished by the government. They didn't give us any warning, so we came to this street two years ago,' he said.

A former fisherman from Bogale Township in the Delta, his arms covered in faded Buddhist tattoos, U Hla Myint had heard our conversation with Htay Htay Myint and walked into her home to join us. With the shanties separated from each other by thin bamboo walls, and often lacking front doors, there is no privacy in Hlaing Tharyar. Bogale was one of the areas worst hit by Nargis, but U Hla Myint and his family survived, only to lose their fishing grounds a year later when the local government sold them to a private company.

Even before Nargis and the economic decline of the Delta, shanty towns were nothing new in Yangon. Nor are they confined just to Hlaing Tharyar: smaller shanty settlements can be found elsewhere in the city, too. But these communities of displaced rural people have always been feared by whoever has governed Yangon, so there are constant efforts to eradicate them. It is a process that began during the colonial era. Then, the shanty towns were regarded by the British as potential recruiting grounds for Burma's nationalists.

By the 1950s the shanties were seen as disfiguring Yangon's aesthetic and 165,000 squatters were summarily moved to new townships in the east and north of the city by the army. In 1989 more squatters were ousted from Yangon, punishment for their support of the pro-democracy protests of the previous year. A decade later, the junta started offering free homes to shanty dwellers willing to relocate to villages in northern Rakhine State, an effort to boost Buddhist numbers in a region where Rohingya Muslims made up the majority of the population.

Now, it is the NLD who want the shanties gone, viewing them as incubators for both crime and discontent with the government. Ambitious plans have been announced to create eight extra townships in Yangon to cope with the expected influx of people from rural areas over the next two decades, although there is no guarantee that they will be provided with affordable homes. It is a development which, if it happens, will result in Yangon expanding even further west, almost to the point where the Delta begins.

Some of the squatters have been radicalised by their experiences of living and working in Hlaing Tharyar. The area has become the centre of Burma's fledgling trade union movement. Banned, unsurprisingly, by the generals, unions only became legal in Burma in 2012. Hlaing Tharyar is now the site of frequent demonstrations, sometimes of ten thousand people or more, protesting against poor conditions, unpaid overtime and the arbitrary sacking of workers.

Most of the factories prefer to employ women aged between eighteen and twenty-five, partly because they used to be able to pay them less than men. These days, though, the workers are represented by shop stewards, who are typically women of the same age who left school in their early teens and moved to Yangon from the Delta or other rural regions. Men in the area tend to look for jobs on building sites, road construction crews, or as porters in the giant fish market Thida and I passed on the way to Hlaing Tharyar.

U Hla Myint is sixty, an old man in Burma where the life expectancy for males is just sixty-four. Unfit for hard physical labour, his youngest daughter supports him and his wife by working in one of the garment factories, despite being only sixteen, two years below the legal age for such work. She earns 4,800 kyat a day (£2.70), the official minimum daily wage in Burma. 'I rented an identity card from an eighteen-year-old neighbour so she could show it to the factory to get the job. I don't think the factory cares and we need the money,' said U Hla Myint.

Security guards man the gates of the factories and their owners don't welcome curious foreign visitors, so I had no chance of getting inside one of them. But Thida knew a woman in the area who ran a small independent garment workshop. Hundreds of such sweatshops supplement the factories in Hlaing Tharyar. On the other side of the highway to the factory zone, it consisted of two semi-open-air, one-storey buildings housing thirty-odd women operating sewing machines, cutting fabric or pressing the finished clothes.

'We make whatever the customers want: *htamein, longyi*, shirts, dresses, all for the local market,' said the owner, a brisk woman in her fifties with dandruff-flecked short hair. 'But it's hard. Sometimes, it's a struggle to pay the salaries. The workers want higher pay, but they don't want to work hard. Often, we have a set delivery date from the customers and if we don't make it, we don't get paid all the money. The young people are lazy.'

Retaining workers is becoming increasingly difficult in Hlaing Tharyar. 'There are so many workshops and factories now, so the workers move around all the time looking for more money,' said the boss. 'Girls who can sew get 120,000 kyat [£63] per month, other workers get 70,000–80,000 kyat [£37–£42]. They work eight in the morning to six at night, six days a week. The girls have to be eighteen and I check their identity cards. But often they say they don't have one or that they've lost it. So many excuses.'

Looking around the workshop it was clear that while the women at the sewing machines were over eighteen, many of the others weren't even close to that age. Thida and I approached three girls sitting at a table piled high with cheap-looking cotton dresses. I said 'Hello' and they started giggling, a sure sign in Burma that they were embarrassed. 'They probably haven't spoken to a foreigner before,' said Thida.

Khine Hmin Wai was the youngest, just thirteen. She sat cross-legged on a plastic stool in pyjama bottoms and a grimy white t-shirt, her long hair plaited down her back and *thanaka* on her cheeks, cutting loose threads off the clothes and sometimes sewing on buttons. 'It's an easy job and not tiring,' she said. I asked her if she'd rather be at school but Khine Hmin Wai was happier working. 'I didn't like school. I went until I was eight. I don't miss it. My parents couldn't afford for me to go anyway, they needed me to work. But I can read and write.'

From Bogale, the same township as U Hla Myint, her family had come to Hlaing Tharyar four years ago. 'We didn't have our own farm. My parents worked on other people's farms, or on construction sites. Now, me, my sister and brother work to support them. My sister is a sewer here and my brother works at the big market. I like Yangon more than Bogale. There are no jobs in Bogale.'

Yadana Lwin, whose pale oval face and delicate features made her stand out from the other girls, looked as young as Khine Hmin Wai but said she was sixteen. Her father worked at the market, too. She had been born in Hlaing Tharyar and it was the only place she had ever known. 'I want to be a dressmaker like my older sister,' she said.

May Thin Zar was from a village near Pathein, the largest town in the Delta. Her family had moved to Hlaing Tharyar when she was nine. She was fifteen now, darker and livelier than the others with her thick hair in a pink bow. Had the boss asked to see her identity card before hiring her? 'No,' she replied. 'I don't have one anyway. I'd have to go back to my village to get one and I'd miss work. I'd have to pay for it too. It cost my sister 50,000 kyat [£26.50] when she applied for one.'

She had been employed in a nearby food market before coming to the workshop. 'My job was to put salads into bags. It was boring. Here, I can learn how to sew,' she said. Alone out of the three May Thin Zar missed education and had ambitions beyond Hlaing Tharyar's factories and workshops. 'I'd like to have stayed at school, but my parents couldn't afford it. I want to be a policewoman. I like the idea of catching thieves,' she said with a cheeky grin.

All three lived close to the workshop and we accompanied Yadana Lwin as she returned to her home during the lunch break. I wondered what she normally ate each day. 'Bread in the morning and a fish curry at lunchtime. I don't have rice or meat in the evening. Maybe some instant noodles,' she told me, as we turned onto a narrow dust track lined on both sides with shanties and strewn with discarded food packaging and plastic bags. I thought we should buy her lunch. 'Where?' said Thida. 'There are no restaurants here.'

Halfway down the track Yadana Lwin stopped outside two one-room bamboo shacks. 'Ten of us live here, my uncle and his children too,' she said. Her mother was sitting under an awning at the front of one of the huts, cooking cubes of tofu which she sold in batches for a few hundred kyat. Inside the hut, men were playing cards and drinking local whisky. Yadana Lwin's mum had the same oval face as her daughter, but her teeth were stained red from betel nut and she looked older than her age of thirty-six. 'I've been here twenty years,' she said.

Prior to that, the family lived in a shanty settlement in Sanchaung, a now fashionable area north-west of Yangon's downtown. 'The government wanted to build a bridge, so we had to move. We lived in a house across from this one at first. That's where my daughter was born.' Now there were rumours that all the shacks in the area would be demolished to make space for more factories. 'We'll find out soon,' she said. I asked her what she would do if they had to leave. 'I don't know,' she replied, and went back to frying tofu.

5

Crime and Punishment

The main cell at Hlaing Tharyar's police station was like something out of a western. Thick metal bars stretched vertically across a wide corridor, a gate in the middle, secured with a heavy chain and padlock, providing access. Behind the bars were around thirty men in t-shirts, singlets and *longyi* squatting on the floor or sitting against the concrete walls at the back and sides of the cell. Some were obviously drunk.

'Lots of visitors today,' joked the policeman guarding the gate. 'They're mostly in for fighting.' Given the archaic nature of his lock-up, I thought he should have a cowboy hat on his head and a sheriff's star on his chest. Instead, he was in the grey shirt and blue trousers that is the uniform of Burma's police. Nor did he have a revolver strapped to one of his legs. 'We rarely have to carry or use our guns. Hardly any of the criminals here have them. If they use a weapon, it's almost always a knife,' he told me.

A few miles past the factory zone, set back from the main road that leads to the Delta, the Hlaing Tharyar police station is a typical Burmese government building. It is ramshackle and run-down, with pale green paint peeling off its walls, dirty white-tiled floors – concrete in the three cells – plastic chairs for staff and visitors and a distinct lack of modern technology. I spied only a couple of computers but an awful lot of paperwork.

Files were stacked a foot high on U Thein Naing's desk. 'There's no time to be bored in Hlaing Tharyar,' he said cheerfully. 'This is the busiest police station in Yangon. We have the most crime because the area is very crowded: there are too many people here, most of them from the Delta. We need more police really.' About 230 officers patrol an area that is home to 700,000 people, based out of the station we were in and twelve smaller outposts spread around the township.

I was here to discover if the media's portrayal of Hlaing Tharyar as the unofficial headquarters of the Yangon underworld is true. For the newspapers, the shanty settlements are the gang-infested haunts of delinquents who terrorise their neighbours and roam far and wide across the city robbing, raping and murdering as they go. In that narrative it is the squatters, rather than native Yangonites, who are responsible for the crime wave that many locals believe Yangon has been experiencing ever since the junta stepped down.

My initial request to accompany the police for a day and a night as they patrolled the township had been refused. I was told that my safety could not be guaranteed. And I was a foreigner. But U Thein Naing, the senior detective on the Hlaing Tharyar force, had agreed to meet me to discuss the policing and crime issues he and his fellow officers faced.

Gap-toothed, with a lined face, close-cropped greying hair and glasses perched on the end of his nose, U Thein Naing's plain-clothes outfit consisted of a white shirt and black trousers. He has been a policeman for thirty-five of his fifty-five years, stationed first in Mandalay before being posted to

Yangon ten years ago. With her instinctive distrust of male authority, Thida was immediately suspicious of him. 'He drinks. Look at his hands shaking,' she muttered.

Boozer or not, I thought U Thein Naing was genial enough for a big-city copper. He sprang his first surprise by telling me that detectives aren't allowed to detain criminals in Burma. 'You have to be in uniform to arrest people, so we can only do surveillance.' Like most law enforcement in Asia, though, the police in Burma are essentially a reactive force: crimes happen and then they try and solve them. Far less time is spent preventing illegal activity from occurring in the first place.

Much crime in Asia is prompted by drug abuse, but not in Hlaing Tharyar. 'People here can't really afford to buy drugs. Some people take "WY" but heroin is very rare,' said U Thein Naing. 'WY' is the local name for yaba, a cheap methamphetamine pill found all across Asia, but manufactured mostly in the frontier areas of Shan State in eastern Burma. The initials 'WY', said to stand for 'World's Yours', are sometimes stamped on the pills.

Instead, it is gambling that is the cause of most wrongdoing in Hlaing Tharyar. 'Gambling, whether cards, dice or betting on the lottery numbers, is the big issue. People gamble and lose money and then they either have to borrow or steal money to live. That's when the problems start,' said U Thein Naing. 'There are secret gambling clubs all over the shanty areas. If you see any, let me know.'

U Thein Naing was unusually frank for a Burmese official in asserting that it is poverty which is at the root of almost all common crime in the township. 'The people are poor and worried about money all the time. They drink, get angry and confused and fights happen, even if there is no real reason for them. People get very angry here. They're under so much pressure, always wondering if they have enough money to feed their families. We detain them only if the fight involves weapons or someone gets badly hurt.'

Khin Zaw Lwin, a 25-year-old market porter, had already told me how the shanty settlements become more menacing at night, when the female factory workers scurry back to the relative safety of their shacks and the men wind down with alcohol after a day spent labouring. 'There's a lot of drinking and a lot of fighting,' he said. 'Mostly we drink local spirit because it's cheaper than beer or whisky. A small bottle costs 400 kyat [20p].'

More serious offences occur as well. 'We get quite a lot of murders. There's been a couple this month, as well as a few rapes,' said U Thein Naing in the offhand, dispassionate tone of the veteran policeman. There were around 200 murders and 270 rapes in Yangon in 2017, although sexual violence remains hugely under-reported in Burma, a consequence largely of the stigma associated with being a victim of it.

Nationwide, the number of murders has increased by over 40 per cent since the junta stepped down. With the notable exception of the Philippines, Burma's homicide rate per capita is higher than most other countries in Southeast Asia, according to the United Nations Office on Drugs and Crime. And those statistics do not include the casualties of the country's continuing civil wars.

Present-day figures, though, pale into insignificance compared to the murder rate in the colonial era and the period immediately after independence. Once the British took control, the constraints of traditional Burmese society began to loosen as the centuries-old system of indirect rule by local authority figures was replaced abruptly by direct rule from foreigners and their subordinates. Arbitration as a means of settling disputes was replaced by an alien legal system. The bonds tying people to the already vague idea of the state in Burma frayed quickly.

Most grew poorer, too, as new taxes were introduced and people in the Delta lost their land. Many people in lower Burma ended up living in rural slums not dissimilar to the shanty settlements of Hlaing Tharyar. Nor were there jobs for the locals in Yangon and the other cities, as Indian and Chinese immigrants dominated the urban labour market.

What resulted was a rapid rise in crime. Between 1886 and 1930, the already high murder rate more than doubled and robbery rates tripled. When Ritchie Gardiner arrived in Taungoo in 1926 he was astonished to be told that Burma had the highest murder rate per capita in the world. In one district of lower Burma alone, home to half a million people, there were eighty-seven murders in 1927, the same number as there were in Chicago that year, a city of over two million people at the time and in the grip of an Al Capone-inspired gang war.

Dacoity was an especial problem. 'Dacoit' is a Hindi word meaning a member of an armed gang of robbers. Such bands were present in Burma long before the British arrived. The teak stockade that surrounded Yangon in King Alaungpaya's time was there to keep out villains as much as tigers. Vincentius Sangermano, an Italian Catholic priest who lived in Yangon between 1783 and 1808, wrote of how, 'Our ears are constantly assailed with the intelligence of robberies and murders.'

During the colonial period, though, dacoity was endemic in Burma. The robbery rate was almost four times higher than India's, and any armed band of five or more people was automatically classified as a dacoit gang. Often shot on the spot when captured, dacoits were subject to harsher penalties than individual armed robbers. But that didn't dissuade them. Armed with the *dah*, the Burmese equivalent of the machete, spears and the odd home-made or stolen gun, dacoits were still plaguing rural Burma long after the Second World War.

In part their presence reflected how little real control the British exerted beyond Yangon, Mandalay and the major towns, for all the new laws they introduced. Colonial rule over all Burma lasted for sixty-two years, only three years longer than the time it had taken to conquer the country. But huge swathes of Burma, in the east, west and north especially, were governed by a smattering of officials whose main preoccupation was collecting taxes. Even in lower Burma, the lack of adequate roads made governance difficult.

Many Burmese had their first encounter with the colonial state in a police station, as Britain responded to the country becoming the crime capital of their empire by locking up the locals. Insein Prison, the largest jail in the empire, was built in the far north of Yangon. Like almost all of the prisons constructed in the colonial era, Insein, pronounced 'insane', is still in use today: criminals convicted in Hlaing Tharyar are sent there. It has always housed political prisoners as well. Aung San Suu Kyi was jailed there on three separate occasions.

Sixteen thousand inmates were occupying Burma's jails by 1910. Yet the crime wave continued and the prison population kept on increasing. By the time George Orwell was posted to Insein Township in 1925 as an assistant district superintendent the British were imprisoning 20,000 Burmese annually. Ritchie Gardiner's memoir describes the frequent sight of shackled prisoners from Taungoo's jail being employed as labourers in the town.

Floggings were increasingly used in an attempt to deter crime, too. The 1909 Whipping Act allowed for thirty to fifty strokes to be laid on the backs of the unfortunate recipients. The law was only repealed by Burma's parliament in 2014. Executions became more common as well. There were 113 hangings in 1923. Four years later, the number had jumped to 191. Orwell's 1931 essay 'A Hanging' offers a vivid description of an execution he witnessed, with the shaken officials downing whisky at eight in the morning to steady their nerves after it was over.

Burma maintains the death penalty today, although no one is believed to have been hanged since 1988. Under the junta almost all of those who went to the gallows at Insein Prison were dissidents, including one of the leaders of the 1974 Rangoon University protests, or members of the ethnic minority armies fighting the *Tatmadaw* in the borderlands. Hangings were at least more merciful than the punishments meted out in seventeenth- and eighteenth-century Yangon. Criminals could be crucified, disembowelled or impaled at the execution grounds in what is now the west of downtown.

Not all crime in the colonial era was committed by the locals. Michael Symes, the emissary of the East India Company, had noted as early as 1800 that Yangon attracted 'foreigners of desperate fortune'. As more Europeans arrived during the nineteenth century, the city became known as a bolthole for chancers who had exhausted their credit elsewhere in Asia and were looking to roll the dice one more time. Entertainment venues catering for them soon began to open.

By the early twentieth century the concentration of brothels, dive bars and nightclubs in downtown ensured that Rangoon rivalled Shanghai – then known as the whore of the Orient – for licentious living. Russian, Japanese, Chinese and Indian sex workers were present in the city, alongside Burmese and ethnic minority women. Sexually transmitted diseases were rife and Rangoon was the equivalent of Bangkok today: a place where sex could be bought easily and foreigners believed themselves released from the codes of behaviour and morality that bound them elsewhere.

Cocaine and opium were widely available as well and Rangoon's reputation as a sin city began to seep into the popular literature of the time. In B. M. Croker's not very imaginatively titled 1917 novel *The Road to Mandalay: A Tale of Burma*, a young English woman in Rangoon gets caught up with a gang of dastardly cocaine-trafficking Germans, before the Burma Police in the shape of a handsome Irishman ride to the rescue.

Another English novelist, Sax Rohmer, created the arch villain Fu Manchu in 1913, the most evocative expression of the xenophobic fear that western civilisation was under threat from the Chinese hordes: the yellow peril. But long before Fu Manchu and his nemesis Nayland Smith confronted each other in the foggy streets of an imaginary London, they had first crossed swords in Burma, a country that, according to Rohmer, was 'a plague spot, the home to much that is unclean and much that is inexplicable'.

Rohmer didn't visit Burma or China. But Rangoon's Chinese community of the time was involved in crime, especially drugs, gambling and prostitution. Chinatown was home to nightclubs and brothels on 19th Street, opium dens on 23rd Street and illicit gambling joints everywhere. The different Chinese secret societies – the Rangoon branches of the triads that had originated in mainland China and followed the Chinese diaspora – clashed sometimes in downtown's streets, chopping each other with knives and axes.

Chinese shopkeepers maintained a near-monopoly on the legal outlets for alcohol and opium, too, not just in Rangoon but across Burma. That was something of an irony, as the

East India Company had pioneered the Asian opium trade by selling Indian poppy to China. Later, the British fought two wars with the Chinese in the mid-nineteenth century for the right to flood their country with the sticky black drug.

Opium could be bought from licensed shops, a useful source of income for the colonists. George Orwell's father worked in the department of the Indian Civil Service charged with collecting the revenue, although addicts were invariably forced to turn to the black market to supplement the official allowance. Cocaine fiends, too, could obtain legal supplies, with dubious preparations containing the drug advertised in the newspapers as 'liquefied energy'.

Alcohol and opium were illegal for the locals until the British arrived; those caught indulging risked execution. The more astute colonial officials wondered if the new and easy availability of liquor and drugs might have something to do with the huge leap in violent crime. Certainly the Burmese believed that. Chinese shopkeepers were sometimes driven out of villages because their stocks of beer, whisky and opium were viewed as corrupting the youth.

Drugs were the downfall of one of the more colourful British ne'er-do-wells of the period and the likely inspiration for Flory, the lead character in *Burmese Days*. Herbert Robinson was an officer in the Indian Army who first came to Burma in 1915, before serving in present-day Iraq during the latter part of the First World War. By 1921 he was back in India and broke, so he applied for a posting with the Burma Military Police.

Spending two years in a remote part of Burma with the military police was one of the favourite options for India-based army officers looking to save money. In *Burmese Days*, Flory's rival for the hand of the ghastly Miss Lackersteen, who has come to Burma in search of a husband, is the superbly obnoxious Lieutenant Verrall. No longer able to afford his polo-playing lifestyle in India, Verrall has been forced to downgrade to the police.

Robinson was posted to Putao in the far north of Burma. He could not have chosen a better place to cut his costs, because Putao was and is as remote as it gets in Burma. In the colonial era it was part of what was known as the North East Frontier, the region where Burma meets the north-east of India, south-eastern Tibet and the south-west of China. Less storied than its equivalent on the other side of colonial India, the North West Frontier with Afghanistan, there was nothing to do in Putao except fish for Himalayan snow trout.

C. M. Enriquez, another British officer who served with the police in the far north, wrote of how dull life was in a region populated largely by ethnic minorities and a handful of foreigners, all male as European women weren't allowed to reside in the frontier areas. 'So we get rich, or pay our bills, but we do not live – we merely exist,' moaned Enriquez in his 1916 book *A Burmese Enchantment*. He went on to list the drawbacks of life on the North East Frontier: 'Solitude, fever, dirt, lice, mails that miss, goat's meat for months on end, and chicken in all its hideous disguises.'

Responsible for a vast area consisting mainly of mountain villages that could only be reached by lengthy journeys on horseback or foot, Robinson spent much of his time travelling and settling arcane disputes, while keeping an eye on the Chinese traders who came across the border from neighbouring Yunnan Province. But he made the mistake of sleeping with a local woman accused of poisoning her husband, a case he was required to adjudicate. She was found not guilty and Robinson was cashiered for consorting with the natives.

Ordered to Mandalay in March 1923 to await his dismissal from the army, where Orwell was doing his training at the city's police college, Robinson smoked opium for the first time in the back room of a Chinese restaurant. Almost immediately he gave himself over to the narcotic, becoming a nightly visitor to the opium dens. He dabbled with cocaine, too, which he took in the local style: mixed with lime and smeared under the lower lip as if it was betel nut. Before long Robinson acquired a reputation as the most debauched Englishman in Mandalay.

That was enough for Orwell, ever the contrarian, to make a beeline for him. Their friendship cannot have impressed Orwell's police superiors, but it provided him with valuable material for *Burmese Days*. Robinson's sojourn with the Putao police gave Orwell the reason for Verrall's presence in Burma. And Robinson's dreamy personality – he fancied himself a poet when he wasn't on the opium pipe – found its fictional equivalent in the misfit Flory's fantasies of abandoning Burma to lead a bohemian life elsewhere.

Flory's ignominious end was also inspired by the way Robinson was ruined by his affair with a local lady. After Flory's Burmese mistress reveals their relationship to the entire British community while they are at church, Flory shoots himself. Robinson attempted suicide in 1925, by which time he had briefly become a Buddhist monk in a failed attempt to kick opium and was penniless, having sold all his clothes and possessions to fund his habit. Unlike Flory, Robinson botched the job and succeeded only in blinding himself with his gunshot.

Repatriated back to the UK by the authorities, Robinson lived out the rest of his days in south London. In 1942 he published an elusive and grandiloquent memoir of his time in Burma, *A Modern De Quincey: Autobiography of an Opium Addict*. Orwell gave it a kind review in the *Observer*, the least he could do after appropriating so many of Robinson's experiences for *Burmese Days*.

Rangoon's louche reputation began to fade in the 1950s, as the city entered a much-romanticised, so-called 'golden era' when Burma had a seemingly democratically elected government, a relatively free media and jobs were plentiful. But for the first time it was the Burmese, those who could afford it anyway, rather than foreigners who got to enjoy those bars and clubs that stayed open, or who went to the races and sailed on Inya Lake.

It didn't last. Rangoon's days as a party town were ended for good by the puritanical junta. After 1962 nightclubs and brothels were shuttered, beauty contests banned and the Rangoon racecourse closed. The generals were so fearful of pernicious western influences that they didn't even allow people to watch TV for two decades: a nationwide television service was only introduced in 1981. When I first came to Yangon in 2010 you could count the number of western-style bars, outside of hotels, on one hand.

Yangon is still more straitlaced than other major cities in Southeast Asia. Even predominantly Muslim Jakarta and Kuala Lumpur are livelier than Buddhist Yangon. There are just a few nightclubs and music venues. Alcohol is widely consumed – Burma has never gone back to the prohibition that existed before the colonial era – but the beer stations close at ten and almost every bar in town is shut by midnight.

After that, the stray dogs dominate the streets and only a few simple tea shops cater for insomniacs and night workers.

This is a poor city, too, and that limits its entertainment potential as much as any inherent, Buddhist-inspired modesty in the locals. The average monthly income is around 360,000 kyat (£190), but millions of Yangonites survive on far less than that, not just in the shanty settlements, and are faced with a higher cost of living than anywhere else in Burma. One of the reasons the pagodas in the city are always busy is that they are free to enter.

Poverty is all too apparent almost everywhere in Yangon: the ten-year-old tea shop waiters working twelve-hour days because their families need their tiny salaries, or children scavenging rubbish to recycle it for small change. Cigarettes sold individually because many people can't afford the 600 kyat (30p) needed to buy a pack of Burmese smokes, the roadside food vendors for those who aren't rich enough for even a noodle dish in a cheap restaurant, people on the street buying and selling stained second-hand pairs of flip-flops.

Little has improved financially for ordinary people since Aung San Suu Kyi and the NLD came to power, and there is no sign that will change in the near future. More than anything else, Burma's spluttering economy ensures that Yangon's crime rate remains high. More than 52,000 people were charged with various offences in Yangon in 2017, a roughly 20 per cent increase on the year before. Mandalay experienced a sharp rise in crime in 2017 as well, including over forty murders. But homicides apart, most of the crimes being committed – bag-snatchings and muggings, thefts of mobile phones and car break-ins – are indicative of people stealing to find the money to live.

'If you can't earn a couple of thousand kyat a day, you and your children don't eat. That's a problem across Yangon, not just in Hlaing Tharyar,' U Thein Naing told me in the police station. He was sceptical about the scapegoating of the shanty dwellers as criminals by the media and other Yangonites. 'The bad reputation Hlaing Tharyar residents have isn't really deserved. Actually, I don't think many people leave the township to commit crime. Most people here work in factories or are labourers. They're too busy to be committing crimes elsewhere.'

Nor can the spate of robberies of taxi drivers be attributed solely to the squatters. 'When the taxi drivers get robbed that's mostly people from outside the area telling the driver to take them to Hlaing Tharyar because it's a long journey from downtown and they can rob them on the way. It's not really Hlaing Tharyar crime,' explained U Thein Naing.

He was also dismissive of the theory that the township is overrun with criminal gangs. 'There's not much organised crime. If there was then people wouldn't be so willing to give us information. They'd be intimidated. Local people often help us or call us anonymously.' More often it is the factory owners and the absentee landlords who recruit groups of thugs from the area to collect rents or evict other squatters so they can take over the land on which the shanties are built.

Yet none of U Thein Naing's smooth answers explained Yangon's current murder rate, let alone the staggering number of killings in the near past. Burma led the world in homicides well into the 1950s. There were almost 12,000 murders, or about four a day, across the country in the first nine years after Burma gained independence. And those were the crimes that were officially recorded. It was only after the junta imposed its draconian rule that the figure started to drop.

Such a propensity for violence stems perhaps from the impact of the never-ending sequence of conflict that has characterised the last millennium in Burma. The country's recorded history starts with rival kingdoms and fiefdoms battling for power and moves on to armies invading Thailand or fighting incursions from Mongol, Chinese or British forces. Then came the rebellions against colonial rule and the appalling impact of the Second World War, resistance to the generals and now the continuing wars between the *Tatmadaw* and the ethnic minority armies in the borderlands.

Under the junta, little bad news, whether crime or natural disasters, was ever reported by the media. Censorship made people feel safe from criminals, while a wide-ranging state surveillance operation, along with the regime's willingness to employ violence against anyone seen as a threat, left many too scared to break the law. Now, just as the British fatally loosened the ties of traditional Burmese society, the replacement of the junta with an elected government means the country has entered a period where the certainties of the last fifty years are no more.

Violent crime came close to home only once during my time in Yangon. A 26-year-old civil servant who lived down the street was raped and stabbed to death while on her way home one evening. Her parents set out chairs and tables, with soft drinks and snacks, under a temporary awning outside their apartment building. At first I thought a wedding was imminent, until I heard about the murder and realised it was for people coming to mourn the victim. But her killer wasn't a shanty dweller from Hlaing Tharyar. He was a taxi driver from the adjoining township to mine who had murdered her after an argument over the cab fare.

6

Christmas in Chin

Christmas was coming. Tinsel was draped over the imitation trees installed in the shopping malls, while seasonal songs and carols played at a subdued volume in the supermarkets catering for the middle classes. A 'Happy Christmas' sign in fairy lights had even been rigged up above one of the main streets in downtown. In Yangon, like elsewhere in Asia, Christmas is now firmly on the calendar, not as a religious festival but as a shopping opportunity, a chance for retailers to boost their sales with some Yuletide kitsch.

Celebrating Christmas in Burma in the traditional manner is easy enough. Christianity is the second-most popular religion, with around 6 per cent of the population practising it, and Yangon has many churches. But for all the steeples and spires, Christianity is very much a fringe faith across lower and central Burma, where the country is most fervently Buddhist.

Instead you have to travel to the borderlands to experience Christian Burma. In Kachin State in the far north and Chin State in the west, as well as parts of Kayin State in the southeast and Shan State to the east, the different ethnic minorities who make up the majority of the population in those regions are predominantly Christian. Around 80 per cent of them are Protestant, overwhelmingly Baptist and split between a disorientating array of denominations, with the remainder Catholic.

Most were introduced to Christianity by the missionaries – American, British, French and Portuguese – who started arriving in Yangon in the seventeenth century, but who found the greatest number of converts from the early nineteenth century onwards among the animist hill peoples living close to Burma's frontiers. Missionaries remained active until 1966, when Ne Win expelled them, but local evangelists continued proselytising, while their American counterparts have made a stealthy comeback since the junta stepped down, travelling under the guise of ordinary tourists.

Chin State was a particularly tempting place to celebrate the festive season, because around 90 per cent of the Chin people are Christian and their homeland is the only one of Burma's states and regions where Buddhists are not a majority. Sixteen centuries of Buddhism in Burma have left little mark on the Chin Hills. Instead, the Chin stayed mostly animist, worshipping the spirits they believed to inhabit the forests, mountains and rivers around them, until American missionaries began arriving in 1899. Even today, the most remote parts of southern Chin State are the last significant strongholds of animism in Burma.

Occupying the far west of the country, Chin State was closed to foreigners under the generals and remains little visited today. Pushed tight against the border with Bangladesh in the south of the state and India in the north, it is home to almost half a million Chin, who refer to the territory as 'Chinland', and is the least-developed and poorest of Burma's states.

A mountainous, heavily forested region spotted with villages that perch precariously on the hillsides or by the side of the mainly unsealed roads that connect the few small towns, Chin is almost completely untouched by industry. It is home to subsistence farmers whose lives are made harder every forty-eight years when the bamboo forests that cover a third of the state flower at the same time and black rats emerge to feast on bamboo seeds, before multiplying and fanning out across Chin to ravage grain, corn and rice stocks. The inevitable result is a famine, the last of which occurred in 2006.

I had been to Chin before but only in the rainy season, when clouds descend low over the hills, creating a near-permanent white-out that can reduce visibility to a few metres. With most of Chin at well over a thousand metres above sea level, the locals shiver through the rains, which last longer there than anywhere else in the country. They don woolly hats, fleeces and even socks – a rare sight in Burma and still worn with flip-flops – and generally act as if they are in the Arctic. The endless drizzle reminded me of England in November.

Travelling in Chin becomes a laborious process during the monsoon, as the dirt roads turn into a dark brown morass, studded with rocks flushed off the hillsides by the rains. The jammed jeeps and minivans serving as public transport lurch along at no more than ten miles an hour. Sometimes we all got out to push our vehicles to a point where the wheels could gain some traction. So bad are the roads that the *Tatmadaw* takes to patrolling on horseback during the rainy season.

For Christmas I decided to go to northern Chin, the least-known area of the state. With no airport in Chin and no railway running even close, the gateway to the north is Kalaymyo, always abbreviated to Kalay, in neighbouring

Sagaing Region. A low-rise town of mostly wooden houses, bisected by two main roads and surrounded by rice paddies, Kalay sprawls along a fertile valley, overlooked to its west by the foothills of the mountains that dominate Chin.

The bus to Kalay departed Yangon at noon. All the other passengers were Chin people returning home for Christmas. In honour of its regular route the bus had a biblical name, 'Solomon', emblazoned across the top of the windscreen. The in-bus entertainment consisted of Christian music videos played on a loop and featuring an earnest Chin band fronted by a chubby girl who sang in a high, sweet voice. I couldn't wait to get off when we pulled into Kalay twenty-odd hours later.

Despite being in Sagaing Region, Kalay has a valid claim to being the true capital of Chinland, because its Chin population is more than double the 25,000 people who live in Hakha, the actual capital of Chin State. Hakha sits at almost 1,900 metres and is located on either side of a road that runs around the lower slopes of a mountain prone to devastating landslides in the rainy season.

Thousands of residents were left homeless in 2015 after part of the mountain collapsed following torrential rain. So dangerous is Hakha's location that geologists have recommended rebuilding the town in a more stable place. On my one visit at the tail end of the monsoon the sight and sound of rocks tumbling down the hillsides onto Hakha was all too frequent for my liking. I wasn't surprised so many Chin have moved to Kalay. At least you can live there without the fear of being brained by a random boulder.

Returning to Kalay after trips to Chin is always a pleasure, as dull and nondescript as the town is. It is a chance to be reacquainted with what in the West are regarded as the essentials of civilisation: showers, electricity, a mobile phone signal, ATMs, shops that stock more than only the most basic items, restaurants that don't just offer noodles and rice. And while Kalay, like all towns in Burma, isn't clean, in Chin you're permanently dirty: either covered in mud in the rainy season or coated with fine yellow dust the rest of the time.

Kalay offers more than just a measure of comfort and material pleasures to the Chin. Employment opportunities are as limited in Kalay as elsewhere in provincial Burma, but the Chin living there have the prospect of more than merely subsisting on a hill farm. Unknown numbers of Chin have left their homeland to work elsewhere in Burma, with far more overseas in India and Malaysia as migrant workers. 'There's no money in Chinland,' a girl told me on the bus from Yangon.

During the Second World War Kalay was a key staging post on the British retreat to India. The Japanese invaded Burma in January 1942, advancing swiftly from Thailand into Kayin State in the south-east. With them was the former student leader Aung San, now commanding the few hundred men of the newly formed Burma Independence Army. Aung San and other leading nationalists, including future junta leader Ne Win, had joined forces with Japan in their efforts to rid Burma of the British.

Lacking the numbers to check the Japanese advance, the British forces fell back. A month after the invasion, civilians were told to evacuate Rangoon. 'It is difficult for anyone who has not experienced this to realise what it meant,' wrote Ritchie Gardiner, by now an army officer, in his memoir. 'A previously prosperous and bustling city of some 600,000 people became empty at a stroke.' The few remaining people were mostly criminals. The jails were emptied and law and order, always precarious in Burma, broke down completely.

By March it was clear that Rangoon could not be defended. Anything of potential value to the Japanese – the port and oil refineries – was blown up and the British left. It was the effective end of their rule in Burma. Gardiner was one of the last men out, clambering aboard a boat bound for Calcutta at midnight on 8 March. As they sailed downriver he witnessed the destruction of the city's infrastructure. Later, he struggled to find the words to describe the sight of the Rangoon riverside ablaze, the giant clouds of smoke billowing northwards across the rest of the city.

'Large parts of the residential and to a smaller extent the industrial areas had already been burnt, either in the bombings or by arson. But that was nothing to the demolition of the wharves and the refineries,' wrote Gardiner. 'The Burmah Oil Company's tanks were said to contain 18,000,000 gallons and there were others beside that, so perhaps the size of the fires can be imagined. The smoke and fires from the oil was almost unbelievable.'

Gardiner was fortunate to be on a boat. The bulk of the British forces retreated north-west and attempted to hold the oil fields at Yenangyaung, south of Mandalay. Outflanked by the Japanese, a headlong overland flight to India began. Trailing behind the soldiers were over half a million refugees, mostly Indians who feared both the Japanese and mistreatment from the Burmese now that they were free of the British.

Up to 50,000 civilians are thought to have died fleeing either to Manipur State in India via Kalay, or across the high mountain passes of the North East Frontier in Kachin State to Assam. The dirt tracks were a clogged mass of the sick, wounded and dying, with bodies littering the route as people dropped dead. Many more died of disease or from the effects of the journey once they reached India.

There are no reminders of the Second World War in Kalay now. The only place that looks like a bomb site is the bus station, a rocky, cracked forecourt surrounded by distressed tea shops and cement-walled ticket offices that lack doors. They look as if someone started building them, only to give up halfway through the job. I was there soon after dawn, when most transport to Chin departs, and nabbed a seat in a minivan going to Tedim, where I intended to spend Christmas.

We headed west along one of Kalay's two main roads for a few miles, before stopping at a police checkpoint. After a cursory inspection we rattled across a small bridge, turned left and then we were in Chin State. Almost immediately the road narrowed, so that the trucks coming in the opposite direction were squeezing past us, and began to ascend the hills in tight bends. From now on, the road would run straight or flat for no more than twenty or thirty metres at a stretch.

Soon after we started the climb the driver pulled over. He turned to face us, held out his hands palms up and said, 'Let's pray'. A passenger recited the Lord's Prayer, before everyone said, 'Amen'. All bus journeys in Chin State start with an invocation for safe passage, and when you first see the near-vertical drops of hundreds of metres on one side of the road, the uprooted trees and telegraph poles leaning at forty-five-degree angles after being struck by landslides, you understand why.

Hamlets of houses built out of wooden planks occupied the left-hand side of the road, with the rear of the homes hanging over the cliff edge, supported by skinny stilts. In Chin it is safer to site your home over a sheer drop than to place it directly under the turbulent mountains. Every so often we ran through more substantial villages with the odd tea shop and general store, where the hillside had been partially excavated, allowing for houses to line both sides of the road.

God was everywhere. Just as Buddhists maintain a shrine outside or in their homes, shops and places of work, so in Chin State the image of Jesus is painted on houses, or his name invoked in slogans, 'Jesus Love Me', 'In God We Trust', 'Hosanna', daubed on their walls. Rough wooden crosses were planted to the side of homes. Sometimes there was a reference to a biblical text written on a door. 'Exodus 9:26' – 'Only in the land of Goshen, where the children of Israel were, was there no hail' – was popular and very appropriate given the risk of falling rocks.

Other houses had a nameplate above the door inscribed with their denomination or congregation, a handy way of avoiding the attention of any passing missionaries. Many people, both the passengers around me and those in the hamlets, wore t-shirts or hoodies proclaiming their church and their love of God. Conspicuous by their absence were the monasteries and golden pagodas found in the villages and towns far below, as well as the packs of stray dogs. We had left Buddhist Burma behind and entered a Christian hill country.

Beneath us Kalay was fading in the haze – the dust that swirls in the Chin State air whenever it isn't raining – becoming an indeterminate huddle of trees interspersed with a few flashes of white indicating concrete buildings. Ahead, the road curved incessantly as it traversed the mountainsides, winding ever higher, the vehicles in the far distance looking as small as a child's toy cars.

Two hours' driving brought us to a simple crossroads. Another few hours forward was Falam and then beyond it Hakha. Falam had been the administrative headquarters of Chin State in the colonial period, when the region was known as the Chin Hills.

Along with the rest of the borderlands – the areas now occupied by Shan, Kachin, Kayin States and parts of Rakhine State and Sagaing Region – Chin was governed separately from the rest of the country by the Burma Frontier Service.

It was a practical decision for the British, but one which has proved to be disastrous for the subsequent relationship between the Bamar, the mostly Buddhist majority ethnic group, and the minorities. The colonial civil servants reasoned that as the frontier areas were so remote, it would be costly and inefficient to oversee them in the same way as the rest of the country. They did not foresee that the result would be to make ethnicity the key political issue in the future independent Burma.

Inland Burma experienced direct rule by foreigners, with the monarchy discarded and a new governance model imposed on the Bamar. But once the borderlands were pacified, a process that took decades in some places, the British formed alliances with the clan chiefs and hereditary rulers. In return for keeping a diminished form of their authority they could collect the new taxes and maintain the peace, thus allowing the British to staff the frontier areas with a skeleton crew of officials and avoid the expense of policing them.

Bamar resentment over the way the minorities were experiencing a milder form of colonialism began to be voiced from the 1920s onwards, as the nationalist cause gathered pace in Yangon and lower Burma. Adding to their ire was the fact that while the Bamar were mostly barred from joining the army of the colonial state, the Chin, Kachin, Shan and Karen were all recruited to the Burma Rifles, the regiment raised to fight alongside the British in the First and Second World Wars. In the eyes of many Bamar, the minorities were traitors for signing up with the colonial oppressors.

Being ruled separately meant that the peoples of the borderlands missed out on the economic and political developments occurring elsewhere in Burma. The Chin Hills in particular were barely touched by progress. Crucially, too, the minorities anticipated that their reward for fighting with the British against the Japanese and Aung San and his Bamar army would be self-rule for their areas after independence. The British government in London, however, didn't seriously consider that possibility, even if some British officials and soldiers who had served in Burma believed that the minorities had earned the right to autonomy.

Those fault lines between the Bamar and the other ethnic groups have never been bridged. In February 1947 Aung San met the leaders of the Chin, Kachin and Shan peoples at the now notorious Panglong Conference in Shan State. He persuaded them to join the future Union of Burma by acknowledging their right to self-determination over their regions, as well as the principle of a separate state for Kachin.

February 12th, the date of the agreement, is still celebrated in Burma as Union Day, although few of the ethnic minorities join the party. When Burma became independent in January 1948, by which time Aung San had been assassinated, the Chin, Shan and Kachin didn't get their own self-governing states. Within months, the Karen minority was fighting the *Tatmadaw* and the civil wars that continue today had begun.

Along with most of the major ethnic groups, the Chin formed their own armed movement, the Chin Independence Army, to fight for self-rule. It was succeeded by the Chin National Army, the military wing of the Chin National Front, one of a number of Chin political organisations dedicated to achieving autonomy for Chinland within a genuine federal union.

Never as active as the ethnic armies in Shan and Kachin states, and always smaller, the Chin militia broke ranks in 2012 and signed an official ceasefire with the *Tatmadaw* after more than a decade when no fighting took place. The Chin haven't forgotten that they were promised self-rule, but most are no longer prepared to wage war to get it.

My minivan didn't carry on towards Falam and Hakha. We turned right, for Tedim, the largest town in the north and the second biggest settlement in Chin State. Now, the sheer drop was on the right-hand side of the road and stretching away as far as the eye could see were ravines, their hunchbacked hillsides a mass of forest in different shades of dark green, plunging down to a meandering, steel-grey river. Desultory clouds hung above the hills in a radiant blue sky, creating a natural palette of primary colours.

Apart from a few sand-coloured scars running horizontally across the hills, indicating tracks wide enough only for a motorbike to travel them, the landscape looked as if it had never seen any humans. Closer to Kalay, just a few trees survive on the slate-rock hills, the rest either harvested or destroyed in landslides. But while logging is increasing throughout Chin, and the locals consume a lot of wood for cooking and construction, the lack of roads ensures the forests are still far more plentiful than almost anywhere else in Burma.

When we stopped for a break it was only a few metres' scramble down shifting soil to pine trees and ferns, amidst which pale red orchids grew. I knew that barking deer, boars, wild goats and jungle cats were somewhere nearby in the forests, still hunted by the locals, while above me, circling in the near distance, was a hawk, its eyes scanning the ground as it searched for prey.

Five hours after leaving Kalay the road dipped and we descended into Tedim. Like every other settlement of any size in Chin its shops and open-air market run along the ridgetop road, while wooden houses raised up above the yellow earth on stilts and roofed with corrugated iron are dotted down the hillside on one side, or amble up it on the other. White and pink cherry blossom blooms around the homes, which are accessed by steep dirt paths, and clumps of banana, bamboo and pine trees form natural barriers between them.

Off in the middle distance, beyond further galleries of green gorges that rose and fell in uneven order, was Kennedy Peak, named after its surveyor and the second highest mountain in Chin State. Towering a thousand metres above Tedim, itself over 1,700 metres above sea level, and covered in tightly packed pine trees, Kennedy Peak was the scene of a vicious battle in October 1944. Japanese troops dug in on its slopes were wiped out by British and Indian soldiers, who had returned to Burma along the same route they had retreated down two years before.

From 1943 the area around Tedim became a war zone. A year later the Japanese were being chased out of Chin State to inland Burma. With Chinese and American soldiers invading from Yunnan in China, the Japanese were pushed back to Rangoon, until they were forced to abandon it in May 1945, a little over three years after the British had evacuated the city. By then Aung San's soldiers had switched sides, joining the Allied armies after it became clear that Japan would not grant Burma any form of real independence.

Hidden in the forests on Kennedy Peak are a few relics of the fighting. Fort White, a colonial outpost, was taken over by the Japanese and then flattened by bombing, although the faint outlines of the building can still be seen and the odd tank and shell case remains. But almost all the detritus of the war has been scavenged and sold for scrap and there is no memorial. For the Chin the fort is an unwelcome memory of how they were subjugated by the British, no matter that some of them fought here against the Japanese, too.

At the guest house in Tedim there were box-like rooms, separated from each other by thin wooden partitions, with ill-fitting windows and a bed and a chair for furniture. It was typical Chin State accommodation and I knew I was in for some cold nights. Hot water for washing had to be heated in a giant, blackened kettle and, as usual in Chin, there was electricity only between six and ten in the evening and on alternate days. 'But I think we'll get power on Christmas Eve and Christmas Day,' said the guest-house owner. 'It's a special time.'

Out on the main street, which slopes sharply from south to north before ascending again on the outskirts of town, the festive spirit was apparent. Trucks with people standing in the back wearing Santa hats clattered past, kicking up the dust, their speakers blaring out 'Hark the Herald Angels Sing' and other carols, as well as an assortment of seasonal hits. Wham!'s 'Last Christmas' was a favourite, and there was even a Spanish entry with the song 'Feliz Navidad'.

Walking uphill, the houses of God were all around me. In Chin State the churches of the major congregations are always the most substantial buildings in any town. But there are much smaller house churches scattered throughout Tedim, too. They have names like 'Jehovah Shalom' and 'Messianic Brotherhood Fellowship'. Some have no more than fifty members, led by a single, charismatic preacher. The early missionaries attracted a similar cult-like following, just as the Chin were in thrall to village shamans until most of them abandoned animism for Christianity.

Tedim's most renowned missionary is Joseph Herbert Cope, who gave his name to the Cope Memorial Baptist Church. A white- and red-tiled building with two red steeples that rises above the main road through town, the church dates back to 1910, two years after Cope arrived in Chin from Philadelphia. He is legendary for devising a Roman alphabet for the Tedim dialect – every town and area in Chin State has its own local language – and translating the Bible into it.

Before arriving in Tedim I had already decided to attend the Christmas Day service at the Cope Memorial Church. But I discovered that there would be competition for my presence from other churches. 'Brother, I see you are writing.' I looked up to see a short, stocky, broad-faced man standing by my table in a tea shop. His hair was in a topknot and he wore round glasses. 'I think you are a journalist or a writer. My name is John. I am a writer too.'

'Brother' is the standard greeting in Chin State between men who don't know each other. We shook hands and I invited John to join me. Like many Chin he spoke good English. For the older generation it is often the consequence of a missionary education. Younger Chin pick up English from working in India and Malaysia. A familiarity with the gospels helps their grasp of the language as well. The Bible also provides the Chin with a stock of names to go along with the local ones they are given at birth.

John, though, had learned his English while studying to be a Catholic priest in Yangon. 'I went to St Joseph's Seminary for four years. Then I realised it was not my vocation to be a priest. My vocation was to have a family.' There was no hint of regret or resignation from John over his decision to leave the priesthood, just a placid acceptance of his fate, signalled by a calm gaze. He was originally from Tonzang, a town north of Tedim and fifty miles south of the border with India's Manipur State. Now John was thirty-one, married to a Tedim woman and father to two young daughters.

His writing career involved translating religious tracts from English into Burmese. 'I've translated five books. The last one was a life of Mother Teresa. I'm translating *50 Questions about Catholicism* now.' His publisher was in India and I wondered if he got royalties, the question all writers ask. 'No,' he said with a brief grimace. 'Some of the books are on their second and third editions now.'

He invited me to meet his family and asked where I was going to church at Christmas. He shook his head when I told him. 'You don't want to go there,' said John. 'Come to midnight Mass with me. The bishop is coming from Kalay. I'll introduce you.' I explained that I had never been to a Baptist service and so wanted to attend the Cope Memorial Church, but promised to come and meet the bishop on Christmas Day.

Rivalry between the different churches in Tedim is fierce, and there is some poaching of souls. John told me how one of his friends had fallen out with the local Catholic priest and so in a fit of pique had crossed over to the Evangelical Baptist Conference, the second largest Baptist congregation after the Cope Memorial Church and known by its initials 'EBC', and got himself rebaptised.

Another John, who I referred to privately as John the Baptist to distinguish him from John the Catholic in ecumenical matters, attempted subsequently to get me to join him at the EBC service. I wasn't sure what the difference between the EBC and the Cope church was. 'In the EBC we believe salvation is by grace alone. If you accept Jesus as your lord and saviour that is enough,' explained John the Baptist.

'The Cope Memorial Baptists believe you have to do some good works too. But we do good works anyway.'

Leaving John the Catholic at the tea shop, I went in search of lunch. Food, or rather where to find it over Christmas, was already occupying my thoughts. I had learned to my cost on previous visits to Chin State that there are hardly any restaurants and they are closed on Sundays and any Christian holiday, as are all shops, apart from those run by the handful of Buddhists. I hadn't seen any Buddhist places in Tedim and I couldn't rely on the few remaining animists either, as they all lived out in the surrounding villages. I made sure lunch was a big meal.

Glory laughed when I told her that I was stockpiling instant noodles for Christmas Eve and Christmas Day. We had met on the bus from Yangon to Kalay. She had just flown in from Singapore, where she worked as a nanny, to return to Tedim for the holidays. I found her in her sister's clothes shop, almost obscured by the racks of cheap shirts, dresses and jeans imported from India. Glory is tiny even by the standards of Burma, where many women are super-slight. 'I am small size,' as she put it succinctly.

She invited me to join her family for Christmas Day. But Glory is a member of the Bible Presbyterian Church, with a small congregation of 150 people. And I didn't want to interrupt her reunion with her family after a year away in Singapore. She is one of seven children. Chin families are large, not only due to the high infant mortality rate – 9 per cent die before their fifth birthday – but because they are required to support their parents once they are too old to farm.

Her father had passed away when she was ten and four years later Glory was on a plane to Singapore for the first time. 'I had an identity card that said I was seventeen,' she recalled. 'I wasn't scared. Most of my friends went away to work at the same age, or a bit older, to Malaysia or India, some to Yangon, a few to China. My mum didn't want me to leave school, but I wanted to. I knew she needed help. My mum is very old. She is sixty and can't work.'

Now twenty, Glory has been employed by the same family for the last six years, initially as a maid. 'The first time I went it was arranged through an agent in Yangon. He took seven months of my year's salary,' said Glory. 'I deal with the family direct now. They are Chinese, rich. He owns a company making keys and she works for a bank. They have two kids, three and one and a half. They're nice. I earn five hundred Singapore dollars [£270] a month. If I was working here in my sister's shop, I'd earn maybe thirty dollars [£16] a month.'

Glory's life in Singapore is mostly work. 'I get one day off a week. I go to church and then go home. Sometimes, I'll go shopping. I miss my family and friends often. Sometimes, I am crying. Then, I'll call my mum. It was harder when I was younger. I cried a lot then.' Her annual holiday at Christmas is the highlight of her year. 'Christmas in Singapore is nothing. It's Chinese New Year that is big,' said Glory. 'But here we'll go to our church on Christmas Eve and Christmas Day and sing and pray and see our friends.'

Enveloping Glory was a vague melancholy which seemed at odds with her age, but which I had observed in other girls from Burma and China separated from their families at a young age to go to work. She would fall suddenly silent, as if some uncomfortable memory had muscled in to the present to harass her, or maybe my questions made her think of her imminent return to Singapore for another year away from home.

With the ease of youth, though, Glory's personality could switch from the pensive to the animated in a moment. Her eyes flashed into life and her features became mobile when she talked about her love of playing guitar and singing – 'My dream job is to be a musician' – or her family and church and the children she looked after. 'I can't sleep when they're ill or sad,' she told me.

All the money being remitted back to Chin State by its migrant workers is having an impact. 'Chin is definitely developing. Each time I come back I see new buildings. It is already very different from when I was young,' said Glory, unaware that I thought she still was. John the Baptist had already mentioned the new houses that have sprung up on their stilts across Tedim in recent years, all financed by Chin children in far-off cities. 'We call them dollar houses,' he told me.

That night the power was off and Tedim was black by six in the evening. Only a few houses were showing lights, run off rare generators owned by people who must have had every child in the family working overseas to pay for them. Outside, the headlights of passing motorbikes lit up the potholes and the ditches that ran on either side of the road. But the darkness did allow for fine stargazing, the constellations arcing high over Kennedy Peak, a fitting portent for the onset of Christmas Eve.

Long before it was light I was woken by someone nearby blasting 'Love Potion Number 9' at full volume, drowning out the roosters that were beginning to stir. Within a couple of hours Tedim was busy. Carols and hymns floated out of open doors, as choirs and bands rehearsed, while in front of one church there was the sight of pigs being hacked up, their heads and trotters on display alongside the meat. In Chin, where turkeys are unknown, it is customary to eat pork at Christmas.

Invited for lunch with John the Catholic and his family, there was little to do after that but wait for the evening, when the churches held services, before people gathered at home with their families and friends. Fireworks popped and whooshed into the sky and the sound of 'By the Rivers of Babylon' and 'Jingle Bells', playing everywhere in town it seemed, reverberated across the Chin Hills until late.

Early morning on Christmas Day and the clouds were hovering above the valleys, a white sea of mist waiting to be burned off by the rising sun which bathed half the hillside in soft yellow light, while casting the rest into shade. The dawn chill in the air was long gone as I made my way to church beneath a gloriously blue sky. People were in their Sunday best, some in suits and western-style dresses, but many in traditional Chin clothing.

Women wear a version of the *htamein*, with bold horizontal or vertical stripes, and a close-fitting blouse. For men, it is loose fitting shirts and trousers, accompanied by loud striped jackets, waistcoats or a wide scarf around the shoulders, topped with a turban-like hat. Just as there are more than fifty different dialects in Chin State, though, so clothing styles vary in each district. All that is ubiquitous are the red, green, white and black stripes – the Chin colours – that decorate many of the garments.

Beijing was the last place I had attended a church service, when I went to midnight Mass at the Catholic cathedral one Christmas. But from the moment I arrived at the Cope Memorial Church I was made to feel welcome, shaking multiple hands and being wished 'Happy Christmas' over and over. I was offered a seat in a pew at the front, which I declined for a place at the back.

Inside, it was a full house with children wriggling on laps and latecomers standing. Light streamed in through the double rows of windows set in both sides of the white walls. Instead of an altar there was a stage for the choir and band, the five pastors and the most honoured members of the congregation. Two Christmas trees flanked either end of the stage. Above it hung a banner with a biblical text in the capitalised Roman alphabet invented by Joseph Cope.

Preach, pray and sing: the form of the service soon became apparent. There wasn't much mystery to it. The pastors took it in turns to read from the New Testament and offer their own Christmas sermons, and we were down on our knees a lot. But the choir was excellent and everyone sang wholeheartedly. A high proportion of people in Burma have good voices, regardless of their ethnicity.

Towards the end of the service, as some of the congregation were being invited on stage to receive presents for good works performed during the year, I slipped out. Back on the main road I turned onto a dirt path and headed down the hillside to join Tedim's Catholics at St Mary's Church. Smaller than the Cope Memorial, there were three rows of plastic chairs outside the open doors to accommodate the Christmas overspill. The Mass was almost over and it ended with a rousing rendition of 'Happy Birthday'.

Perplexed, I wondered if it was perhaps a Chin custom to sing the song in honour of Jesus's arrival in the world. Then John introduced me to the bishop, Felix Lian Khen Thang. 'It's my birthday today too,' he said with a smile. The song had been for him. Silver-haired, bespectacled and beaming, Bishop Felix was surrounded by people waiting to greet him but extended a generous invitation to me to join him for dinner that evening.

Back at the guest house, I was preparing the latest batch of instant noodles, happy at the thought of a real meal to come, when John the Baptist arrived fresh from the EBC service with a Christmas present of a large avocado, a kind gesture. He declined my offer to share it and the noodles, saying he had to get back to his family's celebration. I ate outside on the guest-house deck, gazing out on the valley below, smoke rising from homes across the hillside as Christmas lunches were prepared.

Later, as dusk was falling, I returned to St Mary's for dinner with Bishop Felix. John the Catholic was there, along with the NLD MP for Hakha, who, confusingly, was from Tedim, and various local dignitaries. We tucked into a decent pork curry, accompanied by a spicy salad. Bishop Felix enjoyed a modest birthday glass of red wine. Everyone else drank beer or whisky.

Bishop Felix's diocese has Kalay as its headquarters, but extends south across northern Chin State towards Hakha. 'It's big geographically but not in people. Catholics are a minority here. There are far more Baptists,' he said. 'I try and get around the diocese as much as I can. I have a land cruiser and a driver for that.' Bishop Felix had spent time in Rome as a young priest and, less than a year after we met, he oversaw Pope Francis's visit to the country, the first by a pontiff to Burma.

After dinner, I thanked Bishop Felix and he wished me well and departed to stay with the local priest. Everyone else dispersed to their homes. The electricity was on and Tedim was bright and lively for the second night running as I walked back to the guest house. The same songs I had been hearing for the last three days were being given one last airing, before they were put aside for another year. Christmas in Chin was almost over.

7

The Road to Heaven

None of my Tedim friends advised visiting Siangsawn Village. When I asked Bishop Felix about the place, he rolled his eyes and said he hadn't been there and would never go. Glory thought Siangsawn's residents were 'strange'. The mere mention of the village's name made John the Baptist look sorrowful, as if he was including its benighted pagan population in his daily prayers. 'It's not that Siangsawn people don't like Christians,' said John the Catholic. 'They don't like anyone who isn't from Siangsawn.'

Unique in Chin State, Siangsawn is neither Christian nor animist. Instead, its residents follow their own religion: the Pau Cin Hau Sect. Dating back to the late nineteenth century and named after its founder, its adherents believe in a deity whom they call 'Pasian', the Chin word for God. He sent his son, Pau Cin Hau, to earth as a prophet in human form to save the Chin from worshipping the animist spirits.

Pau Cin Hau was in fact born in Tedim and gained a reputation as a seer from an early age: he is said to have predicted the British invasion of the Chin Hills. But it wasn't until he was forty, in 1899, that he realised he was the son of

God. From then on, he toured the local villages searching out followers for his religion. His key selling point was that it didn't involve ritual sacrifices.

Traditional Chin beliefs required animals to be sacrificed if someone was ill – to appease the evil spirits causing the sickness – and whenever there was a death, so the spirits of the dead animals could guide the departed to animist heaven. As there was no conventional medical treatment available in the region, and fighting between different villages was common, many locals were constantly in debt from purchasing beasts for sacrifices.

So persuasive was Pau Cin Hau that by the 1930s over 35,000 people believed him to be the son of God, and the British recognised his sect as an official religion. Around 4,000 Chin still adhere to it today. With its founder long dead, the mantle of leadership has skipped a generation and passed to a new prophet, Kam Suan Mang, the grandson of Pau Cin Hau. In 2007 he established a headquarters for the sect in Siangsawn, whose name translates as 'heaven', a village an hour's walk north-east of Tedim.

One afternoon I took the road to heaven, striding away from Tedim's centre. This was also the route to Tonzang, John the Catholic's hometown, which, after the road leaves Tedim and descends into the valleys, follows the Manipur River as it runs south from its namesake state across the border in India. But after forty-five minutes of heading uphill past a succession of house churches, I turned right onto a steep path that tumbled down the hillside before rising up again on the final ascent to Siangsawn.

A sign next to the gate guarding the village read, 'No Alcohol, No Drugs, No Tobacco'. It reminded me of flying into Brunei, where the customs officers confiscate your duty-free and the only stimulant legally available is coffee. Once inside the gate, though, it soon became obvious that not only is Siangsawn different to other Chin villages, it was unlike any place I had ever been to in Burma or elsewhere.

Wide and long dirt lanes are lined with square, hollowed-out stones painted white, with plants for decoration inside them, and the bungalow-like houses on both sides of the streets are mostly built of brick rather than wood. They are spaced evenly apart from each other, their gardens neat vegetable patches of black beans, tomatoes and avocados. Villages in Burma are not known for their order or cleanliness and Siangsawn appeared unnaturally tidy: not a speck of litter to be seen, no chickens pecking about, no dogs, goats or pigs nosing around.

Looking down on the village's main street, up a slight rise, was a noticeably larger house painted pink, its second-storey terrace commanding views across the valley to Tedim. Subsequently I learned that it is the home of Siangsawn's prophet, Kam Suan Mang, built and paid for by the other villagers. I wondered why his house needed to be so much bigger and more luxurious than anyone else's.

At first it felt as if I was wandering around a smaller Chin State equivalent of an English new town, soulless and uniform, and in fact Siangsawn is officially designated as a 'model village'. But there was no one about and it was strangely silent – villages in Burma are always noisy, with children playing, people chopping wood, making repairs or revving motorbikes. I began to think I had strayed into the sort of sinister settlement featured in John Wyndham novels, a Chin Midwich, a hill country Village of the Damned.

Finally, I found someone to talk to. Mang Son Pau was twenty-five and on a return visit to Siangsawn from his new home in Waterloo, Iowa, where he ran a grocery store. Looking sharp in a smart jacket and *longyi*, he had come back in search of a wife. 'It's difficult, as there aren't that many followers of Pau Cin Hau,' he told me. 'Only here and a few other places in northern Chin.' But Mang Son Pau was a catch anywhere in Burma: a US resident with his own business, and he was newly married to a girl from Tek Loi, a village nearby split between Christians and Pau Cin Hau sect members.

'Lots of visitors come here from around Chin and Sagaing Region,' he said, asking me what I thought of Siangsawn. I told him I was impressed by how immaculate it was, and inquired about the reason for the sign at the village entrance. 'We are clean. Tedim is dirty. If people come here trying to drink or smoke or be rude, we tell them to leave, that they cannot do that here. We are clean,' repeated Mang Son Pau. Do they ever get missionaries visiting? 'No. We've never had a missionary here,' he said with a faint smile.

He explained that each family gives one-seventh of their income to the community. Siangsawn is largely self-sufficient and contact with Tedim is kept to a bare minimum, to avoid any chance of Christian contamination. 'We have our own electricity and our own water supply from down the hill, where our fields and animals are. We grow corn and bananas mostly.' The money pays also for their school, as well as supporting the sect leader who, like a proper village squire, doesn't do any farming himself.

I asked Mang Son Pau if I could meet the prophet. 'I think he's busy,' he said. 'I just want to say "hello". It won't take long,' I promised. Reluctantly, Mang Son Pau got on the phone and a few minutes later Kam Suan Mang came walking down the street. Middle-aged, squat, like many Chin men, and portly in a fleece and *longyi*, he looked at me quizzically, as if he was trying to guess what my game was. We shook hands and he led us into a nearby house, where he was greeted with reverence by the owner.

Over cups of green tea, Kam Suan Mang described his duties as the Siangsawn sage. 'I speak to Pasian and he speaks to me,' he said. 'I spend most days reading and writing and I wait for Pasian to communicate with me. Sometimes, it is in a dream.' He was on his guard, gloves held high. Kam Suan Mang wasn't used to having to justify his role or actions. Mang Son Pau offered the information that the prophet's dreams had started when he was twelve, and that he had flown around the world guided by an angel in one of them.

Their religion has some superficial similarities with Christianity – it has its own equivalent of heaven, populated by angels, and a hell overseen by a devil. But its scriptures are thin and vague, with much talk of harmony and a notable insistence on the primacy of the prophet. And I didn't believe it was a coincidence that Kam Suan Mang had inherited the role of sect leader from his grandfather. Would his own grandson follow in his footsteps and become the next prophet? 'I don't know,' he replied. 'Pasian hasn't said yet.'

What did he think of the Christians in Tedim? 'If they truly believe in their faith, then that is fine.' I asked if he tried to convert people to his religion. 'No. It's the opposite. Many people come here and say they want to join us. But we accept very few. Most betray themselves by their actions as not being faithful or genuine,' said Kam Suan Mang.

Tea finished, the prophet returned to his home to await the next message from his God. Mang Son Pau took me to a building that housed a statue of the sect's founder Pau Cin Hau, as well as portraits and photos of both him and Kam Suan Mang and their families. He bowed low to the effigy. By now, with the cult-like nature of the Pau Cin Hau religion apparent, I was in full agreement with Glory's assessment of the village's residents.

The road to Siangsawn isn't the only highway to heaven from Tedim. Another road leads to Rih Lake on the frontier with India's Mizoram State. For the Mizo people, who can also be found in northern Chin, the heart-shaped lake has immense spiritual significance as the gateway to Pialrâl, their traditional animist interpretation of a seventh heaven. Pialrâl is a place reserved only for those whose lives have been so exemplary that they deserve to reside in an exalted state of happiness forever.

Making a pilgrimage to Rih Lake is a must for the Mizo and I wanted to see it, too. The lake lies close to Rihkhawdar, a border town thirty-four miles due west of Tedim and a four-hour drive on Chin roads even when it is not raining. I was faced with hitching there. It was a Sunday and no public transport runs on the Sabbath in Chin State. But trucks heading to Rihkhawdar and India pass through Tedim, so I sat at the junction of the road to Mizo heaven hoping for a ride.

Waiting with me were two of the town eccentrics, just about the only people who weren't in one of Tedim's churches for the Sunday services. The two men weren't going to Rihkhawdar, but they had nothing else to do except sit next to me and gleefully repeat over and over again that no trucks would be travelling west today. One had a lolling head and a speech impediment, the other an off-kilter smile and nails caked in thick layers of pink varnish.

After an hour a heavily laden lorry appeared, groaning on its axles. I offered 10,000 kyat (£5.50) for a lift. The driver, his left cheek stuffed full of betel nut, nodded and I climbed in. Waving goodbye, my new friends appeared unconcerned by the inaccuracy of their transport information. As we pulled away the driver's teenage assistant started showing me photos on his phone of crashes they had witnessed previously on the route: crushed jeeps and trucks that had gone off the edge of the road and cartwheeled to their doom.

Perched high in the cab between the two of them, I had a crow's-nest view as we left Tedim and reeled downhill on a dirt and gravel track. In the valley beneath us were villages of one-room houses surrounded by small fields of rice, corn and millet, through which slender streams sidled. In the distance thick forest covered the hills on the other side of the valley.

Wooden churches were prominent in the bigger settlements, proof that it has taken little over a century for Christianity to supplant the ancient animist beliefs in all but a handful of villages in northern Chin. Followers of the traditional folk religion are more common in the hills of the south of the state, where elderly women whose faces are tattooed with intricate patterns of dots and lines can still be found. It is a tradition that supposedly started as a means of preventing Chin ladies from being kidnapped by marauding bands of Bamar men looking for wives.

Pointing ahead, the driver indicated a thin yellow strip that switchbacked up the mountain beyond us. It was in the shape of a rough 'Z', as if Zorro had slashed at the hillside with his rapier, carving his symbol into the earth. 'That's the road to Rihkhawdar,' said the driver. I asked what he was carrying and where he was going. 'Coconuts to Chennai.' I thought that was quite a drive from Kalay. 'Not really,' replied the driver. 'The roads are much better in India.'

Reaching the bottom of the valley, we began the climb up the mountain, the truck's engine whining in low gear as it zigzagged slowly uphill, grinding through the potholes, while we bounced against each other's shoulders as the truck swayed from side to side. It took almost two hours to reach the summit, where a woman sat outside a miserable shack selling energy drinks, fuel for the passing drivers.

Descending the other side of the mountain was quicker and easier and Rihkhawdar came into sight after an hour, a cluster of buildings by the side of the Harhva River, which separates Burma from India here. Two bridges, one for vehicles and one for pedestrians, link the countries. On the outskirts of town the driver stopped at the customs area to declare his cargo and then we drove down Rihkhawdar's hectic main street, lined with scruffy shops and teahouses, where he dropped me near the pedestrian bridge before driving on to India.

Rihkhawdar's sole guest house accepting westerners was run by a family of friendly Muslims, the only ones I ever met in Chin State, who were watching Indian TV when I walked in. As a border town Rihkhawdar has one foot in India and the rupee is as common a currency as the kyat. Most of the goods in the stores are Indian imports too, which means more choice than is usual in Chin.

Not long after arriving I received a visit from the police, a middle-aged Chin officer who had come from his post by the red and white pedestrian bridge. He wanted to know what I was doing in town. I said I was here to visit Rih Lake. 'OK. No problem.' The guest house had told me that locals can cross over to India for the day, as long as they return by 6 p.m. I asked the policeman if I could do the same and take a look at Zokhawthar, the town on the Indian side of the border. 'No,' he said, and got up and left.

Following him to the bridge, I discovered a string of bottle shops cum bars close to it. They were rough and crude: Chin imitations of a Wild West saloon in a one-horse town. There was a single counter where the alcohol was bought, and tables in the darkened rear occupied by people who looked like they had been drinking for a while. The shops were surprisingly well stocked with western beers and spirits and I discovered that they cater mostly for Mizo people from across the border in India, rather than the Chin.

Mizoram was one of India's dry states, where alcohol is illegal, until 2015. Even now, drinkers require a liquor card to purchase booze and are rationed to no more than ten beers a month. Most of the customers in the bottle shops had crossed over from Zokhawthar for the day to take advantage of Chin State's less censorious attitude to beer and whisky. But just as Rihkhawdar's residents have to be back in Burma by six in the evening, so the Mizo must return to India at the same time, only after a day spent imbibing.

As the deadline approached they started to stagger off, some supported by their more sober friends. But not everyone made it by six, when the gate at the Chin State end of the bridge is closed. The latecomers had to swing out onto the side of the structure and climb along it from spar to spar, until they reached a point where they could squeeze between the bars and be pulled onto the bridge proper by the Indian border guards, who walked down from their post to assist them.

With a thirty-foot drop down to the mud-brown river, it wasn't a manoeuvre I would have liked to perform when I was sober, let alone drunk. But I suspected that many of the Mizo inebriates had done it before. The police on the Burma side found the spectacle hilarious, and didn't lift a finger to help. To me, it just confirmed the futility of prohibition. Some people will do anything for a drink.

In the morning, the teenage son of the guest-house family drove me the fifteen minutes to Rih Lake on his motorbike. We shot down the main street, past the bridge for trucks, and then accelerated up through the main residential area of Rihkhawdar, where homes are ranged across the hillside, struggling for space amidst the trees. On the other side of the river Zokhawthar looked far more substantial and wealthier, its buildings bigger and sturdier, with many cars visible on the paved roads.

Rih Lake appeared almost out of nowhere, as we bumped along a muddy trail lined with ferns and bamboo on one side and on the other by rice paddies. The lake was smaller than I expected but almost perfectly heart shaped, the sunlight reflecting off water a deep blue colour that barely rippled in the breeze. Rice fields ring much of the lake, running close to the water's edge, while beyond its northern shore hills of ink-green forest climb towards the border with India.

For the souls bound for Pialrâl, the Mizo heaven, ascending those slopes was the final part of their journey. After crossing the lake they drank from a spring hidden in the trees whose waters erased all memories of their earthly lives, before plucking a flower that prepared them for nirvana. Like the Chin, the Mizo are now largely Protestant, but the utopian ideal of Pialrâl has been blended with the Christian concept of paradise, allowing Rih Lake to maintain its sacred and mystical status.

No homes surround Rih Lake, with only a few houses barely visible from ground level looking down on it from the east. Nor are there any temples to indicate that it is a portal to a higher existence. Animists believe only in the water, trees, earth and sky, all alive with unseen spirits. The landscape itself is holy here and I could almost hear it breathing as I walked, the grass, ferns and foliage waving in the wind as if trying to communicate a message.

To travel to Pialrâl is to dog the footsteps of Hermes, the Greek god of travellers and borderlands whose duties included escorting souls to the afterlife. It is to depart the mortal for the celestial, taking flight into the sky that hangs above Rih Lake like a brilliant blue banner speckled with white clouds. But even at ground level the colours here appear more enhanced than elsewhere, especially when the rice paddies glisten lime-green before the harvest, or the forested hills take on a brooding, almost ominous shade after rain.

Sitting at the centre of this potent terrain the lake itself is supremely serene, the limpid, placid water a challenge to those who would dive in and disturb the spirits. That the lake's banks form the outline of a heart is almost too serendipitous. It is as if the lake has been carved by hand into the land, one last natural wonder for the departed to see before they float off to an eternity of joy.

Returning to the glorified truck park that is the centre of Rihkhawdar was to be reintroduced to the unwelcome temporal world. Smaller than Tedim and Hakha but busier, thanks to the cross-border trade, Rihkhawdar's main street is fume-filled and loud during daylight hours, as the lorries creep towards the bridge to India or jam the sides of the road as their drivers grab one last meal in Burma. It makes an unlikely pathway to paradise.

Later that day I joined Michael and Mr Mang in one of the tea shops on the street, a basic affair where a woman used her bare hands to scoop noodles into dirty, chipped bowls and then ladled a dubious broth over them. I had met Michael and Mr Mang briefly in Tedim over Christmas. Now they had returned to Rihkhawdar and their jobs as teachers at its high school. They were twenty-five, graduates of the University of Kalay, and the fiercest advocates of an independent Chinland that I met in my time there.

'Every ethnic state wants independence, whether it's Rakhine, Shan, Kachin or Kayin. We're no different. Article 5 of the Panglong agreement said Burma would be a federated state,' stated Michael with the certainty of the true believer. With his roving, inquisitive eyes, green camouflage trousers and a black leather jacket zipped to the neck, Michael was the more belligerent of the pair. Mr Mang had betel-stained teeth and was slighter and quieter in a hoodie and skinny jeans.

Article 5 of the 1947 agreement signed by Aung San and the Shan, Chin and Kachin leaders accepted the principle of autonomy for the frontier areas after independence. The subsequent failure to deliver on that promise sparked the civil wars still going on in the north and east of Burma. But the Chin militias stopped skirmishing with the *Tatmadaw* in the 1990s. These days the only armed rebels in the area are Indian militants from Manipur State, who are believed to maintain bases in the far north of Chin.

Instead, the Chin have turned to politics to achieve autonomy. The Zomi Congress for Democracy, the dominant party in northern Chin, campaigns for Burma to become a federal union. But Mr Mang was unhappy with the party's name. 'Zomi is a place name. It should be the Chin Congress for Democracy,' he insisted. In fact, 'Zomi' is mostly used as the generic term for the hill peoples of Chin State, north-east India and south-east Bangladesh. But the word 'Zomia' has been coined in recent years to describe the entire upland area of Southeast Asia.

Mr Mang voted for the NLD in the 2015 election, like many minority people. Removing the military from power took precedence over everything else. There was also a belief in the borderlands that the NLD would be more sympathetic to the minorities demands for self-rule. But that optimism dissipated quickly, as it became clear that Aung San Suu Kyi wasn't going to do anything that might lead to the break-up of the country her father led to independence, no matter how disunited and unrealistic a nation it actually is.

'We believed what the NLD said before the election. Not now,' said Mr Mang. Michael expressed the dissatisfaction of the minorities more eloquently, and virulently. 'Aung San Suu Kyi is like a kite. She is flying in the air and that's what the countries in the West see. But who is holding the strings? The army. Aung San Suu Kyi is nothing to us. She doesn't care about the minority people.'

Yet neither of them was eager to see a return to guerrilla war in Chinland. 'This isn't the right time to fight. The first option is non-violent: put pressure on the NLD. If that doesn't work, then we may have to hold a gun. As Chin we are Christians, so it is difficult for us to use guns. But some young people want to. But it is still too early for that,' said Michael.

Above all, it is the economic disparity between the borderlands and the rest of Burma which feeds the animosity of people like Michael and Mr Mang. The frontier regions were neglected by the British, and little has been done to remedy that since independence. The United Nations estimates that there are still only around sixty doctors in Chin, a state with almost 500,000 people. And many of them can't afford the cost of medical care anyway.

Almost as infamous as Aung San's failed promise of autonomy was his guarantee to the ethnic leaders at Panglong that 'If Burma receives one kyat, you will also get one kyat'.

There would be far fewer angry people in the borderlands had successive governments over the last seventy years made good on that commitment, or at least invested some money in the frontier states.

Like so many Chin, Michael and Mr Mang had done their time overseas, two years working as waiters in a Bangalore restaurant, earning the money to pay for their studies. 'In Kachin they have jade. The Shan sell drugs. Here in Chin we have to go abroad to India and Malaysia and do the lowest jobs to make money. It's not fair that our young people have to do that,' said Michael.

It seemed pointless to tell them that the jade deposits in Kachin State, like the opium and methamphetamines produced in Shan State, benefit only a small minority. Many Shan and Kachin people are just as poor as the Chin. But Michael and Mr Mang were convinced of the injustice their people were suffering, and they were right. We had simply to look outside at the rutted excuse of a main street in Rihkhawdar to see the paucity of development in Chinland. Perhaps one day the road to heaven will be paved.

8

The Buddha Belt

Back in Kalay after a gruelling jeep ride from Rihkhawdar I decided to return to Yangon in stages. The plan was to follow the course of the Ayeyarwady River from Pakokku, a town close to the point where the Ayeyarwady is joined by the Chindwin River, its largest tributary. From then on Burma's major waterway makes stately progress south through a wide valley surrounded by flat plains, before innumerable tributaries branch off to feed the Delta Region and the river empties into the Andaman Sea.

Rising beneath the Himalayan glaciers of Kachin State in the far north of the country and formerly known as the Irrawaddy, the Ayeyarwady travels almost 1,400 miles before it reaches the coast. I had cruised its northern reaches before, making day-long hops on ageing government ferries and faster wooden speedboats south-west from Bhamo in Kachin State to Katha, the town George Orwell used as the setting for *Burmese Days*, and on to Mandalay. There is little romance in the journey: the vessels are overcrowded and uncomfortable and the scenery a never-changing panorama of rice paddies and maize fields.

From Pakokku on, though, the final 700 miles of the Ayeyarwady's course takes on a new significance, because it cuts through the heartland of the Bamar, Burma's majority ethnic group. Immigrants from China started settling in the central basin of the Ayeyarwady 3,500 years ago, clustering close to the river that guaranteed life. By the ninth century CE, the ancestors of the Bamar were joining them there after migrating south-west from Tibet and Yunnan Province in China.

It is the towns on either side of the Ayeyarwady here – Pakokku, Magwe, Pyay, Tharrawaddy, Hinthada – that are the true repositories of Bamar identity and culture, rather than the foreign-influenced and multicultural Yangon and Mandalay. Pagodas and monasteries dominate the landscape, stationed along the Ayeyarwady like lighthouses, with Christians and Muslims a tiny minority.

This is the Buddha belt, a place where ethnicity and religion fuse so that the terms 'Bamar' and 'Buddhist' become interchangeable. Buddhism reached parts of the Ayeyarwady valley as early as the fourth century CE, with Pyay established soon after as a city of pagodas. Bagan, across the Ayeyarwady from Pakokku, was home to 10,000 temples and 3,000 monasteries from the ninth century to the thirteenth century CE, and the capital of the first kingdom to unite what is now inland Burma.

Buddhist-inspired nationalism has a strong and proud history here. During the colonial period, the region was the scene of the biggest rebellion against British rule, when monks joined forces with farmers in a Burmese peasants' revolt. Belligerent Buddhism remains a powerful, sometimes unwelcome, force in the Ayeyarwady valley today. Monks from Pakokku provided the impetus for the 2007 Saffron

Revolution protests against the junta, marching in their thousands, while attacks on Muslims are a recurring theme.

The *Tatmadaw's* ominous rallying cry – 'One voice, one blood, one nation' – resonates the loudest in this part of Burma, an expression of solidarity that excludes anyone who is not Bamar. The military recruit many of their soldiers from the towns and villages close to the Ayeyarwady. And when the generals decided to rename Burma in 1989, they chose Myanmar because the ancestors of the Bamar who settled along the river called themselves '*Myanma*', or the 'strong and swift'.

Despite the Ayeyarwady being a permanent presence as it flows towards the Andaman Sea, much of the country here is part of what is known as the dry zone: the cauldron of Burma. It is an area of scorching temperatures that can top forty-five degrees centigrade in the final weeks before the monsoon breaks. Then, the heat is conducted by relentless thermals so dry they are almost incendiary and you broil, the moisture sucked out of your body and evaporating so quickly that it seems like you are not sweating at all.

Baking everything beneath it, the sun dries up the land so that it splits apart in protest. The earth crumbles and becomes fine and sand-like. Just a few crops can be grown in the dry zone: chickpeas, beans, sesame and tobacco, with rice in the rainy season, while only the hardiest trees like the toddy palms survive, their short, sharp, sword-like leaves guarding small patches of green beneath them. The toddy palm produces sugar and gives its name to a mild alcoholic drink, as well as being the source of jaggery, a teeth-rotting sweet sometimes served as an after-dinner delicacy.

Pakokku, where I began my journey south along the Ayeyarwady, lies in the west of the dry zone. A few hours farther west are the verdant hills of southern Chin State, but Pakokku itself is surrounded by tobacco fields that provide the weed for Burma's best cheroots, the hand-rolled, cone-like smokes wrapped in a green leaf that dangle from the lips of farmers, labourers and trishaw drivers across the country.

I had been told that Pakokku is the most Buddhist place in Burma and monks are said to make up a third of its population. At first sight the town is little more than a collection of uninspired buildings set along and away from a main street that runs parallel to the western banks of the Ayeyarwady. Pakokku is intensely hot and dusty, and has always been a hard place for foreigners to like. C. M. Enriquez, the Indian Army officer turned policeman who found the North East Frontier intolerable, described the 1914 incarnation of Pakokku as 'bare and brown and beastly'.

Concealed down poorly paved lanes where tamarind trees flower, their drooping branches and abundant foliage offering much-needed shade, are eighty-odd monasteries and many Dhamma schools. They provide a free Buddhist education for children whose parents cannot pay the unofficial fees charged by public schools starved of government funding. In September 2007 the monks from those monasteries and schools emerged to help fire the Saffron Revolution.

Like the 1988 pro-democracy demonstrations, the 2007 protests were prompted initially by a failing, barely managed economy. Steep rises in the price of basic commodities, especially cooking oil, natural gas and petrol, left people struggling to afford to eat. Nor were they able to commute to work, as bus fares rose by up to 500 per cent in the space of a few weeks.

Marches began to take place across the country from the middle of August. But the most infamous demonstration occurred in Pakokku on 5 September, when hundreds of monks rallied in support of activists who had been arrested. Confronted by soldiers, police and thugs hired by the junta, three monks were captured, tied to lamp posts and beaten with rifle butts and bamboo canes.

Burma is home to around half a million monks. Every Buddhist male in the country is expected to spend some period of their life in a monastery. Most become novices as young boys or teenagers, some staying for as little as a week in their local temple during the school holidays to make merit for their families, who are honoured by having a son who is a monk. Others remain for years, often because their parents cannot afford to support them. But senior citizens become novices, too, as my friend Tim's father had done after retiring as a government lawyer.

Only adults can be ordained, and even then they are free to disrobe and return to secular society whenever they wish. Those who do devote their lives to being monks are hugely respected. And despite attacks on their status in the recent past – the Sangha, the Buddhist clergy, were marginalised under British rule and sometimes persecuted by the junta – monks maintain a central and highly visible position in Burmese life.

While the monasteries are not as powerful as they were when Burma's kings habitually consulted with their spiritual advisers before making decisions, senior government officials, as well as ordinary people, continue to visit them in search of advice. Burma's Buddhists are among the most devout people anywhere in the world, and it is the monks who guide and educate them in the religion's precepts.

Some of my neighbours spend their days watching Buddha, a television channel where senior monks intone scriptures or deliver sermons from the most venerated pagodas and monasteries, while it is common to hear its radio equivalent in taxis and on buses. In a culture where lay people are not supposed even to touch a monk, attacking one physically is unthinkable for almost everyone. When news of the assaults on the monks in Pakokku leaked out, people across Burma were enraged.

Local officials and policemen were held hostage at the Ashae Taike Monastery in Pakokku the day after the beatings, the monks burning the cars they had arrived in. The Sangha demanded an apology from the generals, as well as the release of Aung San Suu Kyi from house arrest. When neither were forthcoming, tens of thousands of monks and ordinary people started protesting in every major town in Burma. Monks also refused to perform rites for government officials, army officers and their families, an excommunication devastating in Buddhist culture.

So many monks were involved in the demonstrations that they were dubbed the 'Saffron Revolution', a reference to the colour of their robes, although most monks in Burma wear crimson ones. But like all public opposition to the junta the Saffron Revolution ended in bloodshed and failure, with around 130 people killed when the army broke up the protests and many more arrested, as monasteries were raided and some forced to close.

Militant monks were absent when I visited Ashae Taike Monastery, a complex of wooden and stone buildings grouped around two courtyards. Most of the ones I saw reciting their scriptures or performing domestic duties were boys, novices who knew nothing about the protests of ten years before. The few older clerics were reluctant to revisit the past. I wasn't made to feel unwelcome as I wandered around, but nor did

I detect a willingness to reveal anything. The monastery was a closed shop for non-Buddhists, a place for believers only.

Throughout the Ayeyarwady valley people can be wary of foreigners, eyeing them not with suspicion but a shyness that reflects their general lack of contact with westerners. Despite the region's proximity to Mandalay in the north and Yangon in the south the Ayeyarwady valley is its own enclosed society and, when you travel through it, Burma's largest cities feel much farther away than they actually are.

People are conservative and traditional by instinct and upbringing. Local dress is the standard attire, except for the young country hipsters, and there are almost no western-style eating and entertainment venues. Yet residents of the Ayeyarwady valley are also overwhelmingly hospitable, once they have got over the shock of speaking with a foreigner, often ready to suspend their daily lives for a while to show off their towns and villages.

At Hinthada, a pleasant town of teak houses and pagodas surrounded by lush vegetation that was my final stop on my way back to Yangon, I was taking photos of a striking three-storey colonial-era mansion when the family living there emerged to invite me inside. They pressed tea, water and mangos from their overgrown garden on me, while explaining the history of their home, built after the First World War for a rice magnate. Such a warm welcome is less common in Yangon or Mandalay.

Across the Ayeyarwady from Pakokku is Bagan, reached by the longest bridge in Burma. If Pakokku is a vital seat of Buddhist learning, Bagan is a fossilised one, a vast, parched plain peppered with the remains of 2,000 or more temples. They are the remnants of the 10,000 that were mostly built in a 200-year-long rapture in the eleventh and twelfth centuries

CE, as Bagan's kings embraced Theravada Buddhism with the heady fervour of any new convert.

Practised across Southeast Asia, Theravada Buddhism is the oldest and most doctrinally conservative branch of the religion, with its scriptures written in Pali, an ancient Indian language, rather than the Sanskrit used by most other Buddhist sects. Sri Lanka has long been the stronghold of the Theravada school, and monks from there started arriving in Pyay from the fifth century CE to spread the word. By the time the Bagan Kingdom began its frenzy of temple-building, Theravada Buddhism was already dominant in what would become inland Burma.

For the tourists that flock to Bagan, the temples, some imposing red-brick or white stone structures whose terraces rise high above the alluvial soil they sit on, others no more than stubby, blackened stone pillboxes, are simply Instagram fodder. They are backdrops for people to pose, arms outstretched at sunrise or sunset, before the pictures are shared, liked and then forgotten. Even for the locals, Bagan is somewhere to tour more than a place for pilgrims, no matter that a few of the temples do still function as places to pray.

Yet this was one of the great Buddhist cities of the world, as well as the place where the Burmese language began to be formalised with a written script borrowed from the Mon people who now inhabit southern Burma. Bagan is where Burma's history really starts. Not only did the Bagan kingdom briefly unite many of the regions which now constitute the country, but prior to Bagan's founding much of Burma's past is no more than a mask of myths, legends and fantasies, part-purloined from classical Indian texts.

All that can be said with any real certainty is that the Mon people were the first arrivals in Burma from across the border in what is now Yunnan in China, migrating first to the Ayeyarwady valley before establishing a series of kingdoms in southern Burma. They were followed by the Pyu, who founded the city of Pyay on the banks of the Ayeyarwady, and finally the *Myanma*, the forerunners of the Bamar.

Bagan began its life in 849 CE as a humble *Myanma* settlement, much influenced by the Buddhist culture of the Pyu state farther south. But by the time King Anawrahta ascended to the throne of Bagan in 1044 CE, the kingdom had already expanded to include much of present-day central Burma. Anawrahta is the first of a trio of kings revered by the *Tatmadaw* for their warrior prowess, and he pushed Bagan's boundaries yet further: west into what is now Rakhine State, east to the foothills of Shan State and south to Pyay.

His greatest achievement was to defeat the Mon kingdom in lower Burma, and Bagan's reach extended subsequently to the Ayeyarwady Delta and the sea ports of the far south. For the first time a country that resembles the interior of modern-day Burma had emerged. Equally significant for Burma's future was Anawrahta's adoption of Theravada Buddhism, which he made an integral part of his embryonic state. It was on his watch that Bagan became a city of pagodas and monasteries and Buddhism spread ever further through his land.

Just like the Burma of today, though, the Bagan kingdom was an incoherent state, held together by the threat of force from its centre. And as Bagan's influence spread the realm attracted the attention of the ferocious Mongol empire. In the late thirteenth century CE, Kublai Khan's armies invaded from Yunnan with their legendary, brutal efficiency and the Bagan kingdom collapsed. But the Mongols did not sack the city of Bagan in their customary style. Instead, over the next few centuries, the earthquakes to which the region is still prone reduced Bagan to little more than the village it had been before Anawrahta's time.

Petrifying slowly, Bagan became home to only a few outposts of diehard monks and their followers. They could not maintain the temples and the majority of them disappeared over the years, subsiding slowly into the dust of the dry zone. Treading the vanished city now, surrounded by tour groups and backpackers, is a forlorn experience, the surviving pagodas standing as a teasing, unsatisfactory reminder of a long-vanished glory.

Crossing back over to the western bank of the Ayeyarwady, I continued south past the oil fields of Yenangyaung to Magwe. Bigger than Pakokku but just as unmemorable architecturally, Magwe is a sprawl of streets occupying both sides of the Ayeyarwady. It is a city with an unpleasant recent history. The tiny Muslim community in Magwe and its surrounding townships was attacked by Buddhist mobs in 2006, 2013 and 2017.

Magwe and the region around it is 98 per cent Bamar and Buddhist and hostility towards Muslims and people of Indian descent dates back to the colonial era, when many of them came here as economic migrants. The friction is such that something as trivial as the failure of a Muslim bus driver to drop a Buddhist woman at the correct stop is enough to cause rioting, as happened in 2006. Then, the violence spread to different areas leaving three people dead, while mosques and Muslim-owned homes and shops were burned to the ground.

Of all the towns along the Ayeyarwady, however, it is perhaps Pyay that is the most stridently Buddhist. Pyay is the cradle of Buddhism in the region, the religion arriving in the fourth century CE with Indian traders who sailed down the Ayeyarwady, to be followed later by monks from Sri Lanka.

Soon after, Sri Ksetra – the 'field of glory' – was established by the river in what is now Pyay's eastern outskirts. This walled city of pagodas and palaces was the largest settlement of the Pyu people, until they and their state were subsumed by the *Myanma* and the Bagan kingdom.

Pronounced 'p-yay' or sometimes 'pi', Pyay lies alongside the eastern banks of the Ayeyarwady. The scrubby foothills of the Pegu Yoma range, the source of the teak that is still shipped downstream from Pyay to Yangon, undulate gently to the east of the town. Open drains covered with precarious planking run along the sides of the main streets, with palm trees lining the less odorous lanes off them. Dust flies everywhere, collecting at the edges of the roads in mini-dunes imprinted with the flip-flops of passing pedestrians.

Pyay's skyline is dominated by the Shwesandaw Pagoda. Taller even than the Shwedagon, its golden *zedi* is surrounded by smaller stupas and topped with two elaborate *hti*, umbrella-like decorations that encircle the top of the stupa linked by dangling golden chains. The Shwesandaw is said to enshrine two of the Buddha's hairs, enough to make the pagoda one of the most visited temples in all Burma.

One month before I arrived, Pyay was the scene of the latest confrontation between Buddhism and Islam in the region. It was a Sunday and the town's Muslims were preparing to celebrate the birthday of Muhammad, the founder of their religion. Around 10 per cent of Pyay's population are Muslims, a big community for the Ayeyarwady valley. Almost all are the descendants of Indian labourers imported by the British, for whom Pyay was an important riverine link between lower and central Burma.

Less keen on the celebration were a shadowy faction of extreme Buddhist activists and monks calling themselves the

Nationalist Coalition Group. They arrived from Yangon the day before and complained about the event to the local government. In response, officials asked the organisers to limit the party to thirty minutes. But that wasn't enough for the protestors, who decided that they would stop it from going ahead at all.

'Eight cars and two trucks full of monks arrived outside the Eid Ka Mosque at eight in the morning, maybe a hundred people in all,' Kaung Myat Min, a local journalist, told me. 'Most of the Muslims were already inside and the celebration was about to start. The nationalists went in and forced them to cancel it. The nationalists were very angry and the Muslims were worried that there would be fighting. Some of them were crying and saying, "We do this every year." They couldn't understand why this was happening.'

Kaung Myat Min tried to interview some of the monks to find out why they were stopping the party. 'They refused to speak to me. They said the media were all liars. They were very aggressive. Some of the younger Muslim men were obviously angry too, but their leaders told them to go home, that they had to show their love and not fight.' I asked if there had been police present. 'Yes, about fifteen of them,' said Kaung Myat Min. 'But they were just sitting on their motorbikes playing with their phones.'

Everyone who was present at the Eid Ka Mosque knew about Pyay's history of religious conflict over the last three decades. Less than a mile from the Shwesandaw Pagoda, the Eid Ka dates back to the nineteenth century and the reign of Thibaw, Burma's last king, but its salmon-pink minarets are much newer than that. 'The mosque was destroyed in 1988 and again in 1997. The Buddhists just came in and tore it down,' one of the caretakers told me when I visited.

Later I discovered that the hotel I was staying in had been Muslim-owned, until it was attacked by monks from one of Pyay's monasteries in another bout of violence in 2001. After that, the owner sold up and moved to Yangon. 'Pyay is a very Buddhist place and it has a history of incidents between Buddhists and Muslims. I think that is why the nationalists from Yangon chose to come here last month,' said Wai Yan, a 21-year-old Muslim engineering student and friend of Kaung Myat Min's.

We were talking at a restaurant by the Ayeyarwady. Below us the river was fat and sluggish, its green-brown waters lapping softly on the sandy banks along which barges and dredgers were moored side by side, anchored for the night. The red disc of the sun was slipping behind the Arakan Hills on the opposite side of the river, where Kaung Myat Min pointed out the Shwebontha Muni Pagoda, which he said was a favourite of Khin Nyunt, the much-feared chief of military intelligence during the junta era.

Close to the restaurant, occupying prime position as they looked down on the Ayeyarwady, were still-fine teak and brick mansions from the colonial period. 'A lot of them are empty,' said Kaung Myat Min. 'People think they are haunted.' Stout in a *longyi* and striped shirt and sporting a 1950s-style rocker's quiff, Kaung Myat Min was in his early thirties, the son of a Chin father who had served in the *Tatmadaw* and a Bamar mother. He had worked for Radio Free Asia in India, before returning to his hometown of Pyay in 2012 after the generals stepped down.

Both he and Wai Yan believed that the disruption of the celebration of Muhammad's birthday was a political decision. 'There were no protests last year,' pointed out Wai Yan, floppy fringed, his hair fashionably shaved at the sides. 'But since the NLD won the election there are people who want the government to fail and so they are stirring up trouble. They can say the NLD is protecting Muslims.'

Wai Yan was adamant that relations between Buddhists and Muslims in Pyay were better now than when the last communal riots broke out in 2001. 'I have many Buddhist friends at college and I did at school. It is the people coming from outside the town who are making trouble.' But Wai Yan was also eager to see some legal safeguards for non-Buddhists. 'There should be proper laws banning discrimination against all religions. A law on freedom of worship.'

Technically, Burma's constitution does protect religious freedom. But it also emphasises that Buddhism has a 'special position' as the faith practised by most people. In 1961 the then prime minister U Nu attempted to make Buddhism the state religion. The law was never passed. Nevertheless, after the 1962 coup new decrees ensured the religion's supremacy. Missionaries were expelled, the religious schools of other faiths nationalised and Muslims were barred from serving in the *Tatmadaw*, making the institution even more Buddhist and Bamar than it already was.

More recently it has become near-impossible for any new church, mosque or Hindu temple to gain the official approval needed for their construction. And despite Ne Win's policy of keeping what he described as the 'bearded fellows' (Muslims) away from the 'bald-headed fellows' (Buddhists), the junta era saw numerous bouts of violence between the two communities and not just in the Ayeyarwady valley. Mawlamyine in the south of the country and Mandalay experienced serious rioting in 1983 and 1997 respectively.

Clashes between Buddhists and Muslims have been taking place since the seventeenth century, when fighting erupted in what is now Rakhine State, and probably well before that. But there is little doubt that the end of military rule and the rise of social media have allowed extreme Buddhist nationalists more space to operate in. Facebook is by far the most favoured means of communication in Burma, and it seethes with hate speech after any incident that can be construed as a criticism or attack on Buddhism.

Anti-Islamic propaganda has increased noticeably since 2012, when the first of a series of outbreaks of violence in Rakhine State resulted in an exodus of Rohingya Muslims to Bangladesh and the confinement of most of those left behind in ghettos or squalid camps for the internally displaced. But the Rohingya have long been vilified and persecuted in Burma, where the majority of people regard them as recent illegal immigrants, despite evidence suggesting that they have been present in the country for hundreds of years.

Muslims in Burma, though, cannot be lumped together into one entity, just as Buddhists are a diverse crowd, with some more secular than others and many living side by side with Muslims and disavowing the diktats of the radicals. Arabs and Persians started coming here in the ninth century CE. Other Muslims were encouraged to move from India by the British or arrived from China. Many have intermarried over the years and identify themselves as Bamar.

Unlike the stateless Rohingya, the rest of Burma's Muslims are supposed to be full citizens of the country. They served as soldiers for Burma's kings and played a role in the struggle for independence. U Raschid was a close friend and associate of Aung San's at Rangoon University, and later a cabinet minister in the 1950s. And when Aung San was assassinated in 1947, his Muslim bodyguard died with him. Another Muslim, Maung

Thaw Ka, was a co-founder of the NLD with Aung San Suu Kyi. Many others were early supporters.

But the NLD did not field a single Muslim candidate in the 2015 election, leaving around 4 per cent of the population completely unrepresented in parliament. Nor has Aung San Suu Kyi's government overturned a highly controversial 2014 law that requires any Buddhist woman to seek official permission before she can marry a man of a different faith. Another law passed at the same time allows the authorities to interview those wishing to convert to another religion.

That pernicious legislation, and much of the increased tension between Buddhists and Muslims in recent years, can be attributed to the activities of an organisation called *Ma Ba Tha*. Taking its name from a rallying cry of the 1930s independence movement – *Amyo Batha Thathana*, or 'Race, Religion and the Teachings of the Buddha' – *Ma Ba Tha* grew out of the earlier 969 movement, which emerged in the 1990s prompted by the belief that an Islamic plot was underway to eradicate Buddhism in Burma.

Now defunct, after the Sangha's leadership criticised some of their activities, *Ma Ba Tha* has splintered into other organisations like the Nationalist Coalition Group, the people who ended the celebration of Muhammad's birthday in Pyay. Its former leader and the most public face of Islamophobia in Burma is a Mandalay monk named U Wirathu. He has a long history of Muslim-baiting, insisting that they are marrying Buddhist women, forcing them to convert to Islam and then breeding like crazy, so that one day Muslims will outnumber Buddhists.

There is no truth in that. Burma's 2014 census revealed that the number of Muslims has barely increased in the last forty years. The Rohingya were excluded from the census, but the

Muslim presence in Burma has declined significantly since it was taken, following the involuntary departure of so many Rohingya to Bangladesh. In fact, it is Christians who are on the rise, their numbers swelling by almost 2 per cent since the 1970s.

Much of the power that U Wirathu wields stems from the links between Buddhist nationalists and the USDP, the main, army-backed opposition party. The USDP has a vested interest in pressuring the NLD regarding any perceived failure to protect Buddhism, while disorder between different communities reinforces the generals' favourite narrative that only military rule can guarantee stability. Daw Suu's silence on Muslim issues is a reflection of the NLD's fear of extremists inflaming public opinion against her government.

Most Muslims believe that the ire directed towards them over the last few decades is inspired by political manoeuvring. Ko Min Nyo, who witnessed the 1988 violence in Pyay, is convinced of that. 'It escalated into a riot because of the army,' he told me. 'The situation was so bad with the Ne Win government that the army was always looking for excuses, something to distract people. We all saw so-called monks with green trousers under their robes taking part in the attacks. They were soldiers masquerading as monks.'

Similar reports of soldiers posing as monks, or gangs of toughs wearing jeans under crimson robes, have emerged whenever there has been violence against Muslims in recent years. Often the Buddhist mobs are outsiders in the towns and neighbourhoods where they strike, like the nationalists from Yangon who showed up suddenly in Pyay, and observers have noted how some appear to be drunk. 'There are lots of unemployed, poorly educated people who can be paid to cause problems,' Wai Yan had told me.

A fight between a Muslim man and a Buddhist over a prostitute prompted 1988's rioting. 'The Muslim guy hit the Buddhist hard. The Buddhist was a fireman and he came back later with his friends for revenge. They didn't find the Muslim,' said Ko Min Nyo, in between digging a spoon into the bony Ayeyarwady fish we were sharing. 'But the next day they were joined by monks and they started destroying Muslim houses and the Eid Ka Mosque.'

Firemen in Burma are officially part of the *Tatmadaw*, adding credence to Ko Min Nyo's claim that the army played a role in the subsequent four days of attacks on Muslim homes across Pyay, their residents having mostly fled. 'It only stopped when a curfew was imposed,' said the 48-year-old. 'But by then, lots of houses had been destroyed and looted.'

Ko Min Nyo might have his own reasons for blaming the junta for the riots. He had been involved with the All Burma Students' Democratic Front, an armed opposition group formed after the failure of the 1988 pro-democracy protests. Arrested in 1996, he served seven years as a political prisoner. 'Military intelligence came for me. They said I was going to bomb the Kaba Aye Pagoda in Yangon and that I was in touch with the All Burma Students and the Karen. I did have contact with them, but I am not a terrorist and not violent.'

He could have been lying. As a Muslim, though, I suspected Ko Min Nyo would have been kept in jail for much longer if he was truly planning to blow up one of Yangon's better-known temples. But he didn't give the impression that he cared what I thought. Ko Min Nyo shielded himself with an invisible carapace, a manufactured self-assurance expressed in his cool, deliberately vague recollection of his militant youth.

Along with many Muslims, his faith in the NLD has been shattered by the party's unwillingness to speak out against the Buddhist nationalists and their blatant lies. 'I used to support the NLD, but no longer,' he said. 'I still like Daw Suu. I trust her. I think she is honourable. She isn't doing anything for Muslims, but she can only do so much with a quarter of the parliament army officers. At least now there is some freedom and democracy.'

South of Pyay a narrow two-lane highway curves towards Yangon, running roughly parallel to the eastern banks of the Ayeyarwady. The river is an unseen presence from the buses that hurtle along the road, but its waters feed the irrigation ditches that slice through the fields all around, nurturing the crops of rice and beans. To the east is a railway line, bordered by banana trees and tangles of bushes that threaten to overwhelm the track.

Villages of wooden houses and the odd concrete construction indicating a government building go by, shrouded by mesquite trees, palms and thick-trunked tamarinds standing sentry along the highway. Red and yellow archways beckon towards pagodas and monasteries. The horizontal stripes of the six-coloured Buddhist flag fly on bamboo poles outside homes, while women hold metal bowls up to the bus windows in some of the settlements, fundraising for the local temples.

Three hours driving brought us to Tharrawaddy. Unlike Pyay, Tharrawaddy is a relatively new town, established by the British. They built the still-functioning prison, where Ko Min Nyo served part of his sentence. The Tharrawaddy district was notorious for dacoity as far back as the 1850s and would experience a steep rise in crime during the early 1900s. But in 1887, just eighteen months after the British had completed the full annexation of Burma, it was the scene of an early rebellion against the new rulers.

Led by a monk named U Thuriya, a mixed force of dacoits and farmers angered by food shortages and new taxes set out to attack the colonial state. Tattooed with charms designed to protect them from British bullets, the rebels cut telegraph lines and damaged the railway line to Pyay that I had glimpsed from the highway I journeyed down. But that was all they managed to do before the gang was swiftly rounded up.

U Thuriya was one of the many monks politicised by the British takeover of his country. Some took to the hills of upper Burma, leading classic guerrilla resistance that started almost immediately after the overthrow of King Thibaw and would continue for ten years in some areas. Others, like Nga Hmun, who led a rebellion in Pakokku in 1894, and U Oktama, the organiser of a rising in Taungoo in 1906, operated in or close to the Ayeyarwady valley, where the increasing impact of Indian immigration on local livelihoods was another cause for discontent.

Motivated by the removal of the monarchy, which was tied intimately to the Sangha, and the subsequent decline of Buddhist influence on society, radical monks were the forerunners of the 1930s student leaders who led the campaign for independence. The most renowned remain household names in Burma today. In particular, U Ottama and U Wisara, who were both jailed in the 1920s, played pivotal roles in fomenting opposition to colonial rule.

Buddhism and the nationalist movement were inextricably entwined. Buddhist associations and patriotic societies sprang up across Burma from the late 1890s, becoming the focal points for defiance against the British. Monks toured the country advocating sedition. Increasing numbers began to be arrested. One hundred and twenty monks were imprisoned in 1928 and 1929, as much a source of anger for the locals as the beating of the three monks by the junta bullies in Pakokku in 2007 was.

In December 1930 the twin strands of Buddhist nationalism and rural despair over heavy taxation and the loss of land to Indian moneylenders came together to spark the Saya San Rebellion. Starting in Tharrawaddy, it spread across lower Burma and was the single biggest revolt against British rule, lasting almost two years. Tens of thousands of soldiers were required to put it down and thousands of rebels died, were wounded or jailed.

Leading the uprising was Saya San, a novice monk turned traditional medicine healer. He became involved with the Buddhist association movement in the 1920s, travelling the country on its behalf to observe rural conditions. Saya San noted the anger of farmers over taxes and the lack of respect for Buddhism among colonial officials. As the effects of the global depression reached Burma and rice prices dropped, conditions were ripe for a Buddhist peasant crusade with monks acting as the organisers and cheerleaders.

Saya San was hanged at Tharrawaddy prison in November 1931, a few months before his rebellion was finally crushed. But he has not been forgotten. A sign in Tharrawaddy proclaims that this is 'Saya San Town' and there is a statue of him. Most significantly, Saya San's deployment of Buddhism as a weapon set an example to others. In July 1938 Muslims and Indians were the targets of prolonged attacks across lower and central Burma, after monks demanded a response to an anti-Buddhist tract written by a local Muslim.

Present-day nationalist monks like U Wirathu and his fellow Islamophobes are, in one sense, the heirs to the radicalised clerics of colonial times. But instead of resisting foreign invaders they work to provoke violence against citizens of their own country. Nor is the Ayeyarwady valley the birthplace of today's extreme Buddhist ideology, for all its historical significance as the homeland of the Bamar and the incubator of Buddhism in Burma. To reach that dark place I would have to travel farther south to a monastery in Mawlamyine.

9

Mawlamyine

Six hours after leaving Yangon the bus ran onto the bridge that crosses the Thanlwin River, its metal plates clanking under the weight, the steel girders to the sides framing the view ahead of golden stupas on a jagged ridge. Below, the Thanlwin was a dirty blue as it made its way towards the Andaman Sea, the final part of a journey that began in the mountains of Tibet.

Mawlamyine lay on the other side of the bridge. A motorbike taxi took me to the Strand, the riverfront road. As it curled sharply right, before entering a long straight, I passed the main market, across from which long-tail boats were shuttling shoppers to and from Bilu, the island opposite Mawlamyine which sits between the Thanlwin and the open sea. Then came grimy government buildings and finally a string of decaying mansions, their walls blackened by mould, windows lacking glass, gates padlocked. Out on the river, fishing boats and a few rusting cargo ships rode the current apathetically.

Downtown Mawlamyine runs back from the Strand in a grid of lanes and roads that reach up to smarter streets in the hills that overlook the town. The houses and tenements are fronted with balconies with stone, wood or chrome balustrades depending on their era. Splashes of colour – bright red, muted yellow, jade green, rose pink and sky blue – enliven many of the buildings, the paint jobs masking rough plaster and distracting eyes from open drains, potholes and festering piles of garbage.

Trees sprout in defiance of the city around them: tall teaks, tamarinds, rain trees and ferns, coconut and toddy palms, as well as betel-nut palms with their drainpipe-thin trunks and narrow leaves. They march down the Strand in rough formation, cloak the lanes with their fronds and bunch together for protection on the hills above town, a half-colonised forest where frontier homesteads battle with the indigenous timber.

Everywhere are the reminders that Mawlamyine was the original capital of British Burma. It was a prize from the First Anglo-Burmese War, swiftly rebuilt in the image of its thieves and slowly forgotten from 1852 onwards, when Yangon began to supersede it as both the major port and administrative centre of the country. Occupying the lowlands of the town are the houses of God left behind by the colonists and those who followed in their wake: Anglican, Baptist and Catholic churches, mosques with their crescent-topped minarets, Hindu temples stamped with the image of Ganesha, Chinese shrines adorned with mysterious characters, all overseen by the far older pagodas strewn along the ridgeline.

Colonial-era schools function still, double-decker wooden buildings in white and green whose classroom doors open out onto wide verandas. A teak courthouse flanked by a cloister-like arched stone walkway where youthful lawyers in their short black gowns, the tropical version of an English barrister's garb, shelter from the sun, snacking on corn on the cob while waiting for their cases to be heard. And in the centre of town is the prison. Designed on panopticon principles, its cell blocks run away in all directions from a central hub, a red-brick Edwardian spider enclosed by high walls.

Nowhere in Burma evokes the past like Mawlamyine. Getting off the bus here was to tumble down the rabbit hole again, one that led straight back to the nineteenth century and the days of the Raj. If Yangon's latest life is an uneasy existence where the colonial period, junta years and the waning optimism of the present all telescope together, then Mawlamyine is stalled in Buddhist limbo, still waiting to be reborn.

There is a timelessness to living in Burma. It is part of the country's charm that its clock seems to run more slowly than elsewhere, lagging behind with either a genial smile or an atavistic snarl. Everything about Burma, from the heat to its history, conspires to make things happen at a leisurely pace. But Mawlamyine takes that to extremes. It is a soporific city, one in a state of permanent hibernation, apparently not caring when or if it wakes up.

In the late afternoon I joined the sunset rush of tourists to the Kyaikthanlan Pagoda, a shimmering ninth-century CE vision regilded and enlarged over the centuries by both Mon and Bamar kings. Mawlamyine was part of successive Mon kingdoms, until the last of them was vanquished by King Alaungpaya in the mid-eighteenth century, a victory he celebrated by giving Yangon its name – 'End of Strife'.

Now, the Mon people number around 1.1 million and their homeland has been reduced to Mon State, a slim coastal strip at the top of southern Burma. Much assimilated with the Bamar, the Mon retain only their history and a dying language understood mainly by monks. From Mawlamyine it is a short journey east to the hills and jungle of neighbouring Kayin State, home to the Karen minority, and then the border with Thailand, a hundred-odd miles away, where more Mon communities can be found.

Standing as a token of the Mon's past glories, Kyaikthanlan is visible from miles around, the tallest of the temples that run along the ridgeline above Mawlamyine. Immediately beneath the pagoda the hillside has been bricked in and stiffened with concrete to prevent the stupa sliding towards the Thanlwin River. Monasteries, the robes of their monks drying on balcony rails, lie to the left and right of the two unnerving lifts that take visitors to the base of the pagoda.

Gazing down on Mawlamyine from Kyaikthanlan reinforces the sense that the town is trapped in time. The trees rule the hillside below, the farthest away shrouded by the clouds of dust sent skyward by the cars and motorbikes rolling through downtown's streets. In the far distance is the river, shining almost red as the sun sinks towards the horizon. While the people around me waited with cameras and phones for the perfect sunset shot, the harsh white lights of the prison beneath us snapped on in the watchtowers and along the cell blocks.

Only the concrete buildings in downtown and the mobile-phone masts – the tallest structures in Mawlamyine bar the pagodas – act as reminders that this is the twenty-first century. Otherwise I could have been witnessing the same panorama Rudyard Kipling enjoyed when he visited Mawlamyine in 1889. The city was known then as Moulmein. In Kipling's words it was 'a sleepy town', already a fast-fading version of the port that had been the principal exporter of the Burmese teak harvested by Scottish firms until it was displaced by Yangon.

Kipling was returning to London on leave from his job as a journalist in India and spent just three days in Burma, a night at the Pegu Club in Yangon and then a stop at Mawlamyine. But it was long enough for him to rhapsodise about the local women he encountered and to be inspired to write 'Mandalay', the best-known English language poem about Burma. Kipling coined the expression 'the river of lost footsteps', too, about the Ayeyarwady and the men he knew in India who had travelled up the river to fight the guerrillas resisting the recent annexation of upper Burma.

Kyaikthanlan is the temple mentioned in the opening line of 'Mandalay', 'By the old Moulmein Pagoda, lookin' lazy at the sea'. Kipling's poem remains a literary staple, recited, parodied or sung by everyone from Bertolt Brecht to Groucho Marx and Frank Sinatra. In January 2017 the then British Foreign Secretary Boris Johnson attempted his own rendition while visiting the Shwedagon, only to be halted abruptly by the British ambassador, fortunately before he reached the lines, 'Bloomin' idol made o' mud, Wot they called the Great Gawd Budd'.

Despite Kipling's insensitivity towards local beliefs and his unwavering espousal of the empire, he has his fans in Burma. An extract from 'Mandalay' was read at Aung San Suu Kyi's 1972 wedding – 'a neater, sweeter maiden in a cleaner, greener land' – and she named her second son Kim after Kipling's most famous hero. She has spoken of how Kipling's 'If' is 'a great poem for dissidents'. In turn, the junta compared Daw Suu to the Burmese girl who consorts with a British soldier in 'Mandalay', an unsuccessful attempt to smear her as 'unpatriotic' for marrying an Englishman.

George Orwell, too, recognised that he and Kipling had much in common, despite their completely contrary views on colonialism. In a 1942 essay Orwell denounced Kipling as a 'jingo imperialist' and damned him as a 'good bad poet', not least for his unfortunate habit of phrasing some of his poems, like 'Mandalay', in music-hall cockney. Orwell, though, acknowledged the vitality of his writing and in the same essay unconsciously noted the similarities between himself and Kipling.

Both men went straight from boarding schools to jobs in the empire, where they were unpopular, regarded as eccentric and unclubbable. Just as Orwell made friends with outsiders like the hopeless drug addict Herbert Robinson in Mandalay, Kipling spent his nights in low liquor shops and opium dens after a day spent bashing out copy for his newspaper in Lahore, as well as visiting the local prostitutes. It was Kipling who came up with the phrase 'the world's oldest profession'.

At their finest, Kipling's short stories and poems about India are almost stylised reportage and they angered his contemporaries in the Raj after they became immediately popular. A few decades later Orwell would be accused of letting the side down with *Burmese Days*. Its account of the heavy drinking and petty rivalries of clubland, the memsahib watching her husband like a hawk so he can't jump on the maids, reads like a heightened version of colonial life.

Orwell has a Mawlamyine connection as well. His maternal grandmother was born in the city and his mother, Ida Limouzin, spent part of her childhood there. Her French family arrived in 1826, just after Mawlamyine was taken by the British as part of the spoils of the First Anglo-Burmese War. The Limouzin family were swept into Mawlamyine on a wave of immigration as Indian labour, both Muslim and Hindu, arrived to build the port, roads and houses and the Chinese came to trade and run shops.

Establishing themselves as shipbuilders and teak exporters, the Limouzins prospered. Most of the family stayed on even as Mawlamyine began its lethargic decline, and his grandmother's presence in the city is cited as the reason why Orwell applied to join the unfashionable Burma Police. In February 1926 Orwell got the one posting he craved during his time in the country when he arrived in the then Moulmein as deputy chief of police.

Like so many homecomings, Orwell's sojourn in Mawlamyine didn't work out, as the opening line from his 1936 essay 'Shooting an Elephant' makes clear. 'In Moulmein, in lower Burma, I was hated by large numbers of people – the only time in my life that I have been important enough for this to happen to me.' Detesting his job as a colonial enforcer, Orwell was both taken aback and enraged by the resentment he faced from the locals, especially the monks.

'Shooting an Elephant' describes an incident where a British policeman feels compelled to kill a rogue pachyderm in front of a huge crowd to maintain the facade of imperial control. Orwell had been confronted with a similar situation and, although he didn't admit it publicly, he probably pulled the trigger. Certainly, his second wife Sonia believed he did. Working elephants were and are very valuable animals in Burma. Orwell's punishment for killing one was to be posted to the backwater of Katha in upper Burma, the setting for *Burmese Days*.

A small lane in Mawlamyine is named Limouzin. It starts close to the southern end of the Strand, a couple of blocks back from the river. I had visited it before, but when I returned this time there was a new road sign, misspelling the name as Lain Mawzin. It is a dozy street, one half of which is taken up by a monastery. The former Limouzin family residence stood at the top of the lane, on the junction with Upper Main Road.

Their home was destroyed in an air raid during the Second World War and two large wooden houses of indeterminate age occupy the plot of land now. I knocked on the door of one and a bare-chested, middle-aged man in a green *longyi* answered. He invited me in and his wife, daughter and granddaughter looked on curiously as I asked if they knew anything about the Limouzin family. They didn't. 'We've lived here for twenty years. We bought it from an Indian. He moved to Yangon,' said the man. 'But come next door, a very old woman lives there. She might know.'

His neighbours were equally welcoming, smiling at our intrusion and pressing a can of Coke on me. The ninety-year-old matriarch of the family sat in an armchair, a white-haired skeleton in a thin cotton dress, her skin sagging off bare, bony arms. She had lived in the house for sixty years. But she had no memory or idea of who had come before. No one had heard of George Orwell either. I drank the Coke, thanked them and left.

Pirate copies of *Burmese Days* are on sale everywhere tourists can be found, but there is scant awareness of Orwell in Burma. His books were banned under the generals and, while they are on the syllabuses of universities now, he is not widely read. It is Kipling who, for all his jingoism, is better known. Daw Suu has never been heard quoting George Orwell. But, as Orwell observed in his 1942 essay, Kipling's phrases have endured while many more politically correct and once fashionable writers are forgotten.

As for the Limouzins, they intermarried with the locals as the colonial period gave way to the independence era. Some did so in the nineteenth century, too, the reason why there has been speculation that Orwell might have had Burmese ancestry. But with the advent of the junta the large Anglo-Burmese community in Mawlamyine and elsewhere began to face increasing official bias and many, like Orwell's relatives, departed for the UK or Australia.

Leaving Limouzin Street I walked south down Upper Main Road. It was fiercely hot under a cloudless blue sky. No one else was strolling around. Betel-nut vendors and motorbike taxi drivers congregated under the protective branches of trees, hiding from the sun as they waited for customers. Dogs sought the shade of parked cars, lying under them, their tongues hanging out, panting hard.

Soon the castellated, blackened red-brick tower of St Matthew's appeared, behind which the Anglican church stretched back, supported by buttresses and roofed with corrugated iron. At first sight it seems abandoned, stranded in overgrown grounds where palms arch lazily and the grass is bleached brown from the sun. The door was locked, the two clocks on the tower told different times – both wrong – but through the slatted windows I could see teak pews, concrete walls painted pink and a distressed tiled floor.

Behind the church a few families have made homes in huts, their washing slung on lines between the trees. They told me that services were still held on Sundays and that the church shared a vicar with nearby St Augustine's. Both were built in the 1880s, joining the numerous other churches in Mawlamyine, the oldest of which dates back to 1827. Now, though, the Anglican community in the city is much diminished. It is the Baptist churches and the Catholic cathedral that are busier with worshippers.

'When I was young the church would be full, mainly with Anglo-Burmese and Anglo-Indian families,' said Moses, the caretaker of St Augustine's. 'But they have mostly passed away, or they emigrated in the 1960s after Ne Win took over. Now, most of the congregation are Karen. We get about ten people on Sundays, the same as St Matthew's, although more people come at Christmas and Easter.' Around 20 per cent of the five million Karen minority are Christian, and many have moved from their homeland in neighbouring Kayin State to work in Mawlamyine.

Moses was a youthful looking sixty-two, his hair still black, in a white vest and blue *longyi*. He has lived next door to St Augustine's his entire life. It is six years older than St Matthew's, built in 1881, but looks much newer, having been recently renovated. Now boasting a salmon-pink paint job, both inside and out, Moses showed me around after we had taken our shoes off at the entrance. I admired the huge seashell which acts as the font. Moses nodded in agreement at its beauty. 'But the last time we had a baptism was eight years ago,' he said sadly.

The next morning I stood opposite St Augustine's finishing a cigarette before stepping inside the tobacco-free grounds of the Myazedi Monastery. On the other side of the road from the church, Myazedi is the birthplace of the extreme Buddhist nationalist and anti-Muslim 969 movement. The number 969 stands for the nine attributes of Buddha, the six special attributes of his teaching and the nine attributes of the Sangha, the Buddhist clergy.

Burma is a country obsessed with numerology. Major events are habitually scheduled to coincide with auspicious dates, or favourable number sequences like '8888' – 8 August 1988 – the day of the general strike that was the centrepiece of the 1988 pro-democracy protests. The radical Buddhists chose 969 to counter the 786 sequence sometimes displayed on Muslim homes and shops which represents the Basmala, the phrase, 'In the Name of Allah, the Most Gracious and Most Merciful', which begins Muslim prayers.

Inside the monastery, a monk named Sucittasara explained the significance of 786 to me. '786 means this is the Muslim century. Add seven and eight and six and it equals twenty-one, the twenty-first century.' I couldn't fault his arithmetic, but I wasn't so sure that three numbers signified a hundred years of Islamic domination. Sucittasara, a podgy man in his late thirties with a quick smile, was here to vet me. We met in one of the courtyards that make up Myazedi, which is home to over five hundred monks and novices from all over Burma.

Sucittasara told me he had studied Buddhist literature in Sri Lanka, another country with a long history of strident nationalist monks. I said I had been there. He offered me one of his fast grins and then, apparently satisfied, ushered me into an anteroom lined with shelves full of gifts for the monks: mostly hampers of fruit and sacks of rice. Sitting on a mat in the centre of the room was U Vimala, the abbot of Myazedi, a lean 73-year-old with a craggy face, his eyes watchful behind square-framed glasses.

U Vimala was previously general secretary of *Ma Ba Tha*, the organisation led by the arch-Islamophobe monk U Wirathu that grew out of the 969 movement. He is also a prominent supporter of the opposition USDP. Before the 2015 election U Vimala said that Burma wasn't ready for democracy and claimed Aung San Suu Kyi wasn't fit to govern the country. 'There needs to be good control for there to be peace,' he told me in a soft voice.

We sat in a rough circle on the mat, Sucittasara to the left of his abbot. He was his trusted aide-de-camp and U Vimala left him to answer most of my questions, staying silent but keeping his eyes on me all the time. Three kittens appeared from the edges of the room and played around us, one trying repeatedly to snag my pen with his baby claws.

They claimed that 969 and *Ma Ba Tha* had been necessary because Muslims in Asia aren't like those in the West. 'The mentality of Muslims in the East is different. They want to make all Asia Muslim. We are surrounded by Muslims here. Islam has swallowed Indonesia and Malaysia. They were Buddhist countries once: look at Borobudur in Java,' said Sucittasara, referring to the ancient temple complex that is the Indonesian equivalent of Bagan or Angkor Wat. 'We don't want that to happen here.'

For that reason they were firm advocates of the 2014 laws requiring Buddhist women to get official permission before marrying men from other faiths or converting to another religion. 'If you marry a Muslim man, you become a Muslim. We don't agree with that. Prevention is better than a cure, right?' said Sucittasara, flashing me one of his speedy smirks, which were becoming rarer as he got into his stride. 'We have to be watchful. Once there were only ten Arab families in Indonesia. Now there are two hundred million Muslims there.'

Did they regard Christianity and Hinduism as a challenge to Buddhism in Burma? U Vimala rotated his right hand vertically to say, 'No', the most animated he got during the conversation. 'Muslims are different from Hindus and Christians,' asserted Sucittasara. 'If they offer their life to Allah, they go directly to heaven. But suicide is against our law. It is a sin. The suicide bombings they do are all sins. Hindus, Christians and Buddhists respect life very much. This is the teaching of the Buddha and the Lord Christ.'

I mentioned the Rohingya and the oppression they face. Immediately, I knew I had made a mistake. 'There is no such thing as Rohingya,' sneered Sucittasara. 'Rohingya is just a name, not a race. They are just Bengali Muslims. Invaders from Bangladesh. We want them to leave.' He was leaning into me, his face close to mine, his dark eyes alive with the disdain of the true zealot. There was no sign now of the smiley monk who had greeted me thirty minutes before.

'Why are you in the West so optimistic about the Muslims? You let all the migrants come and they cause problems. You haven't been to Mecca, have you? No, because they won't allow you. Buddhists and Christians let anyone into temples and churches. But Muslims won't let you into a mosque because they do political things there. They have secrets. That's why we don't permit them to build any more mosques.'

He was ranting now, and I was struggling to get a word in. There was no reason in us continuing to talk. Even the kittens could sense that something wasn't right, retreating back to their hides in the far corners of the room. I said that I should be going. Outside, we posed for a selfie as if nothing had happened. Then U Vimala placed his hand in mine and steered me around his monastery, decorated with giant posters bearing his face.

Towards the back of the complex, U Vimala pointed beyond the red and white tiled wall. 'There is a Muslim neighbourhood over there. We have no problems with the Muslims in Mawlamyine.' I thought that maybe he was embarrassed by his assistant's loss of composure, although I knew he agreed with what he had said. We parted at the main gate. 'Come for lunch next time,' said U Vimala.

Crossing the road, I found Moses at St Augustine's. I was in need of some Christian charity. He listened attentively as I told him about my visit to Myazedi. 'We've all been under the gun for most of our lives – Christians, Buddhists, Muslims, Hindus – and we all got on OK, more or less,' said Moses. 'But things are different now. I'm not even certain there will be Christians in Mawlamyine in twenty years. There will be fewer of us, for sure.'

Circling the wall that surrounds Myazedi, I made my way to the Muslim area U Vimala had mentioned. It is actually a mixed district, with a minority of Buddhists, centred on the hundred-year-old Shah Bandar mosque. To its side, I met Junaid, a teacher at a nearby Islamic school who was lounging on a chair at his friend's mobile phone accessories store. Skinny, with a wispy beard, he wore a taqiyah, the skullcap of the pious Muslim, and a long white shirt over his *longyi*.

Some of his students, dressed the same, were wandering down the street, or sitting in the tea shops, during a break in classes. 'It's a free education for boys from families who can't afford the government schools, just like the Buddhists who send their children to the Dhamma schools or the monasteries to study. We teach the Koran and Arabic and Urdu too,' said Junaid.

Buddhists and Muslims fought in Mawlamyine's streets in August 1983, when hundreds of Muslims fled across the border to Thailand to avoid the violence. But Junaid was relaxed about current relations. 'Most people around here are shopkeepers and we all get on, Buddhist and Muslim. There are no problems between ordinary people.' Mixed marriages are unknown, though, despite monk Sucittasara's claims that Buddhist women were being forcibly converted. 'Ten, fifteen years ago, a few people were intermarrying, but not now,' said Junaid.

During the lead-up to the 2015 election *Ma Ba Tha* had marched through the neighbourhood. 'The monks came shouting, "Muslims go home." One screamed, "Fuck you" at me. Monks are supposed to be peaceful,' said Junaid, still scandalised. 'I reported him to the police, but they wouldn't even make out a report. They said, "This is a Buddhist country, not a Muslim one. If you don't like that, you can leave." The laws here don't apply if you are a Muslim.'

Unsurprisingly, Junaid and all the Muslims he knew had voted for the NLD in the election, despite Daw Suu's conspicuous failure to condemn the rabble-rousing of the Buddhist nationalists. 'We didn't really have a choice,' he pointed out. 'We voted for the NLD, those of us who were allowed to vote that is, because we knew that the USDP and *Ma Ba Tha* were hand in hand. You know how politics in Burma is a dirty game. The politicians know the country is ninety per cent Buddhist, so Muslims are an easy target.'

To vote in Burma one needs an identity card, the pink document that all people are supposed to carry. The cards record the holder's ethnicity and religion alongside their name and age. Since 1990 Muslims are no longer allowed to identify themselves as Bamar on the documents. New applicants are now mostly described as 'Indian Muslims'. In recent years it has become increasingly difficult for Muslims to get identity cards at all, making it impossible for them to vote or get a passport and much harder to move to different towns and cities for work or study.

'Everyone knows that if you are a Muslim and you want an identity card you have to pay 500,000 kyat [£270]. Most people can't afford that,' Junaid said. 'You can show proof that your family has been here for generations, but you still have to pay 500,000 kyat. I have proof that my family has been here since the nineteenth century, but I still had to pay.' The cost and stress of obtaining an identity card is a deep source of anger for Muslims, and just another sign of how they are being excluded from the mainstream of society.

Later in the day, as the sun started its descent towards the sea, I found myself on the Strand staring down at the

Thanlwin River. The water looked as if it was coming to the boil, rippling furiously in the red-hued light as it eddied around submerged obstacles. That was Mawlamyine, rather less somnolent than it appears at first glance. I was happy to be heading south.

10

On the Myeik Main

An endlessly bumpy road snakes its way from Mawlamyine towards Kawthoung, Burma's most southerly town. The minibus departed while it was still dark, running through silent streets, the Thanlwin River and then the coast out of sight to our right. As the first splashes of pink in the sky announced the arrival of another day and the city fell behind, the Tenasserim Hills began to emerge in the distance to the left, a natural barrier of evergreen forest between Burma and Thailand.

Trapped between the Andaman Sea to the west and the frontier with Thailand in the east, the far south of Burma is a narrow sliver of land no more than ten miles wide in some places. Just inland from the highway are palm oil and banana plantations, floppy leaves spreading expansively as they lure the sun, and betel nut and rubber farms, dark lines of trees in neat order, so closely packed together that their branches shut out the sky. A few tracks disappear into the fields and shade, allowing access for the tappers and the farmers.

Mixed construction crews worked sporadically by the side of the road, almost every inch of the men and women hidden from the sun – long sleeves, some with *longyi* wrapped around their heads in lieu of hats – only their eyes, hands and feet visible. They hauled bamboo baskets loaded with rocks, widening the highway by tipping them at its boundary to await the heavy roller, while oil drums of bubbling pitch stood close to hand.

Leaving Mon State for Tanintharyi Region, Burma's southernmost province, a nondescript border marked by a police post, we shot through the town of Dawei. Heading on to Myeik, the major port of the south, the road was interrupted by narrow bridges guiding us across streams and tributaries. Villages of palm-thatched wooden houses sat close to the waterways, their fishing boats moored and ready for the commute to the nearby sea. Everyone was darker than farther north, their complexions blasted by the unrelenting sun.

The highway became progressively worse as the driver sped us south, barely able to run straight, twisting incessantly as its inadequate camber banked sharply left or right. The boy next to me was fighting to hold down his curry and rice lunch, gulping it back, until finally he admitted defeat and threw it up on the minibus's floor, splattering his flip-flopped feet and my trainers.

Tanintharyi is truly tropical. In the north and west of Burma the mountain ranges of India and Tibet force their way into the country. The central dry zone is almost desert. To the east, the jungle-covered hills of Shan State mimic those of Yunnan Province in China. But the far south is sultry and languid, the heat relieved only by sea breezes. From Dawei down wide strips of sand backed by coconut palms fringe the coast, still awaiting the resorts and package tourists found across the border in Thailand.

Foreigners were barred from travelling overland south of Mawlamyine until 2013. When I got off at Myeik I realised what I had been missing. Mawlamyine is staid and slothful but Myeik was immediately alive, possessed of an energy which seemed to pulse through the sticky air as a motorbike taxi took me from the bus station to its ancient heart. Unlike Mawlamyine, Myeik is a city that has ridden its luck over the centuries, rather than letting itself be snared by its history.

My guest house was a block back from the harbour. It was the busiest port I had seen in Burma, outside of Yangon, fishing boats jammed tightly together, all seeking the shelter of a natural bay between the mainland and an island of two prominent hills a few hundred metres across the water. A giant reclining Buddha at the foot of one of them stretched out, easily visible from the town. Beyond the bay were more islands, some of the 852 that Burma claims ownership of, most of which lie off the Tanintharyi coast.

Come nightfall and the bay was lit up, a low-level floating cityscape of its own, as the fishing fleet prepared to sail to work. Strings of red and green bulbs shone out, slung along the tangles of rigging connecting the wheelhouses and masts or draped around them as if they were Christmas trees. The squid boats had their fluorescent white halogens on, ready to draw the cephalopods upwards to their nets. Shafts of light flickered across the surface of the dark water, creating a pattern of stripes upon which the vessels rocked.

People promenaded along the harbour front, pausing at food stalls to graze on squid impaled on wooden skewers, or sat on the harbour wall talking, laughing, playing guitars. Teenagers on tinny sounding motorbikes accelerated up and down the road, their friends squeezed behind them, two or three to a bike. The beer stations were busy and the palms positioned every few metres looked down on everything in silent approval, fronds fluttering as the wind came in on gentle gusts off the sea.

In the morning I walked up the steep hill which rises behind the harbour. Elegant, detached, well-maintained houses, pillars supporting gabled roofs, their distinctive arched windows guarded by wooden shutters, stood along the winding lane that led uphill. They had been built for merchant families in the Sino-Portuguese style and could have been transposed from the streets of Singapore or Phuket Town 200 miles south in Thailand.

Trailing down the other side of the hill were streets of shop houses – where the ground floor is for commercial use with the upper storeys for living – and substantial wooden homes. Some were given over to breeding the swiftlets that produce the bird's nest delicacy Myeik is famous for. The bird nests are added to soups, giving them a unique flavour popular in southern China especially. This was the port's old Chinese neighbourhood and many houses had characters inscribed above their doors. Wells were sited at strategic points, still supplying some people with water.

I stopped for a noodle breakfast at the Green Eyes Café. Its name harks back to the sixteenth century, when Myeik's streets were already a melee of peoples and cultures, the Mon, Karen and Bamar joined by Chinese, Malays, Thais, Indians and Arabs. Europeans – Portuguese, French, Dutch and British – arrived soon after and everyone mixed, so that even a generation ago it was still possible to encounter locals with green or blue eyes.

Myeik was a thriving port, the western terminus of a trade route that ran from China to Thailand and then on by land and river across the Tenasserim Hills to Myeik. In the opposite direction, from the other side of the Bay of Bengal, goods from India and the Middle East travelled east. Myeik became a hub of global commerce, its overland connection to Ayutthaya, the then capital of Siam – the former name for Thailand – enabling ships to avoid passing through the pirate-infested Strait of Malacca.

Chinese silks, porcelains, tea, silver and copper vessels spread west from Myeik to India and then Europe. Thai elephants, the ancient equivalent of tanks, were imported by the Indian maharajahs for their armies, too, herded over the Tenasserim Hills to the town of Tanintharyi, floated downstream on barges to Myeik and then battened down in ships and sailed to Madras. Indian cotton and scented woods and pepper from the Middle East came to Thailand in return, before travelling on to China and Japan.

At that time Myeik – then known as Mergui – was not part of Burma. The port had been the southernmost extension of the Bagan empire but, after the kingdom collapsed in the late thirteenth century, Myeik came under the control of Siam for the next 500-odd years, providing the Thais with easy access to the Bay of Bengal. Alaungpaya's forces regained the town in 1765, but sixty-one years later Myeik and the rest of southern Burma was ceded to the British after the First Anglo-Burmese War.

Strewn along the top of the hill I had walked up are the remnants of the colonial period. The area behind the harbour had been a fetid mangrove swamp until the 1920s, so Myeik's most prosperous residents lived up or over the hill in an effort to avoid the tropical diseases being nurtured beneath them. I passed the courthouse, where the women squatting on their heels waiting for their errant husbands offered a cheery 'Mingalaba' and their kids high-fived me. Foreigners are still a novelty in Myeik, a result of them being banned from the city for so long.

On a nearby lane I found what I was looking for: the site of the former district commissioner's house. Bombed in the Second World War and rebuilt a number of times, the locals avoid it if they can, believing the current building to have inherited the ghosts that inhabited the previous homes. Many residences in Burma stay empty because they are thought to be haunted. A government office occupies the land now, but the view from the garden remains the same as before, reaching across the harbour to the island opposite and its reclining Buddha.

Two of the more unusual British officials to come to Burma governed Myeik from this location at various times. J. S. Furnivall, who was criticising the lust for riches at the expense of the Burmese as early as 1908, and whose time in Yangon inspired him to invent the idea of the plural society, was district commissioner during the First World War. Myeik had faded into obscurity then, its days as a conduit to East Asia and China over, and the port was regarded as a punishment posting for officials who were 'pro-Burman' or didn't display sufficient enthusiasm for the colonial mission.

Maurice Collis, who served as Myeik's district commissioner between 1931 and 1934, fell into both categories. Like Furnivall, Collis was a member of the elite Indian Civil Service, arriving in Burma in 1912. He reached the high point of his career in 1929 when he became Rangoon's chief magistrate. But Collis was too friendly with the locals and didn't get on with his fellow members of the Pegu Club, quickly gaining a reputation for being soft on Burmese and Indian agitators for independence.

Removed from the post after just two years, Collis was sent to Myeik. He liked the town, bursting into tears when he boarded the boat to leave it for the last time. His fellow British were embarrassed by his display of emotion. The Burmese consoled him. Myeik was Collis's final posting. He retired to London to write numerous books, including one about Samuel White, pirate, emissary of the King of Siam, East India Company renegade and the most extraordinary foreigner to have lived in Myeik.

Arriving 250 years before Furnivall and Collis, White was the first to build a house on the plot of land on which their homes would stand. But while Furnivall and Collis were liberal administrators, White set out to make Myeik his personal fiefdom. He succeeded for a while and, for sheer rapacity, proved himself to be the equal of any of the companies set up in the colonial era to strip Burma of its resources.

Like all the best buccaneers, White hailed from Bristol in England's West Country, a port city indelibly associated with the twin evils of piracy and the slave trade. Bristol is where Jim Hawkins and Long John Silver set sail from in *Treasure Island*, and Blackbeard, Calico Jack – the first pirate to fly the Jolly Roger – Black Sam Bellamy, Francis Drake, William Dampier and Woodes Rogers are just some of the freebooters who grew up in the port or the counties around it.

White is far less well known, but equally deserving of notoriety. Almost single-handedly he turned Myeik into the Southeast Asian version of the pirate haven of Port Royal in Jamaica. The islands beyond the port – the Myeik Archipelago – challenged the Strait of Malacca as the region's equivalent of the Spanish Main, the haunt of the pirates and privateers who hunted the treasure-laden ships departing Spain's empire in Central and South America.

Scattered like green pearls across a 250-mile stretch of the Andaman Sea running south from Myeik to Kawthoung, the Myeik Archipelago is the last untouched island paradise in Southeast Asia. With just a few military bases and a handful of villages in the archipelago, most of the 800-odd islands are uninhabited and undeveloped. Thickly forested limestone formations edged with white sand beaches, they see only fishermen, a few passing yachts and a dwindling number of sea gypsies, the maritime nomads known in Burma as the Salone people.

Until White showed up in Myeik in 1677 the Salone were the pirates in the area, using the remote bays of the islands as hiding places from which they emerged to pounce on small vessels plying the local trade along the Tanintharyi coast. White's arrival ended the buccaneering days of the sea gypsies, their boats no match for ships armed with cannon and manned by crews with muskets.

Employed by the East India Company as a ship's pilot, White was sent to Madras initially. The Company was already enforcing its monopoly on trade between India and the Far East and the UK, despite challenges from individual British merchants known as 'interlopers'. Some of those rogue traders specialised in the commerce between India and Thailand. White joined forces with them and soon received an offer to skipper one of the King of Siam's ships ferrying elephants, betel nut and tin from Myeik to Madras.

He parlayed that position into a far more lucrative one as the king's representative in Myeik. In 1683 White was put in charge of all trade out of the port, responsible for arranging the despatch of goods sent from Siam to India and collecting the revenue they generated. Instead of a formal salary, White received a percentage of the profits. Sitting in his Ayutthaya court on the other side of the Tenasserim Hills, Siam's King Narai might not have realised the potential for corruption, but White did and quickly set about enriching himself.

Making his home on the hill above the harbour and surrounding it with a stockade, White recruited English sea captains and fitted out ships as men-of-war, before sending them out to seize prizes from the kingdoms along the southeast coast of India. White and his minions lurked also in the Myeik islands, many of which White mapped, hijacking ships sailing close to the archipelago and bringing them in to Myeik, where their captains were told they could leave once they had handed over a fee and signed papers saying nothing had been taken from them.

This was simple piracy, even if White did remit some of his ill-gotten gains to Ayutthaya. But he was also robbing King Narai blind, falsifying the figures of the legitimate trade between India and Siam. It was his accountant, a Boston navigator named Davenport captured by White and then put in charge of his financial affairs, who left the only personal record of White from this time. Davenport described him as being suave and cunning, able to switch from moments of gentility to extreme anger in seconds, and noted his fondness for strong drink.

Davenport was more fortunate than the Indian sailors who fell into White's hands, many of whom ended up as slaves in Myeik. White's ships began to hold whole towns on the Coromandel Coast ransom, threatening to burn them to the ground unless they paid up. But by now the East India Company was after their former pilot, as ships under their protection fell victim to his pirate crews. The Company petitioned London to send a navy ship out to detain White and bring Myeik under their control.

Typically intractable, White was in no way cowed by the prospect of arrest. 'Dost thou think I'm to be scar'd with the sight of a king's flag on a boats bow?' he raged at his press-ganged accountant Davenport. 'If ever a king's captain comes ashore and tells me that I must go to Madras, I'll be the man that will pistol him upon the place and wipe my arse with his king's commission.'

Fortunately for White, the Royal Navy arrived just at the time that Myeik's local population decided to rebel against his despotic rule. The British residents of the town were attacked and the men mostly slaughtered, White's house went up in flames and he, along with the navy, was forced to flee Myeik. Taking to his ship, *Resolution*, White convinced the navy captain that he had simply been acting under the orders of the King of Siam and promised to follow his ship to India.

Of course he didn't. Instead, White made his own leisurely way back to England, his arrival coinciding with the confusion of the Glorious Revolution, in which James II, the last Catholic king of England, was overthrown by the Protestant William of Orange. James had been a keen supporter of the East India Company and its trade monopoly. William was not. Samuel White escaped all punishment, despite returning home with an estimated £5 million in today's money from his nefarious activities. But he didn't get to enjoy it. The 39-year-old White died of an unknown fever in April 1689.

Six years later, Henry Every, another West Country boy turned pirate, caused the East India Company more trouble than White ever did by seizing one of the Grand Mughal's ships as it sailed from India to Mecca for the annual pilgrimage. It remains the largest haul in the history of piracy, worth over £50 million. The Company had to promise to pay compensation to the unimpressed Mughal emperor.

Like White, Every never stood trial for his crime. White would have been jealous of his loot. But White was a much more sophisticated pirate. He was a nautical version of his old boss the East India Company, which was plundering India to line the pockets of its shareholders, with every employee eager to gain a private fortune and get back to England before disease carried them off.

Thailand no longer makes any claims on Burma's territory, but Myeik continues to rely economically on its neighbour. Much of the catch brought in by the fishing fleets of Myeik and, farther south, Kawthoung goes to Thai kitchens, or ends up in the fish-canning factories staffed by some of the three million migrant workers from Burma thought to be in Thailand. And under a deal made in the junta era which will last until the late 2020s, almost all of Burma's natural gas stocks in the Andaman Sea are bought by Thailand.

'You can't buy a fish in the villages around Myeik,' I was told at the harbour. 'You go into a shop and they say they haven't got any. Then you see a crate and ask them to open it and it is packed full of tuna, barracuda or red snapper on ice. You ask to buy one and they say, "No, it's already sold to Thailand." And what fish is left for us is too expensive for many people to buy. Twenty years ago, we used to say, "I can't eat another tiger prawn." Now, we can't afford to buy one. They're 2,500 kyat [£1.35] each.'

Boat crews were unloading plastic drums and crates that held the previous night's catch. Groups of women on the quayside were busy gutting the fish. Ice trucks were arriving, and suitcase-sized chunks were being pushed up wooden runways onto the boats preparing to go out again. Some of the vessels were small, no more than large long-tails with a simple awning near the stern for the crew to shelter under.

Others were industrial trawlers, with dozens of blue drums for the fish lashed to the top of their superstructure.

That afternoon I took the ferry to Kadan Island, which Samuel White had sometimes used as a hideout. I was keen to see one of the legendary Myeik islands, and Kadan is the only one which has public transport travelling to it. The ferry was crowded with shoppers returning home. Two young women sat next to me, arranged their bags around them and proceeded to take a series of selfies with me without ever saying a word.

Docking at a jetty above which a pagoda loomed, I followed the other passengers to Kyunsu, the main settlement. Kyunsu is built above one of the mangrove swamps that cover much of the island, the houses in the lowest sections on stilts over pools of stagnant water. Signs warned of the risk of malaria and I thought that I wouldn't want to be here in the rainy season, when the mosquitos double their efforts.

There was no hint of piracy, except for the motorcycle taxi drivers with their special rates for foreigners. Nor were there any of the dreamy white sand beaches untouched by human feet that I had heard so much about. I returned to Myeik, a journey enlivened by the ferry breaking down in sight of the harbour. A coastguard boat came to the rescue. Burmese ladies in their *htamein* aren't the nimblest of people, but they scrambled up the ladder that was lowered for us, bags, umbrellas and all.

It is the islands that lie west and north of Kawthoung, Burma's far southern point, that are the real jewels of the Myeik Archipelago. They are the most stunning and least visited and also the ones where the remaining Salone, the sea gypsies, mostly roam. But no public boats run to any of those islands and hardly any are populated. Only fishermen and live-aboard yacht tours travel through this part of the archipelago, catering to a few thousand well-heeled foreign tourists a year. I set out to hitch a lift on one of them.

Fortune was kind and I made my way south to Kawthoung. Almost directly opposite the Thai town of Ranong, where the local fishermen unload all their catch, Kawthoung is an undistinguished transit point for migrant workers heading to Thailand. The harbour was crowded with the long-tails that run people to and from Ranong. A market, one street back from the waterside, offered Thai goods and alcohol at duty-free prices for the shoppers who come across from Thailand on day trips.

Waiting at the harbour was my ride, *Sea Gypsy*, a sturdy wooden vessel in yellow and green, its two-storey design reminiscent of a Chinese junk. There were no sails on its single mast; an engine would keep us moving. The crew were a mix of Bamar and Karen, the passengers mostly middle-aged Europeans combining a holiday in Thailand with four days of island-hopping in Burma. I boarded to be told that I would be sleeping on the deck in front of the wheelhouse, where the impassive skipper, eyes hidden behind sunglasses, steered the ship.

We departed Kawthoung in the early afternoon, heading north-west at eight knots across a flat sea the colour of royal blue. The cook strung a fishing line off the back of the boat, hoping for a bite from mackerel. An hour out of port, mobile phone signals disappeared and lumpy outcrops of limestone began to rise abruptly out of the water. The islands were small, some no more than islets, green forest erupting out of them, leaving room only for slender beaches of smooth sand, the sea off them turning turquoise over the coral reefs.

By the colonial era the pirates had been driven out of the Myeik Archipelago and some of the islands and the channels between them began to gain names, often those of the mariners who first identified them. But the archipelago remained largely unknown even after Burma's independence, with foreigners prevented from travelling here and only a scattering of permanent settlements.

Even now a permit is required to visit and the southern islands feel particularly remote, despite the most distant being only sixty miles off the coast. Many of the smaller islands don't have names, just numbers to identify them on the charts. The archipelago's obscurity is why the villain in the James Bond movie *Thunderball* chooses it as the place where his $100-million ransom of diamonds is to be deposited. Captain W. E. Johns, the creator of the flying policeman Biggles, a British schoolboy staple from the 1930s to 1960s, set a number of stories in the islands, too.

As we sailed on, the boat's motion barely perceptible, sea kites and eagles with bulbous bodies, broad wings and curved beaks soared overhead searching for their next meal. Occasional fishing boats were our only other company, passing either side of us or anchored off beaches which led to freshwater springs. We were never far from an island. They lay in wait ahead, or faded to indistinct shadows behind our stern, sometimes alone in the sea but more often two or three of them clustered close together.

Before dusk we moored a couple of hundred metres from a beach to catch the breeze that disappears closer to shore. A skinny ellipse of a new moon appeared after dinner. Beyond it the stars congregated in bright constellations. Arching over the island was a faint layer of green light indicating the presence of squid boats on the other side, their halogens mixing with the black of night. The new moon brings the fishing fleet out in force. A full moon is too bright, keeping the fish away and the boats in Kawthoung.

Late at night the breeze grew stronger, rustling the awning above the deck and rousing me from shallow sleep. A rope creaked as *Sea Gypsy* swung on its anchor and turned into the wind. They were sounds I would barely have heard on land, but which are as loud as a breaking window in such a hushed place. The green glow of the fishing boats was the only hint of human life around us. I understood why these islands were so attractive to Samuel White and his fellow pirates, slipping from bay to bay, readying themselves to take another ship, or for a raid on the Indian coast.

Awake by first light, I saw we had company. A couple of hundred metres away was a *kabang*, the traditional Salone boat, a ten-metre-long wooden vessel with a thatched roof covering the rear. For the sea gypsies, the *kabang* is the 'mother boat', their floating home, behind which smaller dugout canoes are towed and used for fishing. Two of the canoes were setting out, each crewed by a lone woman, a small boy in the bow of one, standing up and leaning on the oars to propel the craft forward.

Both *kabang* boats and the Salone are an increasingly rare sight. There are thought to be no more than 3,000 of these waterborne itinerants left in the Andaman Sea, found either in the Myeik Archipelago or, in smaller numbers, the Thai islands around Phuket, where they are known as the Chow Lair. As recently as ten years ago there were 8,000 of them, moving from island to island, fishing for squid, sea slugs, sea urchins and pearls, their children able to swim before they could walk, living on land only in the monsoon season.

Now the Salone struggle to survive by fishing. Their spears and hand-thrown nets can't compete with the trawlers that drag the seabed sweeping in the fish, while there are fewer Salone men these days. Seafaring is a dangerous enough existence – and there are no hospitals in the islands – but with more vessels coming to the area the Salone have taken to dynamite fishing to increase their catch. Many have perished while doing so. Others have fallen victim to drugs and alcohol.

Traditionally a *toke*, a patron, provided the Salone with all their needs – rice, clothes and other essential goods – in exchange for their squid, shells and pearls. But Maurice Collis noted in the 1930s how the Salone were often part paid in opium. Today, activists working with the Salone claim that as many as 40 per cent of the surviving men use either heroin or methamphetamines. There is no lack of narcotics in the region. Some of the fishing boats passing through the archipelago are also smuggling methamphetamine pills to Thailand.

Originally, the Salone lived far from Burma. They are an Austronesian people, perhaps from Taiwan, who migrated east and south to the Pacific and west to the Malay Peninsula, arriving in the Myeik Archipelago around 500 years ago. These days they are far less nomadic with many living in villages and no longer maintaining *kabang* boats, fishing instead close to the shore in their dugout canoes. And with the shortage of Salone men, the women are increasingly marrying the Bamar who have settled on a few of the islands.

A day later we dropped anchor in the north-west bay of Jar Lann. Home to a rare pagoda in the archipelago, manned by just two monks, and a small *Tatmadaw* base, Jar Lann is one of the bigger islands and now has a permanent settlement of about two hundred people, a mix of Salone and migrants from the mainland. It was squalid in the sunshine, a line of mostly one-room shacks on stilts along the shore, discarded plastic bags, packaging, cans and bottles floating in the water underneath them.

Shelves of alcohol were prominent at the village's best-stocked shop, where I found 21-year-old Cham Myae, a slim, pretty girl, her long hair reaching almost to her waist. Her parents moved from Myeik ten years ago. 'It's better business here. We get a lot of fishing boats stopping to make repairs and they stay a while,' she said. But Cham Myae didn't like island life. 'It's boring. There's nothing to do except play computer games at night.'

Nor are there any potential suitors. 'It's hard to find a husband here. It's only Salone men and fishermen and they are not handsome,' she told me with a giggle. 'But I prefer the Salone to the Burmese here. They are natural and simple people and quite polite.' Did she socialise with them? 'Sometimes I hang out with the Salone women, the ones who speak some Burmese. We go swimming, although I can't really swim. And we celebrate festivals together.'

Separated by their different languages – the Salone speak an Austronesian tongue known as Moken which has a number of different dialects – hardly any of the Salone children go to the primary school in the village. 'The school teaches in Burmese,' said Cham Myae. 'But the children of the Salone who marry Bamar people learn to speak Burmese and they go to the school. When they're older, some go to school on the mainland like I did.'

Intermarriage is why the number of Salone is dropping so fast, and the reason why they will probably be assimilated with the Bamar in another generation or two. At a house in the village I found five Salone women, a grandmother and her sister, two daughters and a granddaughter with her baby son. Three of them were widows, their husbands dead from either fishing accidents or drugs, and one had split from her partner.

All but the baby boy, who was suffering from a disability, his eyes vacant, mouth stuck open and dribbling constantly, were born at sea on *kabang* boats. None of them had been to school or knew how old they were. The one woman still married had a Bamar husband. 'That's why I can speak some Burmese. But I can't read or write,' she told me. We sat in a circle on the porch of the house, the ladies dipping frequently into a small bucket holding betel nut. They all reached for cigarettes when I offered them.

Up close, their Austronesian ethnicity was apparent. They were darker than the Bamar, their noses broader, with thick and wiry hair. Their teeth were stained and their *htamein* were worn and filthy. The house, which they shared, the married woman apart, lacked furniture. A cooking pot, fishing gear and a few clothes hung on nails driven into the walls were their only visible possessions.

Their friend Ta Aye joined us with one of her kids. Married to a Bamar fisherman, she didn't know her age either. Ta Aye looked forty-something, but I knew she was probably ten years younger. Like her friends, she spends her days fishing. 'Sometimes we fish all day or all night and maybe catch one or two squid,' said Ta Aye. 'There are many more fishing boats now and every year there are less fish.'

One kilo of squid sells for 4,500 kyat (£2.50) on the island. Nor are the Salone able to supplement their income by hunting for pearls as they once did. 'The government says we can't take the pearls anymore. There are pearl farms now,' said Ta Aye, one hand waving dismissively out to sea. She wanted her children to study rather than fish. 'If they are educated, they will have better lives.' Ta Aye was looking straight at me, almost daring me to ask what would become of the Salone. She knew the fate that awaited her people. 'There will be fewer of us in the future. It is too hard a life for us now.'

Ta Aye missed the old ways, though, as did the other women. 'We prefer to stay on our boats. That's how we lived when I was young, before we stayed on the islands. Now, our culture is disappearing. Young people don't know how to build a *kabang* anymore.' And despite being married to a Bamar man, Ta Aye and the others were uncomfortable living alongside the mainlanders. 'We're not very friendly with the Burmese. But I can't say what I think of them,' she told me. 'I live on the island and there may be trouble if I say what I think.'

Salone canoes were heading out of the bay when we left Jar Lann, the kids on board waving. *Sea Gypsy* set a course south-west through the Investigator Channel, gliding across a wave-free sea. We were on the far west of the archipelago now, close to the maritime frontier with India. A hundred and twenty miles farther west were the Andaman and Nicobar Islands, Indian territory even though they are much closer to Burma than India.

Our destination was Boulder Bay Island. Its horseshoe-shaped bay was the prettiest I'd seen anywhere on the voyage, a vast crescent of a beach backed by thick forest, the white sand so soft and powdery that my feet sank ankle-deep into it. The sea was perfectly clear and I could stare down from the deck of *Sea Gypsy* and watch striped bannerfish mingling with yellow and blue emperors. Beneath them was the silvery flash of torpedo-like barracuda nosing around.

But when I went snorkelling on the other side of the island, I found only a graveyard. The reef had been dynamited, the coral splintered into bone-like ash-white fragments, as if some underwater ritual slaughter had taken place and the butchered skeletons were all that remained. Nature had been overwhelmed here, most likely by the Salone, the people who once lived so close to it, as they fight to survive. Their paradise was gone forever, and soon they would be, too.

11

Hiding in Plain Sight

Noor is as rare as one of the dwindling number of tigers that stalk the Tenasserim Hills, someone as little seen as the handful of freshwater dolphins which survive in the Ayeyarwady River. The son of a Rohingya Muslim father and a Rakhine Buddhist mother, he is a supremely scarce combination of ethnicities. 'There are very few people like me,' Noor told me with a proud smile over a cup of tea in Mingalar Taung Nyunt, a township north of Yangon's main railway station.

Rakhine State, which lies south of Chin State in the west of Burma, has been home to both the Rakhine people and the Rohingya for centuries, shared by Buddhists and Muslims who went to school and worked together but hardly ever married each other. The south of the state, a shallow curve of coastline that kisses the Bay of Bengal, has always been dominated by the Rakhine. In the north, the Rohingya were traditionally the majority in the areas close to the Naf River, which divides northern Rakhine State from Bangladesh.

Maungdaw, a town on the Naf River, was 80 per cent Rohingya when Noor was growing up there. But his dad's family, like most Rohingya, hail originally from what was once known as Bengal, the region which is now Bangladesh and the Indian state of West Bengal. Noor's ancestors migrated first to Mrauk U, the ancient capital of the Rakhine kingdom, before his great-great-grandfather moved the family to a village outside Maungdaw. 'My father's family has been living in Rakhine since 1819 and we have the documents to prove it,' said Noor.

Significant numbers of Rohingya came to Rakhine State – formerly called Arakan – in the colonial era. But Rohingya and Rakhine have been moving across the Naf River in both directions for hundreds of years. Muslims were present in Mrauk U by the fifteenth century, building mosques alongside the pagodas. And Arakan, which was its own independent state until 1784, had a history of commerce with the Arab world stretching back a millennium. Merchants from the Middle East settled in Arakan and some Rohingya claim ancestry from them.

But while Noor, his sister and mother all have the pink identity cards which identify people as nationals of Burma, his father doesn't. 'He is Rohingya, so he isn't considered to be a citizen. It's ridiculous, when you think about how long his family have been in the country,' said Noor. In recent decades, though, all Rohingya, even those with identity cards and passports, have come to be regarded as illegal immigrants from Bangladesh.

'If you're a Muslim from Rakhine, you're really from Bangladesh. If you're a Muslim from Yangon, you're really from India,' one Rohingya woman told me. But unlike people of Indian heritage the Rohingya are officially stateless, a result of the junta changing Burma's citizenship laws in 1982. Since then, only people from an ethnic group recognised by the state, and who can prove that their ancestors were present in the country before 1823, are eligible to be citizens. And the Rohingya are not considered to be an indigenous minority.

Burma's border with Bangladesh was only demarcated in 1985. It has always been porous, prime territory for smugglers and anyone seeking to cross. There is no question that some Rohingya did arrive illegally in the past. But northern Rakhine State, where farmers and fishermen eke out a subsistence living in an intensely malarial region prone to flooding in the monsoon season, is no longer a desirable destination for would-be migrants. 'Why would anyone come? Bangladesh is doing better. It's much more developed on the other side of the border,' said Noor.

So unattractive is northern Rakhine that in the 1990s the generals offered criminals early release from prison if they would move there, as well as trying to entice Yangon's shanty-town dwellers to relocate. The idea was to settle Buddhists in an area with a majority Rohingya population. Those who agreed to swap jail for northern Rakhine State received not only a house and land but free food rations for the first year, as long as they stayed for a minimum of three years. Around fifty villages were built for the convict pioneers. But after the three years were up, almost everyone who could leave did so.

Until very recently northern Rakhine was a little-known pocket of Burma, while the Rohingya were barely thought of by most people outside of the state, mentioned only in crude propaganda that portrayed them as Muslim trespassers from Bangladesh. 'I don't think I heard the word Rohingya until 2012,' my friend Tim told me. 'If we referred to them at all we called them Bengali Muslims. In Burmese "Rohingya" means "Arakanese People" and that's why most Bamar people can't accept the use of that word.'

Now, though, everyone in Burma and the rest of the world is aware of the Rohingya. Since 2016 a campaign of *Tatmadaw*-led terror has pushed an estimated 700,000 Rohingya across the frontier into Bangladesh, where they have joined another 300,000 who fled previous attacks. The 400,000 Rohingya thought to remain in Rakhine State are confined in their villages and camps for the internally displaced, with a few thousand penned in a ghetto in the Rakhine capital of Sittwe.

It is a humanitarian tragedy on an enormous scale, one that Bangladesh is in no position to cope with. But the aftershocks from the violence have had a disastrous impact inside Burma, too, and not just for the Rohingya. The nation's and Aung San Suu Kyi's reputations have taken a battering that they will struggle to recover from. And the actions of the army in Rakhine State have exposed the deep flaws in the country's political system, just two years after the election that was supposed to herald a democratic future for Burma.

Under the 2008 constitution the military retain jurisdiction over border affairs and security, which has allowed the *Tatmadaw* a free hand in Rakhine State. Daw Suu has said nothing about the army's assault on the Rohingya, her only role being to take the global blame for the brutality. 'I am very sad that she is so silent on this,' Noor said. 'We know she can't control the military. But she is a Nobel Peace Prize winner and she shouldn't protect the military, even if she can't do anything for us.'

Sympathy for the plight of the Rohingya is in short supply in Burma, though. There are no votes to be earned or moral high ground to be won by standing up for them. Decades of stigmatisation, a slow-burning persecution, mean that just to use the name 'Rohingya' is enough to provoke a fight with the country's nationalists. And the violence that began in October 2016 was prompted by a militant Muslim group, the

Arakan Rohingya Salvation Army (ARSA), ambushing police posts near Maungdaw.

That attack, and further ones in August 2017, gave the *Tatmadaw* the excuse to sweep through northern Rakhine on an ethnic cleansing crusade, raping and killing, burning and looting, driving the Rohingya out of their villages so they could only flee across the Naf River to Bangladesh. With the United Nations, aid agencies and media almost entirely excluded from the region, the government and military claim the Rohingya left of their own volition, having first decided to raze their own homes to the ground. It is an implausible argument, one voiced initially by the Muslim-hater and Mandalay monk U Wirathu.

One of Noor's aunt's lost her home in the violence, burned down by the soldiers. 'She hasn't got anything now, just the clothes she was wearing when she escaped to my cousin's house in Maungdaw,' said Noor. 'Four people were killed when the army came to my village. Almost everyone has left for Bangladesh now. The people who have stayed can't do anything. They can't leave the village.'

A slight 33-year-old with a greasy, orange-streaked fringe stuck to his forehead, sideburns and a wardrobe of skinny jeans and loud shirts, Noor identifies himself as Rohingya, despite his Rakhine mother, and was raised as a Muslim, although he told me he attended the mosque rarely. He is gay, too, and rather flamboyant about it for a country where same-sex relationships are still illegal and few people are openly out. But Noor wasn't worried about any potential official inquiries into his private life. He was far more nervous about what the authorities might do if he was known to be discussing the government's treatment of the Rohingya with a foreigner.

Growing up in Maungdaw, Noor claimed that there was little tension between the Rohingya and the much smaller Rakhine community. 'There were no problems when I was at school. I knew a lot of Rakhine Buddhists. I'd speak Rakhine with them and the Rohingya language at home,' he stated. Rohingya, while related to Bengali and Chittagonian, the language spoken in southern Bangladesh, is a separate tongue of its own.

Attending university in Sittwe was Noor's introduction to the antipathy many Rakhine have for the Rohingya. 'I had a place at Yangon University, but I couldn't go because at that time I didn't have an identity card. So I went to Sittwe University to study law,' he said. 'It was a real contrast from Maungdaw. There had been some conflict between Rohingya and Rakhine in Sittwe the year before I started, so a lot of Rakhine parents told their children not to mix with the Rohingya.'

All Rohingya are now barred from Burma's universities, but even in 2001 they were a small minority and easy targets. 'We didn't sit next to the Rakhine in lectures. We couldn't hang out on Strand Road in the evening like the other students because people would try and attack us. And on the bus if a Rohingya had a seat and Buddhist didn't, we had to stand up and give up our seat,' recalled Noor quietly, his eyes downcast. 'The discrimination you experience makes you discriminate in your heart. If you're treated like a dog, you start to hate.'

I asked why he thought there was such animosity towards the Rohingya and his answer came in a jumbled flow of reasons accompanied by nervous hand waving. 'I blame the government. The local government officials treated us the worst. They're not well educated, they think Muslims are their servants. And the Rakhine are really Buddhist and the

Rohingya are very Muslim. Both peoples are too religious. And Rakhine and Rohingya look so different. And there's a lack of jobs in Rakhine State. People have time to think about politics and to look for someone to blame.'

Without an identity card, Noor wasn't eligible to receive a degree certificate when he graduated. 'That's when my family started thinking about leaving. It was too hard for us in Rakhine,' Noor said. 'My mother couldn't tolerate the fact that I couldn't even get my degree certificate. She donated a jeep to an official, it cost ten million kyat [£5,300], so that my sister and I could get our identity cards. They gave me my degree then. We moved to Yangon after that.'

They are not alone. Estimates of the number of Rohingya living in Yangon vary; some say up to 200,000 are resident, with many carrying identity cards describing them as Indian Muslims or, in a few cases, even as Buddhists. Shahida is one of the Rohingya hiding in plain sight from the authorities. 'You can get permission to come to Yangon if you pay a bribe to immigration, four million kyat [£2,125],' she told me.

Some Rohingya then move on to China or Thailand via Shan State. Ruili, a border town in Yunnan Province and a node in the jade trade, has a significant Rohingya population. Others head to Mong La, an infamous hub of criminality in Shan State, from where there are long-established people-smuggling routes to Thailand. Once in Thailand, most travel farther south to Malaysia or fly to the Middle East. But many Rohingya choose to remain in Yangon, unwilling to leave Burma while they still have relatives in Rakhine State.

Bright and passionate with an unblinking gaze, gold bracelets dangling on her wrists, Shahida grew up in Sittwe. Unlike northern Rakhine, the Rohingya were always a minority in Sittwe, making up around a quarter of the population. Shahida had also been prevented from attending Yangon University, even though she has an identity card, and was also refused permission to study for a postgraduate degree. 'Muslims aren't allowed to do a master's,' she sighed. Like Noor, she'd made me promise not to use her real name.

Shahida left Sittwe in 2013, a year after the persecution of the Rohingya had begun to make global headlines. The alleged rape and murder of a Buddhist woman by Rohingya men in May 2012 triggered a wave of tit-for-tat violence across Rakhine State in the following months. Rakhine mobs set fire to all but two of Sittwe's Muslim neighbourhoods, despite a heavy army presence. 'It was like a nightmare. I thought I would be killed,' remembered Shahida. Two of her uncles died in the clashes and more than 100,000 Rohingya were herded into camps outside Sittwe.

Around four thousand Rohingya remain in Sittwe now, confined to a small area surrounded by police posts, with no one allowed in or out unless they have official permission. For a year after the 2012 rioting Shahida lived with her family in the ghetto. 'It felt like being locked up. We weren't able to leave the neighbourhood. We mostly stayed in the house. My sister went crazy, she couldn't handle it. A Rakhine family we knew supplied us with groceries, for double the normal price,' said Shahida.

Life has improved since they came to Yangon, swapping a large house for a cramped apartment. 'Yangon was so bright after spending so long hiding in the house,' she said. But Shahida is conscious that her family were able to leave only because they have money. 'The people in the camps outside Sittwe, they can't afford to pay a bribe to get out,' she said. She feels unwelcome in Yangon, too. 'Some of the other Muslims here say, "You're causing trouble for us." Living as a Rohingya is stressful and depressing, because I don't think things will change for us.'

Like Noor, Shahida believes the authorities have deliberately escalated the tensions between the Rakhine and the Rohingya. 'The fuel is always there. It just needs a spark and the army likes to provide it,' she said grimly. 'I think the Rakhine were incited to riot in 2012. Monks were distributing pamphlets saying, "Bengalis will steal your land. You need to protect your race and religion." I feel sorry for the Rakhine. They are just as poor as us and are being manipulated by the army and the monks.'

The Second World War was the first time the Rohingya and Rakhine squared off against each other in significant numbers. The British recruited the Rohingya to fight for them, the Rakhine sided with the Japanese and both indulged in sectarian violence. But there is a long and strong tradition of radical Buddhism in Rakhine, with local clerics prominent in the campaign for independence from Britain. Today, monks form some of the recruits to the increasingly active Arakan Army, the Rakhine separatist militia.

For the Rakhine, like the Bamar, identity is tied to religion. To be Rakhine is to be Buddhist. That would be an asset to the military, once they initiated the process of detaching the Rohingya from the rest of the country after Ne Win's 1962 coup. Prior to that, the Rohingya were regarded as part of Burma's fabric. A number were elected as MPs in the 1950s and one served as Minister of Health under the then prime minister U Nu. In the 1961 census they were listed as 'Rohingya' rather than 'Bengali'.

During the junta period, though, life got progressively harder for the Rohingya, as the generals looked for scapegoats to distract people from protests, the economic malaise and to justify the heavy army presence in the borderlands. The authorities started registering the Rohingya as foreigners rather than locals. In 1978 the first major exodus took place, when around 200,000 Rohingya fled to Bangladesh saying they had been driven out of their homes by soldiers, although most would return over the next few years.

Soon the junta began to claim that Islamic insurgents were crossing from Bangladesh to link up with Rohingya separatists already present in Rakhine. There is a history of extremist Rohingya organisations based in Bangladesh, but they carried out few attacks in Burma. That might change in the future, with so many young, angry and dispossessed Rohingya men now in refugee camps in Bangladesh. But there is little evidence that ARSA, the group who ambushed the police in Maungdaw in 2016 and 2017, have any significant capability or local support.

Such misinformation served to polarise the Rakhine further from the Rohingya. There are around 2.4 million Rakhine, the descendants of people who migrated from China to central Burma before moving to Arakan around the tenth century CE. For the next 800 years various Rakhine kingdoms exerted a power and influence that extended into what are now Bangladesh and India and, through trade, beyond to the Middle East.

Arakan's time as an independent nation ended in 1784, when it was forcibly absorbed into the Burmese kingdom in a notably bloody conflict. The Rakhine are still resentful of their conquerors. It is one of the anomalies surrounding the crisis that the Rakhine dislike the Bamar as much as they do the Rohingya, in some cases more so, feeling that they have long been treated as second-class citizens of Burma themselves. Rakhine only became an official state in 1974, long after the Chin, Kachin, Karen and Shan peoples were given their own regions, even if in name only.

Today, the Rakhine remain ferociously nationalistic and proud of their otherness. I have heard them described as the Sicilians of Burma, separated from the rest of the country not by sea, as Sicily is from Italy, but by the Arakan Mountains. In the colonial period it was quicker to travel to Sittwe from Calcutta than from Yangon. There are still only two real roads leading over the Arakan Hills, reinforcing the sense that Rakhine State is cut off from Burma proper.

With their territory taken from them first by the Bamar, then by the British at the end of the First Anglo-Burmese War, and then once again by the Bamar after independence, the Rakhine are profoundly sensitive about losing land. The junta poked that wound deliberately and the Rakhine were easily persuaded that the Rohingya were flooding in from Bangladesh to displace them.

Further inflaming their sense of injustice was the almost complete lack of investment in their homeland during the junta years, along with the rest of the border regions. After neighbouring Chin State, Rakhine is the most deprived part of Burma. Mixed together, the Rakhine people's deep-seated anger over the annexation of their territory, their history of militant Buddhism, paranoia over the Rohingya and extreme poverty make for a very combustible cocktail.

'As long as Rakhine stays poor, the people will stay angry. Rakhine people want access to their own natural resources. But the government ignores them,' a Rakhine journalist named Ko Min Min told me. 'There's been no real difference since the NLD took over. The roads are a bit better and there's more construction, but that's it. If anything, people are angrier and more set in their attitudes. Rakhine people didn't like Aung San much and it is the same with his daughter.'

Ko Min Min was tall and thin with a quizzical smile playing on his face. He looked as if he doubted everything he heard, an entirely reasonable approach for an investigative journalist in Burma. He set up his own news agency in Sittwe in 2015 after working on local papers. 'In Sittwe the newspapers are biased. They talk only about the Rakhine, just as the foreign media write only about the Rohingya. I set up my own agency to talk about all the ethnic groups, to be balanced.'

Does he think there is a hunger in Rakhine State for such non-partisan reporting? 'I think there are quite a few liberal people in Rakhine, but they don't want to speak out,' Ko Min Min replied. 'Most Rakhine believe in the idea of their own state. They want their own nation and they'll sacrifice other things to achieve that. Caring about the Muslims is far less of a priority.' But Ko Min Min conceded that the progressives are outnumbered by the intolerant. 'At a grassroots level, there's a lot of hatred.'

By his own admission he was once a Rakhine loyalist. 'I used to believe what the nationalists said about Rohingya being an invented name so that the Muslims could establish themselves in Rakhine. I used to fly the Buddhist flag on my motorbike,' he said. It hadn't taken long for his change of attitude to anger his former nationalist friends. Within eight months of setting up his agency, Ko Min Min was receiving death threats on Facebook and a small bomb was thrown at the compound that houses his office.

When we met for a coffee in a Yangon shopping mall, he shrugged off the attack. Ko Min Min was more concerned about one of his former colleagues, who had moved to Reuters and was now serving seven years in prison, after being convicted with another journalist of possessing official documents, which they had been handed by the police immediately before their arrest. Sentenced under a 1923 colonial-era law, the real reason for their imprisonment was their reporting on the killing of ten Rohingya men by the military in 2017, hard evidence of the state's involvement in massacres in northern Rakhine.

Media independence has been another casualty of the violence in Rakhine State. The press have been prevented from travelling to northern Rakhine since 2016, except on stage-managed trips. But even before the Rohingya crisis, legislation passed in the colonial and junta periods was routinely being utilised by extremist monks, politicians of all parties and the *Tatmadaw* to silence the local media. Since the end of military rule people have been arrested for everything from posting satirical comments on Facebook to reporting on the ethnic armies operating in the borderlands.

In March 2012, when I was in Yangon covering the by-elections that resulted in Aung San Suu Kyi taking a seat in parliament for the first time, I visited the cramped and chaotic NLD head office. An emancipated fourth estate was on the party's mind then. 'We still have no free press,' Nyan Win, a senior NLD figure and Daw Suu's long-time lawyer told me. 'We'd be more confident if we did.' Six years on, the NLD appears happy to keep the media muzzled, while mimicking the junta's tactics of closing off the parts of the country they don't want outsiders to see.

Unable to reach northern Rakhine, I decided to travel to Sittwe. I hadn't been there for eighteen months, since just before the 2016 violence, and when I landed at the airport there were police on the runway checking who was disembarking. Others lined the route into town, many more than I remembered from my last visit. The roads had been upgraded, no longer punctuated by potholes the size of small craters, but they still lacked pavements and were choked with motorbikes, with everyone swallowing the dust kicked up by the traffic.

Tensions were high. Two months previously seven Rakhine had been shot dead by the police during a protest in Mrauk U, their historic capital a few hours north of Sittwe. Less than a month before I arrived three bombs had gone off in downtown. The local conspiracy theorists were having a field day. 'It was the government who set off the bombs. They're trying to justify what happened in Mrauk U. They want people to think that the security situation is so bad that the police are under threat,' said the man who drove me into town.

People were feverish and not just because we were all burning up under a sun growing more intense by the day, signalling the approach of the monsoon, the time of year when tempers fray. The twitchy atmosphere served to make the town appear even less attractive than it already is. Sittwe's modern incarnation is low-rise and mediocre, wooden and brick homes set on scrappy lanes that straggle back from the Strand, the riverfront road that winds past the port to a point where the Kaladan River meets the Bay of Bengal.

Many businesses along the main road parallel to the Strand were closed. The rest were general stores or mobile phone shops. There was little sign of economic activity, apart from the large fish market. But much of the catch from Rakhine is taken by trawlers from outside the state and goes elsewhere, principally Yangon, while the natural-gas fields offshore supply India. 'There's no industry and there are no jobs. A lot of us have to go to Malaysia or Thailand to find work. Of course we're angry,' said a man at the market.

Foreigners in Sittwe, almost all of whom are NGO workers, have been on the receiving end of some of that rage. People in provincial Burma are normally eager to stop and talk to westerners, but not in Sittwe. The Rakhine are naturally insular anyway, but now, following the worldwide condemnation of the crackdown on the Rohingya, they feel picked upon by the West and resentful of the aid agencies who come to Sittwe to help the Rohingya and not them.

Walking through the market, pushing through the crowds of people and the trishaws loaded with shopping, I attracted a lot of stares, by no means all friendly, and while some people responded to a greeting, others just ignored me. Circling back to the main road, I stopped outside the Jama Mosque. Surrounded by a high wall, behind which palm trees lean protectively in as a further barricade, the Jama is the oldest mosque in Sittwe, dating back to 1859.

Sittwe was known then as Akyab. It was one of the earliest of the British acquisitions, taken in 1826 after the First Anglo-Burmese War, and later became a key port in the rice trade, with the grain shipped from the Ayeyarwady Delta to Akyab for export. But during the Second World War Arakan was the scene of some of the fiercest fighting between the British and the Japanese, with the Rohingya and Rakhine on opposing sides. Akyab was largely destroyed and never regained its former prominence after independence, the town left neglected and ignored.

Since 2012 that has been the fate of the Jama Mosque. It was closed after almost all of Sittwe's Muslims were moved to camps for the internally displaced, although 'deliberately displaced' is a more accurate description. Now the Jama is falling apart by inches, plaster crumbling off to reveal the brickwork, wooden shutters and doors hanging by their hinges, the plinths on the roof gone, so the minarets stand forlorn at the four corners of the building, the intricate patterns around the windows barely discernible under the dirt and mould.

Standing on tiptoes to peer over the wall at the mosque, I noticed two men looking at me. I heard them shouting as I took a few pictures with my phone, and then a policeman was running up to me. 'You can't take photos here. It's not allowed.' I said, 'OK', and moved off. The two men were grinning now. They had told the policeman I was taking pictures. Sittwe is seeking to obscure its Muslim past and doesn't want any witnesses, so the Jama is being left to collapse discreetly behind its high wall, the authorities looking forward to the day when they can bulldoze the rubble and all memories of it.

'They're trying to make us leave of our own accord. We're not being forced out directly, but they're making life difficult for us, making us hungry,' my Rohingya contact in Sittwe told me. We were talking fifty metres beyond the barbed-wire barrier and police post that guards the entrance to Aung Mingalar, the one remaining neighbourhood in Sittwe where Muslims can be found. A few thousand Rohingya live here, close to the Jama Mosque, unable to leave officially without permission, even if it is a major medical emergency, which is only granted if a bribe is paid.

Aung Mingalar's residents are effectively imprisoned, reliant on food deliveries from outside to survive, with the local officials waiting for their money to run out so they can be transported to join the rest of the Rohingya in the camps outside town. 'They say, "Go to the camp and you will get rations." But I've seen the camps and the conditions are very bad,' said the man. 'It's impossible for me to leave. My house is here. Some Rakhine are still nice and supply food and other things to us, for a profit.'

My contact was taking a risk leaving Aung Mingalar illicitly, even if we were close to the entrance. We were hidden from view, having arranged to meet inside a shop, but I knew I had been noticed by the police as I approached. He had needed to come out, though, to meet with two Rakhine men looking to hire labourers for 5,000 kyat (£2.65) a day. Some Rakhine continue to employ the Rohingya, not least because they are cheap. 'The police won't let them have the men unless they pay some tea money first,' said the Rohingya man. In Burma, 'tea money' is the euphemism for a bribe.

Getting out of the ghetto, if only for fifteen minutes, was the highlight of his day. 'There is nothing for us to do in Aung Mingalar. There is no business, we have no jobs. We sit in the house or the tea shop, we walk and talk and pray. This is the Aung Mingalar life.' He looked older than his age, but he was smart in a *longyi* and patterned shirt over his belly and his eyes were still bright and lively. He wasn't giving up.

Four hours later I sat waiting in a near-empty tea shop a few hundred metres down the road from Aung Mingalar. It was early afternoon and I was sweating in the heat. The teenage waiters were slumped over tables, heads on their arms, or fanning themselves with the plastic menus. My phone rang. 'He's on his way. Wait outside.' A couple of minutes later a Rakhine man pulled up on a motorbike. He offered a smile as a greeting and handed me a helmet, motioning me to pull down the visor. I climbed on the back and we accelerated away.

We were on our way to one of the villages outside Sittwe whose Rohingya residents haven't been driven into the camps. Behind me, out of sight on another bike, was my contact. I hadn't suggested we try and reach a village, knowing that if we got caught he would be in serious trouble and so would I. But he knew I wanted to go, and I understood that it made him happy to outsmart his captors and escape Aung Mingalar for a while.

Whipping through Sittwe's northern suburbs, we went through an archway manned by police who didn't get the chance to see us for more than a couple of seconds. This was the military area of town. For the next two miles we passed a succession of barracks on both sides of the tree-lined road, home to some of the units that deployed to northern Rakhine in 2016 and 2017 to drive the Rohingya across the border to Bangladesh. The garrison is built on land confiscated from Rakhine and Rohingya farmers in the 1980s.

Emerging from the trees, we drove through open fields towards a village that is home to one of Sittwe's universities. After ten minutes I could see the institution and knew that we had missed our turn-off. The driver halted by the side of the road and called his colleague for instructions, while I squatted by the side of the bike hiding from the traffic. A police pickup truck went past, the men in the back in helmets with shotguns on their knees, followed by an army officer in a car that passed so close I could see the rank insignia on his epaulettes.

This wasn't the ideal place to stop. But we were mobile again soon, retracing our way back to a large tree where we found the other bike and a paved path that led away from the road at a right angle. After a couple of hundred metres the concrete gave way to a dust track that wound through a small Rakhine village, haystacks interspersed with wooden homes. The dust was thick and deep, the driver struggling to control his front wheel as we slithered through it.

Then we were sliding around a corner and in the near distance I saw the unmistakeable shape of a mosque with a small dome and two metal crescents atop either side of its entrance. This was the Rohingya village, home to 200-odd families, around a thousand people. A single dirt road led through it, the palm-thatched houses on either side and down small lanes shielded from view by high bamboo fences, something I hadn't encountered in Burma before. 'It is to prevent our women being seen from outside,' the village elder explained when I was introduced to him.

Bald with a white and yellow beard, in a short-sleeved shirt and *longyi*, he sat on a raised platform in a tea shop. Around him were men ranging in age from their late teens to their sixties, some with beards, many wearing taqiyah caps. I saw hardly any women while I was in the village. Those who did emerge from their houses were in black burkas, their faces covered completely.

Two Rakhine men came down the road, driving their cattle ahead of them. 'They are from the next village. We live side by side with the Rakhine here and it has always been peaceful. There was no violence here in 2012. In the rainy season we work in their fields sometimes. Now we have nothing to do, so we stay in the tea shop all day,' said the elder. But the Rakhine village occupies land that once belonged to the men in the tea shop, taken from the Rohingya in the junta era and handed to the Rakhine.

Most Rohingya are traditionally farmers or fishermen. But with their land appropriated over the years many Rohingya around Sittwe used to work as labourers, either on Rakhine farms or in the city. 'We can't do that now. We can't go too far from the village,' said the elder. 'Most of us have relatives working abroad, in Saudi Arabia, Bangladesh or Malaysia, and they send money back to us so we can live.' The money is remitted under the hawala system, an informal banking network first used a millennium or more ago by Muslim traders on the Silk Roads.

Just like the people living in Aung Mingalar, the Rohingya here are being deliberately isolated by the authorities in the hope that they will leave the village, either to move to the camps, which were out of sight south of us, or to go abroad. 'The government knows we are here but they never come. They don't care. The government will do nothing for us. They just want us to disappear,' the elder said. There was no bile in his voice as he spoke. Some of the men sitting with him were sullen, their anger obvious, but more of them appeared resigned to their fate, beaten down by their circumstances.

None advocated armed resistance to the government, or any form of opposition. Their situation is too far gone now for that. 'People here don't support violence. Maybe some villages in the north did. But ARSA can't do anything for us. How can they liberate northern Rakhine with no weapons and no support? Look at the Kachin and Shan people. They have been fighting for seventy years and they still have nothing,' said the elder.

Nearby were a few other Rohingya villages, the only ones left in the vicinity of Sittwe. There are far more in northern Rakhine, but their residents are now also imprisoned in them. Just a thirty-minute drive from the centre of Sittwe, the village has no electricity or running water, just wells and a couple of shops selling basic supplies. 'This is still better than living in the camps,' my contact told me. I asked what happens when people fall ill. 'We take them to the clinic in the camp. If it's serious, we pay to be allowed to take them to the hospital in Sittwe.'

Later, the elder showed me around the village. It was silent, with hardly any passing traffic and no noise coming from the homes. By far the liveliest place was the madrasa attached to the mosque, full of boys and girls as young as three in skullcaps and headscarves sitting beneath a blackboard with Arabic script on it as they studied the Koran. The elder pointed to a wooden hut in the mosque's compound. 'That is our school. Before 2012, the children went to the government school in the Rakhine village. They can't now, so we teach them ourselves.'

Corn fields and fallow rice paddies marked the boundary of the village. They are the last remnants of the land its people once owned and worked. 'My great-grandfather came here first,' remarked the elder, who was sixty-six. 'And my family had land here since then. But the army started taking my land from me in 1988 and now I have none. That is what I miss the most. I am a landless person.'

Asking what he expected to happen to them seemed foolish, given their lack of land and freedom. 'We have no future under these conditions. It is impossible for us to be happy the way we live. Many people want to leave for Malaysia, but it is too difficult now. In the future we will try and leave, like the Rohingya in the north,' he said. 'If we don't, we will disappear anyway. In another fifteen years there won't be any of us left here.'

Returning to Sittwe in the early evening to be confronted with apparent normality was disturbing. Men played *chinlone* by the side of the main road, passing a rattan ball around, keeping it airborne all the time. Food stalls were being set up under the wall that hides the Jama Mosque. Motorbikes weaved their way home. But a few streets away was Aung Mingalar and just outside town were the camps and forgotten villages. Hidden away, or forced into exile, the Rohingya are being erased from the landscape as if they were never here, their history and that of Rakhine State rewritten without recourse to facts or pity.

12

The Dream Factory

Restricting the media's ability to operate, either by censorship, repressive laws or refusing access to sensitive areas, as in the case of Rakhine State and the other conflict-ravaged regions of the borderlands, is a tactic the NLD have adopted from the military. Soon after their coup, the generals set up the Press Scrutiny and Registration Division, housed in a building occupied by the Japanese secret police in the Second World War, to make sure journalists and writers toed the line. Other censors were employed to do the same for artists and film-makers.

Yet the junta was merely following the example set by the British. They were assiduous in their efforts to muffle the local media, banning books, movies, newspapers and pamphlets. Even so, there were more than two hundred local periodicals in circulation by 1940. Advocates of independence were quick to realise the power of both the printed word and celluloid. They politicised those exposed to them, as well as projecting an image of Bamar identity to unite the country, ethnic minorities excepted, against the British.

Colonial Rangoon was a city bereft of art galleries, museums and libraries, but there were plenty of cinemas and film would prove to be highly influential in the struggle for self-determination. The very first film shown in Rangoon was an account of Japan's victory in the 1904–5 Russo-Japanese War. Japan's triumph had a huge impact on nascent nationalists – an Asian country defeating a European power in battle for the first time – and the opponents of colonial rule would quickly co-opt the fledgling movie industry to their cause.

Burma's first film appeared in 1919, a documentary following the funeral of an early campaigner for independence. A year later came the country's debut movie, *Love and Liquor*, a cautionary tale of the evils of alcohol and gambling, vices associated with the colonists. Like all Burmese productions from the 1920s the film is now lost, but its makers would go on to found A1 Film Company, the local version of a Hollywood dream factory.

By the 1930s A1 occupied twenty-five acres in the north of Rangoon. 'We had six sound stages and they were full all the time. We had a separate post-production facility in downtown. We were bigger than anything else in Southeast Asia. We'd shoot comedies, horror, musicals, dramas,' recalled Ko Myint, the great-grandson of A1's founder, when I visited him at the rambling, now dilapidated teak house his ancestor had built.

Realising film's ability to influence public opinion, the British started banning and censoring both Burmese and foreign movies early on. *The Adventures of Kathlyn*, a 1913 American movie serial about a woman lured from California to India and sold into slavery, was probably the first film banned in Burma. 'You will see her bound by fanatical natives,' went the advertising strapline, more than enough for its screening to be prohibited in 1914, the British not wanting the Burmese to get any ideas about tying up foreign women.

Censorship couldn't stop films critical of the colonists from being made, though. In 1937, the revolutionary students at Rangoon University got their close-up when future prime minister U Nu wrote and directed *Boycott*. It starred Aung San and other young nationalists, outlining their reasons for launching yet another student strike the year before. A1 would later film Aung San's speeches, which were then shown in cinemas.

Seventy years after U Nu's foray into film-making documentarians began venturing onto the streets of Yangon again, only this time to capture the realities of life under the generals. Independent film-making was virtually unknown after the 1962 coup, and there is little footage of Burma from the military era shot without the regime's approval, but a loose collective of budding film-makers set out to change that. 'Under the junta documentaries were propaganda, or films about how to do things. But we wanted to show the lives of ordinary people,' Thaiddhi, one of those young pioneers, told me.

Art, like politics and business, is often dynastic in Asia, where children are encouraged to follow in their relatives' footsteps. Thaiddhi is no exception; the son of a well-known musician, his younger brother is the tattooed guitarist of one of Yangon's top bands. But Thaiddhi, whose name comes from the Pali language, chose film as his medium, a much more risky endeavour than music when he started making documentaries in 2005. 'We couldn't shoot on the street, unless it was a location we knew with people we knew. If the police came, we'd tell them we were just practising how to use the camera.'

Sidestepping the censors was the aim of Thaiddhi and his contemporaries. 'The Ministry of Information, which was really the Ministry of Propaganda, was responsible for censoring movies and TV. Film-makers had to submit scripts to get permission to shoot and the film had to be submitted again after it was edited. But we didn't submit our films. We made our films illicitly, then sent them abroad to festivals or distributed them on DVDs. We were able to get around the censorship because documentary just wasn't really a genre here.'

Prematurely plump like many Burmese men, thanks to a diet of oily curries and fried snacks, Thaiddhi chose to meet in a café close to the old Rangoon racecourse in Yankin, the township where he grew up. He was modest about his work, deflecting my suggestion that it took courage to refuse to play by the junta's rules. 'We were afraid of them, for sure. I was born in 1983, so I was five when 1988 happened. I grew up with the fear. We knew people could get arrested and imprisoned,' he said.

Over coffee and pastries Thaiddhi explained how he and a handful of other young film-makers reinvented the art of the documentary in Burma. In doing so they compensated partially for the lack of an independent press. Their films, and the documentaries being made today, cover contentious topics – land confiscations, environmental causes, feminist and LBGT issues, access to education and healthcare – that are still largely ignored by the local media. That is partly out of fear of government reprisals, but also because a free press is still a new concept in Burma.

'We didn't do overtly political films in the beginning. It was more subtle than that. We wanted to hold up a mirror so we could reflect our society. We'd do a day in the life of an artist who had been in jail for supporting the NLD or people in an old-age home. It was quite gentle at first,' Thaiddhi recalled. 'But when you're making documentaries, you're dealing with truth and reality and that was sensitive for the authorities. Under the junta you couldn't show poverty, like a village of bamboo shacks, in mainstream movies. But we did.'

Soon they began to understand the potential of documentaries to achieve what other media couldn't in Burma. 'We realised we could tell stories like a feature film does, but they would be stories about ordinary people and their lives,' said Thaiddhi. 'We could show real life in a way the movies couldn't, because they were so heavily censored. And once you do that, politics is automatically involved.'

Their early experiences would coalesce in 2008 when they started shooting what would become a feature-length documentary about the immediate aftermath of Cyclone Nargis. 'Nargis is one of the most important events in our recent history,' said Thaiddhi. 'So many people died, but the junta only cared about pushing through the new constitution right after it. And it came soon after the Saffron Revolution, when lots of activists were in prison, so it was a key moment for the country.'

Footage of the Saffron Revolution, shot secretly and smuggled out of Burma, had embarrassed the junta. Thaiddhi and his colleagues would shame the generals further by journeying into the Ayeyarwady Delta, which bore the brunt of the destruction when Nargis made landfall in May 2008. 'Nargis hit Yangon hard too. The whole city looked like a war zone, trees down everywhere. Then my journalist friends told me it was worse in the Delta. So we decided to make a film. Two of us accompanied a family going to check on their relatives in Bogale Township,' he remembered.

With the junta providing no assistance to Nargis's victims and initially refusing to allow international aid into the country, many people started making trips to the Delta with donations of food and supplies. Thaiddhi and two other cameramen made repeated visits with some of them, filming as they went. 'We stayed in what was left of the villages with the victims. They helped us so much, hiding us when the army finally showed up. They were very unhappy with the government because they'd had no help and wanted their stories told.'

Having accumulated seventy hours of footage, the decision was made to edit the film outside Burma, well away from the eyes of regime spies. 'We sneaked the footage out to Hamburg,' said Thaiddhi. 'We were going to premiere it at Amsterdam's film festival, which is the biggest in the world for documentaries, but then one of the other cameramen and an editor were arrested back in Yangon, not for making the film but for their part in the Saffron Revolution. They were detained for forty-five days. We freaked out and put false names on the credits.'

Nargis: When Time Stopped Breathing introduced the new documentarians of Burma to the outside world. The film is raw and rain-soaked. There is no commentary, the story of Nargis is told in the voices of the victims, still in shock and left to fend for themselves in a flooded, flattened landscape. The documentary was acclaimed at film festivals in Europe and Asia throughout 2010, but there was no chance of it being shown in Burma while the junta was still in power.

Only in 2012, after the generals had stepped down, was it screened in Yangon. 'It was a test of the new government, and we put our real names on it,' said Thaiddhi. But *Nargis* has still never been broadcast on any of Burma's television channels. 'We've tried to get our films on television here but so far it hasn't happened. They're too scared to show them right now,' Thaiddhi said. Documentaries are shown only at one-off screenings in Yangon or on the Democratic Voice of Burma television station, which was based overseas until recently.

Such self-censorship is a hangover from the junta era, when films were scrutinised by a board that included representatives of the *Tatmadaw* and the Ministry of Religious Affairs and Culture. Those censors continue to operate under Daw Suu's government. Documentaries with LBGT themes, which focus on ethnic minority issues, or are considered too overt in their portrayal of sexuality, have all been banned since the NLD won the 2015 election.

'We're still fighting for the censorship to end. I know a lot of NLD people and I am constantly lobbying them for it to go. Censorship looks ugly in a democratic country,' said Thaiddhi. He was wary, though, of heaping any more criticism onto Daw Suu. 'She gets the blame for the army's actions. It's a really tough game for her,' he emphasised. 'As a film-maker, I am lucky to be living and working in these times. But it's not realistic at the moment to be attacking the government.'

Media ownership in Burma is concentrated in the hands of very few people, too, all with links to the former junta, further limiting the chances of controversial films being broadcast. 'The thing about television here is that the channels are owned by cronies, ex-generals or the sons of ex-generals. It's the same with radio, and television and radio are the two most powerful mediums in this country,' said Lamin Oo, one of the film-makers who emerged in the wake of Thaiddhi's generation. 'People think television is free because they can watch *Myanmar Idol*, but they don't show documentaries or independent news.'

Challenging that monopoly is still too risky for the new documentarians. 'I'd get into trouble if I made a film describing how television channels are owned by cronies. It's easier to interview ordinary people than it is to expose establishment figures,' said Lamin Oo. 'I think it is always in the back of your mind whether or not a subject is too controversial. We still can't make films about the Rohingya or Buddhist extremists, or which are critical of the government. It's not just the authorities, but the backlash we'd get on social media as well.'

Despite these limitations the number of documentaries being made continues to rise. They are much cheaper to shoot than movies and there are more and more film-makers who view them as a way of combining reportage with art, no matter what the government might say. 'When I started making films I was worried about what the authorities would think. Now I don't care,' said Shunn Lei, a 27-year-old director. 'I used footage of police beating women who had lost their land. The censors wanted me to cut that. I refused, so my film wasn't allowed to be screened.'

Shunn Lei is one of an increasing number of female film-makers who have graduated from Burma's sole film school in the last few years. Like my friend Thida, she spurns *thanaka* and the *htamein*, preferring jeans and t-shirts which reveal a couple of tattoos. For Shunn Lei documentaries are a means of questioning the prevailing male orthodoxy in Burma. 'I'm interested in women's rights and I thought film would allow me to inform people in a beautiful way,' she told me in her office in downtown Yangon.

Raising awareness of sexual harassment and violence, under-discussed and little reported in Burma, is one of Shunn Lei's principal goals. 'It's a real issue for women,' she pointed out. 'Even if you get a taxi in Yangon, you can get hassled. If you walk to work, or get the bus, molesting and catcalling is commonplace. Men are never taught that it is wrong. But women are always being told how to avoid harassment. That's victim blaming.'

Commentators in the colonial period were struck by how women in Burma appeared to be more liberated than elsewhere. James George Scott, the most noted of the early foreign interpreters of Burmese society, thought they enjoyed greater legal rights than their contemporaries in Europe. He cited how they retained any property they owned after marriage and kept it if they divorced. Henry Fielding-Hall, who wrote about his experiences in late nineteenth-century Burma in *The Soul of a People*, regarded the local females as 'the freest in the world'.

Today many would disagree with that. 'Burma is a very patriarchal place. I don't think it is true that women here have the same rights as men. People say, "Women have legal rights." But there are cultural limitations. There's sexist language. It is the way people believe women are born subordinate to men. That's why we need feminism in Burma. A Burmese feminism specifically for all women in the country,' said Shunn Lei.

Like other local feminists Shunn Lei does not look to Aung San Suu Kyi for inspiration. Since becoming Burma's leader she has spoken out on gender discrimination and the need to promote women's rights. But even though around one third of the NLD's MPs are female, Daw Suu didn't appoint any of them to her cabinet. And of the fourteen states and regions in Burma, only two have female chief ministers.

'Most people don't think of her as a woman. They think of her as Aung San's daughter,' noted Shunn Lei. 'He died when she was two, but no one ever talks about the role of her mother in raising her. That doesn't mean we don't admire her. We do. But she is a special, privileged case and definitely not a role model for rural women. She's an example of how our identities are defined by our fathers, husbands and work places. Never by us.'

As well as making documentaries Shunn Lei has co-founded a magazine discussing feminist issues, and organises workshops around the country introducing women to the idea of genuine equal rights. But she admits promoting feminism is a struggle. 'Most people in Burma, even educated ones, think it is a dirty word. Even men of my age think feminism means man-hating, which it isn't. They don't think of it as gender equality or empowerment. They think you're challenging the established system.'

That, though, is exactly what she and the other feminists in Burma are doing, just as the Rangoon University students of the 1930s confronted the colonial state. 'We are questioning the whole power structure in our country, so we are kind of revolutionary. It is revolutionary to be a feminist here. There is an element of the "oppressed and oppressors". But I don't think all men are oppressors,' said Shunn Lei.

Buddhism has played its part in entrenching the notion of male superiority over women. Despite Henry Fielding-Hall's extravagant claims about the independence enjoyed by Burmese women, he noted also that Buddhism places a lower value on females than men. The most senior nun in Burma is still regarded as subordinate to any ten-year-old novice monk, while women are barred from some of the most sacred Buddhist sites or confined to separate areas from men.

THE DREAM FACTORY

Taking on the Buddhist hierarchy is beyond anyone in Burma, a country where women might run shops and control household finances but are rarely seen in senior positions in business, as well as politics, and are almost invisible in the all-powerful military. Proportionally, young women are now the majority of students at universities, so there is hope for the future. But only around 7 per cent of the population goes on to higher education in Burma. And more young women than men leave school early to help support their parents, like the girls I met in the sweatshop in Hlaing Tharyar.

For now the best-known women in Burma are actresses, singers and television personalities, a trend that began in the 1930s when local movie stars like May Chin began to emerge. By the 1950s actresses such as Myint Myint Khin, Kyi Kyi Htay, Khin Yu May and Win Min Than, the first Burmese actress to star in a Hollywood movie when she played opposite Gregory Peck in *The Purple Plain*, were the queens of a decade viewed now as the high point of Burma's film industry.

'In the 1950s there were co-productions with India, Japan and Thailand, production values were high and the films were shown across Asia. It was the golden age of Burmese cinema,' Swe Zin Htaik told me. The grand dame of local actresses, she introduced herself as 'Grace', the English name she sometimes uses, when she arrived right on time to our meeting in a Golden Valley restaurant. Elegant in a blouse and *htamein*, with gold jewellery around her wrists and neck and sunglasses atop her black hair, Grace was refreshingly unpretentious and happy to reminisce about her time as a movie star.

She appeared in 200 films between 1971 and 1991, testimony to the punishing shooting schedules imposed by Burma's film-makers. 'One year, I made twenty-four films,' laughed

Grace. 'Sometimes I'd be shooting two or three films at the same time.' She retired at just thirty-seven. 'I felt isolated. Most directors, writers and producers were too close to the generals and I didn't like that. So I stopped acting and went behind the camera and into NGO work.'

Grace was born when the golden age was in full swing. Studios like A1 survived the carnage of the Second World War better than most of Burma's industries and were soon making films again. Even after independence their output remained fiercely patriotic. 'The big genres in the 1950s were period action movies, family dramas and comedies. The period movies were mostly set in colonial times and were nationalist in tone,' Grace recalled.

Growing up in Yangon, she haunted the city's cinema row – a collection of movie palaces near Sule Pagoda in downtown. 'There was the Palladium and the Globe, which showed Hollywood movies. They were air conditioned and very luxurious for the time. On the other side of the road, the cinemas showed Burmese and Indian movies. I used to like watching Hayley Mills in all those Disney movies. But the cinemas were nationalised in 1968, like everything else, and by 1970 they'd stopped showing Hollywood films.'

Just a few of the art deco theatres built in Yangon before and after the Second World War survive now. They have started showing foreign movies again, with Hollywood and Bollywood productions drawing the biggest crowds, but the refined atmosphere enjoyed by Grace in the 1950s is a very distant memory. My first visit to cinema row was to see the James Bond film *Spectre*. Movie-going is cheap in Burma, with tickets on sale for 2,000 kyat (£1.60), but 007 was a popular choice and touts outside were selling marked-up tickets to latecomers.

Inside, whole families ranging in age from babies to grandparents were present. There is no ratings system in Burma, so a five-year-old can watch a movie classified as an '18' in the UK. Everyone had brought food along and when the action scenes stopped the sound of collective crunching drowned out the dialogue. By the time Bond had dispatched the villain the floor was ankle-deep in discarded chicken bones, bottles and packaging and the resident rats were stealthily probing the detritus.

Back in the early 1950s, though, the glow from the golden age of Burma's movie industry helped light up Yangon, then in much need of some glamour. The city was pummelled during the war, its port and oil refineries destroyed by the British when they left, then heavily bombed after the Japanese occupied it. In May 1945 the Japanese pulled out, but not before randomly wrecking as much of downtown as they could, while leaving the bodies of locals hanging from lamp posts and lying in the streets as a grisly welcome for the arriving Allied soldiers.

The war inflicted more damage on Burma than any other nation in Asia, and the country has never really recovered economically from its impact. Around 80 per cent of Yangon had to be rebuilt after 1945, a figure mimicked by Mandalay. Other cities such as Meiktila and Myitkyina were completely destroyed, while roads, railways and bridges across the country were in ruins. With the amount of land for rice cut in half and the number of cattle reduced by two thirds, much of the population of inland Burma struggled to feed itself.

Rangoon was little more than a shanty town in 1945, a much larger version of the squatter neighbourhoods found in Hlaing Tharyar today, its residents sheltering where they could, while British and Indian soldiers took over the remaining buildings. When George MacDonald Fraser, the author of the Flashman novels, arrived with his platoon in June 1945, they slept on the marble floor of the local branch of the Hong Kong and Shanghai Bank.

Close to 100,000 soldiers from Britain and its imperial allies were killed, wounded or died of disease in Burma, the bloodiest theatre of the war for the UK. But any goodwill the British earned for ejecting the Japanese dissipated quickly. The colonists banned the use of the currency introduced by the Japanese, thus wiping out what savings people had managed to accumulate, while their efforts to introduce an executive council to rule the country ran into immediate opposition from Aung San and the Anti-Fascist People's Freedom League (AFPFL), the coalition he led.

From 1946 a campaign of disobedience began with a series of strikes and the AFPFL calling on people to refuse to pay rents or taxes. With the country awash with discarded weapons and the British struggling to impose any sort of order, crime and dacoity soared once again. Ritchie Gardiner, back in Rangoon four years after he fled the city ahead of the Japanese, took to sleeping with a shotgun under the pillows, much to the discomfort of his wife.

Gardiner had been as successful in wartime as he was in peace. Twice decorated for his bravery and leadership, he rose to be head of the Burma branch of Force 136, the Southeast Asian arm of the Special Operations Executive, a clandestine organisation dedicated to creating havoc behind enemy lines. Gardiner's men parachuted into remote areas of the borderlands to link up with the Kachin and Karen minorities, launching hit and run raids on the Japanese, before disappearing back into the jungle and mountains.

Along the way Gardiner had clashed with Orde Wingate, the legendary commander of the Chindits, a force of soldiers who also operated deep inside Japanese-held territory. Gardiner had disagreed with the strategy of sending British troops who knew nothing of local conditions so far behind enemy lines, and he was borne out by the appalling casualties the Chindits suffered. When recruiting for Force 136 Gardiner sought men like himself, who had lived in Burma, knew the jungle and could speak the different languages.

His job in 1946 was to get Macgregor's timber business underway again. But there would be no going back to the pre-war days of afternoon tea on well-watered lawns, nights at the Pegu Club and the easy exploitation of Burma's resources. The war had changed everything, transforming Aung San from a mildly threatening nationalist agitator into the commander of an army and leader of a political party who had to be included in any negotiations about the country's future.

Britain tried to delay granting Burma independence, offering dominion status within the empire first and then a plan leading to self-rule in 1953. But after a visit to London in early 1947 Aung San insisted the British depart within a year. There was no appetite in the UK for another fight in Burma so soon after the war and Aung San got his way. On 4 January 1948 Burma became independent. Ritchie Gardiner and his family left for Scotland, never to return.

Almost immediately Burma was at war again. Four months after independence, communist groups rose up against the AFPFL's coalition government. It was led now by U Nu after Aung San's assassination by a rival politician in July 1947, a stunning event that revealed how Burma's nationalists were united only in their dislike of the British. The communist insurrection was followed soon after by the rebellion of the

Karen, who had fought so effectively against the Japanese as part of Force 136. Their soldiers reached the suburbs of Yangon before being forced back.

Newly independent Burma was a mass of competing parties and organisations, all jockeying for position and power and unwilling to compromise. Ominously, Ne Win was appointed head of the *Tatmadaw* and then deputy prime minister in 1949. Just one year after independence and the military were already part of the political system, with U Nu dependent on the army's support to survive. Struggling with a devastated economy, Burma had all the dice loaded against it; a barely functioning state whose huge structural problems were compounded by infighting and inefficiency.

Some people in Burma look back on the U Nu era with a nostalgic fondness now, a pleasant contrast to the junta years that followed. The 1950s is seen as a time when there was an unshackled press, a democratically elected government and a revival of the arts and literature. The reality was rather different. Today, the elections of 1951–2 and 1956 would not be viewed as free and fair, while the media was always at the mercy of politicians and the military. And if the capital was peaceful, much of the rest of the country was grappling with insurgents and dacoits.

But the movie industry was thriving, sprinkling its stardust over Yangon especially. It is hard to judge how good the films of the golden age were because, like much of Burma's history, they exist now only as names and ageing, unreliable memories. Most are lost. The national film archive holds just twelve black and white movies, all in poor condition. When I first saw a Burmese film from the 1960s, the print was so scratched and faded that I might have been watching a 1920s silent.

'AI made over three hundred movies but hardly any of them have survived,' Ko Myint told me. 'We gave a lot of our films to the television channels when they started so they could show them, but they're all gone now. They didn't know how to store them properly.' Nor is there anything left of AI's studio, the twenty-five-acre complex sold off long ago. All that remains is the house Ko Myint's great-grandfather built for the family, the lane it sits on named 'A One' in honour of Burma's premier dream factory.

Technically, AI gave up the ghost in 1983, but the studio had been struggling for years before then. 'It was too hard to get anything made,' said Ko Myint. 'The junta didn't like film people. They'd say, "We don't want to see this kind of movie." We couldn't make horror movies at all because Ne Win didn't like them. We had to submit our scripts to the censors. Worse, they held all the film stock. You couldn't get film to shoot unless you had official permission.'

There was an air of decaying gentility inside Ko Myint's once grand, now run-down, house, repairs neglected and the furniture ancient. Even the awards on display that AI won over the years were dusty. Ko Myint was seventy, bald with bushy eyebrows. He had started appearing in AI movies as a child, before moving behind the camera as an adult. 'It was the family business, so it seemed natural to be in films,' he said. 'I feel sad when I look back at that time. I saw the golden age of Burmese cinema and now there's nothing left of it.'

After the 1962 coup, Ne Win brought the movies under the junta's control, all part of his scheme to build a utopian state via his masterplan, 'The Burmese Way to Socialism'. It was as much of a disaster for film-makers as it was for every other sector of the economy. 'The movie industry isn't like a factory making trucks,' Grace told me. 'Ne Win wanted all actors and directors to make propaganda and, of course, people didn't want to see those movies so they didn't go to the cinemas. We're very good at silent punishment in Burma.'

Occasionally A1 fought back against the restrictions. In 1972 the studio made *Journey to Pyay*, a comedy about a one-day drive from Yangon to Pyay that turns into a ten-day road trip after repeated breakdowns. The censors hadn't picked up that the movie was satirising the collapse of the economy under the junta's mismanagement. But the generals understood the meaning when they saw it. 'It was banned for two years and we got into trouble. But it was worth it,' said Ko Myint.

Sanctions and shortages did as much to cripple Burma's film studios as overbearing state control. 'In the 1970s the industry was still pretty intact. But by the 1980s the lack of equipment and film was really affecting it,' said Grace. 'We'd have to wait six months for film sometimes. The government couldn't afford to buy it and so everything started to switch to video.' The much-delayed arrival of television in 1981 presented a new test and cinemas started to close. From a high of 450 in the 1950s, there are now around seventy across the country.

Movies are still made in Burma, but only a few are released theatrically. 'I make comedies and horror movies. That's all they want here,' Thein Thut, Ko Myint's older brother, told me. 'I'll shoot a feature, up to two hours long, in two weeks and edit it for a month. So from start to finish it takes two months maximum. The highest budget would be US$100,000, lower end is US$50–60,000. They go straight to DVD.'

Poor production values, stereotyped plots and actors who learn their trade on soap operas combine to make most current Burmese movies barely watchable, especially in the face of competition from Hollywood and Bollywood blockbusters. It is Burma's documentarians who offer the best hope for a revival of the country's film industry, and a few are now venturing into independent movie-making. One day, Burmese movies may draw the crowds to Yangon's cinema row again.

13

Astrology and the Abode of Kings

Ne Win's grandiose plan to transform Burma – 'The Burmese Way to Socialism' – had its genesis in the 1930s, when student nationalists were in thrall to Marxism. For Rangoon's revolutionaries, capitalists and colonists were one and the same and both were enemies. Before he was assassinated, Aung San spoke of how Burma would never be dominated by capitalism again. He wanted a socialist nation where industries and infrastructure were nationalised. It was a popular vision. Leftist parties and communist insurgent groups provided the main opposition to U Nu's AFPFL government throughout the 1950s.

Marxism's appeal in the newly independent Burma prompted politicians and, later, the military to announce various programmes to create the ideal state, none of which came close to being realised. Dreams of nirvana, and a preference for looking to the future, have a natural resonance in a nation where the construction of new pagodas takes precedence over upgrading the roads. Burma is a place where the prime minister – U Nu – could announce to his cabinet that he was going to meditate for a month and was not to be disturbed, 'Even if the whole country goes up in flames'.

Dealing with the detail that comes with governance was too much for U Nu. His administration's efforts to resuscitate the economy misfired, hampered by the dreadful damage Burma had suffered in the Second World War, as well as the constant fighting with rebels. The inability to enact any meaningful economic reforms was a source of major frustration by 1960. 'We've had twelve years of independence and what have our politicians given us? We still cannot manufacture even a needle,' lamented Aung Gyi, Ne Win's right-hand man at the time of the 1962 coup and, later, briefly the first chairman of the NLD.

U Nu's politics blended socialism and Buddhist precepts. Unlike Aung San, who argued for a separation of politics and religion, U Nu was an ardent advocate of Buddhism, viewing it as a unifying force in a country divided politically and ethnically and pushing for it to be made the official state religion. But he maintained a belief in *nat* spirits, too. Literally 'celestial beings', the *nats* are a remnant of the animist faiths which held sway across much of Burma until Bagan's kingdom became entwined with Buddhism and King Anawrahta started spreading the word as his empire expanded.

Nat shrines can be found in many villages in Burma, as well as in some urban neighbourhoods, and U Nu always paid his respects at them when he visited rural areas. It was a wise decision. The *nat* spirits are mischievous, often malevolent, genies who live in trees – *nat* shrines are invariably located under the spreading branches of banyan trees – and act as the local guardians. If they are not appeased with regular offerings, disaster is sure to follow.

Thousands of these spirits inhabit Burma, almost all of whom were once human before being anointed as *nats* after their deaths. They were no fans of the British, according to Henry Fielding-Hall. 'All the *nats* seem to have been distressed at our arrival, to hate our presence, and earnestly to desire our absence. They are the spirits of the country and the people, and they cannot abide a foreign domination,' he wrote in *The Soul of a People*.

Just as Buddhists make the pilgrimage to the Shwedagon, *nat* believers flock to Mount Popa every December for an annual celebration. An extinct volcanic plug that erupts out of the dry zone in central Burma, Popa is populated by bold monkeys and the thirty-seven most important *nats*. King Anawrahta conquered much of what is inland Burma today. But he couldn't vanquish the *nat* spirits. Having failed to outlaw their worship, Anawrahta compromised, drawing up a list of thirty-seven official *nats* and enforcing a syncretistic merger with Buddhism.

While the *nats* have shared spiritual space with the Buddhist deities ever since the eleventh century CE, *nat* worship is scorned by many locals today, at least in public. 'It's only villagers who believe in *nats*,' said Thida. 'They think they have to give them gifts or something bad will happen.' But given the prevalence of *nat* shrines across the country, plenty of people are clearly still wary of the capricious spirits.

After the 1962 coup U Nu's homely, ineffective brand of government gave way to 'The Burmese Way to Socialism', Ne Win's authoritarian vision of the future. Cherry-picking Marxist economic theories and ruling under the Orwellian-sounding name of the 'Revolutionary Council', the junta declared all political opposition illegal and the universities and media were quickly placed under state control. Every sector of the economy was nationalised, while army-run committees oversaw all aspects of life.

Eradicating foreign influences was another priority. Western-style entertainment venues were closed down. Faced with rising official prejudice, Indians and Chinese began fleeing. Around 300,000 Indians and 100,000 Chinese had departed by 1967, as well as many Anglo-Burmese, an exodus which had an immediate and deleterious effect. Indians and Chinese were shopowners and wholesalers, the middlemen of the economy. Driving them out did nothing for Burma's financial prospects.

Part-Chinese himself, Ne Win's xenophobia didn't prevent him from making a half-Australian woman one of his six wives. He was also a gambler and a regular at the Rangoon racecourse – where he met one of his brides – before he banned horse racing. Nor did Ne Win let his socialist beliefs interfere with his own life of luxury. Reputed to bathe in the blood of dolphins, he is said to have amassed a personal fortune of £2.8 billion during his time in power.

More than anything Ne Win enjoyed a round of golf, the sport introduced by Scottish expatriates in the colonial era. Nervous about being assassinated, he would take to the links in a steel helmet and with a battalion of soldiers guarding him. Golf became the favoured sport of *Tatmadaw* officers keen to ingratiate themselves with their leader – Ne Win once slapped the chief of military intelligence because he didn't play. Now, golf courses can be found close to army bases across the country, even in the conflict-torn borderlands, often built on land confiscated from local farmers.

Abandoning the name he was born with, Shu Maung, Ne Win chose a moniker which reflected his revised perception of himself. Ne Win means 'Brilliant as the sun', and he adopted the name when he became one of the Thirty Comrades, the founding members of the Aung San-led Burma Independence Army, the organisation that would become the *Tatmadaw*. From 1949 Ne Win was its commander and he oversaw the battles against the Karen militias and communist rebels in the 1950s.

Deeply duplicitous, paranoid and ruthless – U Nu described him as 'more terrible than Ivan the Terrible' – Ne Win unleashed the vicious war against the ethnic minorities in the frontier areas that continues today and had thousands of dissidents imprisoned and tortured. He survived protests and plots against him to run Burma for decades. Even after stepping down as head of the regime in 1988 he continued to rule as the power behind the throne for many more years.

Building a new Burma was beyond Ne Win, though. 'The Burmese Way to Socialism' was an abject failure, like every other attempt at remodelling the state. Three years after his coup even Ne Win was forced to admit that the already precarious economy was unravelling, as Burma lost its status as the world's leading rice exporter and the country became ever more isolated from the rest of the world. The generals and cronies were adept at enriching themselves, far less proficient at managing a country.

Yet Ne Win did not turn Burma into a totalitarian state on his own or single-handedly put its economy on life support. He did it with the help of astrologers and numerologists. On Ne Win's watch Burma was a nation ruled as much by soothsayers as generals. U Nu may have tipped his hat to the *nat* spirits, but the junta governed in a fantastical fashion that defied logic, reliant on occult mysteries to steer the country.

Burma has a long history of whimsical rule. It is a profoundly superstitious nation, a land where a still potent spirit world coexists with Buddhism and fortune-tellers wield an influence that would be unimaginable in the West, and it has always been that way. Ne Win set up an official board of astrologers to advise on the timing of state events, but he was simply reviving a body that had done the same job for Burma's kings.

When the Union Jack was run down the flagpole in Yangon for the final time on 4 January 1948, it occurred at 4.20 in the morning. Eminent astrologers had agreed that was the most auspicious time for Burma to begin its life as an independent nation. Sir Hubert Rance, the last British governor, didn't question the decision. He made sure only to get up very early to be at the ceremony in downtown.

Under the junta, though, rule by necromancers was taken to extremes. The Japanese government funded a planetarium which hides in a corner of Yangon's People's Park. Locals were barred from stargazing. Instead, the planetarium was used by Ne Win's astrologers for their calculations. Burma's leader could also sometimes be seen walking backwards across bridges late at night, apparently on the advice of his seer.

In 1970 Ne Win switched the side of the road people drive on to the right, after his astrologer indicated that Burma was drifting to the left politically. He devalued the country's currency deliberately by introducing forty-five and ninety kyat notes in 1987, because they were variables on his lucky number nine, while at the same time withdrawing the seventy-five kyat note issued to mark his seventy-fifth birthday, along with the twenty-five and thirty-five kyat notes. Ne Win gave no warning for this substitution, thus rendering around two thirds of the money in circulation worthless.

Than Shwe, who led the junta from 1992 to 2011, also sought the advice of soothsayers. He was a keen follower of *ket kin*, a form of fortune-telling where letters of the Burmese alphabet correspond to a day of a week that indicates a number and planet. Than Shwe and his wife were also practitioners of *yadaya*, rituals undertaken to prevent future misfortune. *Yadaya* can mean nothing more sinister than building a pagoda to make merit, but the junta employed its own rites in an effort to neutralise Daw Suu's appeal.

Magic was not an effective way of stymieing political opponents. The junta's astrologers picked 27 May as the day of the 1990 general election, because the date was a multiple of nine, a lucky digit in Burma. The NLD still won 80 per cent of all seats, even if the generals refused to accept the result and simply carried on ruling. Than Shwe had more success in ensuring that the prison sentences handed down to pro-democracy activists were variables of eleven. Known as the 'master number' by numerologists, the auspicious double one in the number eleven is believed to represent both male and female energy, a combination of power and intuition.

Most startling of all, Than Shwe relocated the capital from Yangon to the new city of Naypyidaw in November 2005 after his fortune-teller told him that Burma faced an impending attack from the West. The sight of foreign navy vessels in the Bay of Bengal during the 1988 pro-democracy uprising had focused the regime's mind on the possibility of being overthrown by overseas forces. Than Shwe is thought to have reasoned that moving the capital inland to the centre of the country, away from the sea, would make it harder for any invading army to capture him.

Soothsaying is a risky profession at the highest level. Many astrologers to the generals, such as Ne Win's, were imprisoned after their patrons died or were purged, their wizardry seen as a threat by the men who succeeded their former clients.

Astrologers and numerologists are less prominent now than they were under the military. But the dates of important events, like the signing of ceasefires with ethnic armies, continue to be chosen because they are variables of nine or add up to the number eleven.

Not everyone in Burma is as obsessive about attempting to predict and control the future as the generals were, but consulting a fortune-teller is not considered unusual. Many people possess personal astrological charts, usually drawn up soon after they were born, and it is an important reference point for them. Visiting an astrologer or *ket kin* specialist to discuss a favourable date for a marriage or a change of name, to check your job prospects or to see if romance is in the air, is regarded as prudent rather than eccentric.

As a proud iconoclast Thida is, of course, as dismissive of divining destiny as she is of *nat* worship. But she is also superstitious, insisting on the existence of ghosts, and I knew she had met with astrologers in the past. Thida admitted that her cynicism was actually the result of an unpalatable prediction about her former husband that came true. 'A fortune-teller told me that I had no future with my first love. I didn't believe him, but he was right. Now I hate fortune-tellers,' she said. Nevertheless, Thida agreed to accompany me to one.

Astrologers and numerologists can be found all over Yangon, many congregating near prominent pagodas. Others squat on pavements in downtown, their charts laid out in front of them, waiting for passing trade. The most successful soothsayers have their own premises, or make house calls to the wealthy housewives of Golden Valley, as well as to politicians and senior army officers. A few commute between Yangon and Naypyidaw, home to parliament and the government.

Thida recommended a seer named Zay Yar San, the regular fortune-teller to one of her friends and family. We met at the apartment of the friend, a young doctor who told me she worked at home. 'People call in with their symptoms and I tell them what they should do. What drugs they should buy, or whether they need to go to hospital,' she said. Medical consultations by phone were a new phenomenon to me and she didn't seem busy, soon sitting on the floor with Thida and I and listening to the fortune-teller.

Zay Yar San was middle-aged with thick hair and flyaway eyebrows. The pocket of his check shirt bristled with pens and after bowing to the Buddhist shrine in the room he got straight to work, extracting a notebook from his bag and asking my date of birth, as well as the day and time I was born. He started making calculations, referring periodically to a row of numbers I could see in his notebook.

'You want to explore new things. You have a different mind. Most people go from A to Z, you go from Z to A. It's hard to read your mind,' Zay Yar San began. 'Don't wear red at important meetings or rent an apartment facing east. Try to eat less beef, it is not good for you. Don't sign contracts on Thursdays or Sundays. You can't rely on some of your close friends. Strangers are better for you.'

It was a barrage of advice, unleashed so fast it was hard for Thida to translate Zay Yar San's predictions before he had moved on to the next one. 'Your lucky colour is black, your lucky day is Wednesday. Thailand and China are lucky countries for you. I think you'll be living in Buddhist countries for the next eight years,' he continued. 'You should think about taking up meditation. It will improve your thinking skills. I think you will become interested in religion and write a book about one. You'll do that when you are fifty-eight.'

I was grudgingly impressed. He didn't know that I was a writer, or a former resident of China and Thailand, although I was aware that the most talented fortune-tellers are adept at telling people what they want to hear. I was keen to know if Zay Yar San pulled his punches sometimes, keeping his prophecies positive rather than upsetting his clients. 'I'll tell people bad news if they need to know and I think they can cope with it,' he said. 'Some people like to test the fortune-teller. If they do that with me I won't spare them bad news.'

An ability to read people is part of the job description for any astrologer, but I was curious how he had got into the business of predicting the future. 'I studied and studied and then I became one,' grinned Zay Yar San, who had clearly encountered doubters before. 'I didn't believe in it at first, but I studied with a monk from the age of eighteen and also from books and meditation. I've never done any other job as an adult.'

Now, he is normally only available to regular customers. 'I'll see ten to twenty people a week. Some of my clients are senior officials and they'll come for advice before making big decisions. Other clients want to see me when there is a specific issue. Should I start a new business? What's the best day for my child to marry? But I work with a football team also and today is a Friday, so they'll be asking later what is the best colour for them to wear this weekend to increase their chances of winning,' said Zay Yar San.

Tradition plays a part in the enduring appeal of fortune-tellers, as does the close connection between numerology and Buddhism. 'Nine is a significant number because it comes from Buddhism. There are so many nines, or variables of it, in the history of Buddhism, like the forty-five years he was Buddha,' said Zay Yar San. 'The numerology derives originally from India, but it was adapted long ago for Burma'.

Ket kin is the most complex form of fortune-telling and I struggled to follow Zay Yar San's explanation of 'numbers magic', as it is sometimes known in Burma. 'In our alphabet sounds and syllables are related to numbers and days of the week, and in turn planets. There are good number combinations and bad ones,' he told me. Reversing or manipulating the combinations is believed to be a way of influencing the fate of people, which is what Than Shwe is thought to have tried to do with Aung San Suu Kyi.

Employing numerology in an attempt to crush a nationwide democracy movement is both odd and optimistic. But Than Shwe's reliance on fortune-tellers took on a more serious tone with his unexpected decision to create a brand-new capital at a cost estimated at almost £3 billion, a huge amount for cash-strapped Burma. On 6 November 2005 Naypyidaw became the country's administrative centre and the first government departments to move there left Yangon the same day at 6.37 a.m., a time judged favourable by the junta's astrologers.

Moving the capital to a purpose-built city was the ultimate hubris. The last local to relocate Burma's government was King Mindon, who founded Mandalay in 1857 as his royal capital. Naypyidaw, which means 'abode of kings', was Than Shwe's attempt to match Mindon. He viewed himself as the modern-day incarnation of Burma's sovereigns, with the *Tatmadaw* as the inheritor and defender of their traditions. Both Than Shwe and Ne Win were fond of dressing up in antique royal costume at private parties.

The *Tatmadaw* idealise three kings in particular: Anawrahta, Bayinnaung and Alaungpaya. They were the most imperial and aggressive of the country's monarchs, carving out what is now inland Burma as well as briefly creating an empire that pushed into present-day Thailand, India and China. Three giant golden statues of these warrior kings sit in Naypyidaw, overlooking the vast parade ground where the *Tatmadaw* marches on important national holidays.

Naypyidaw is above all an army town, and the military control everything from the sole taxi company to access to the neighbourhoods where senior officers and politicians live. Much of Naypyidaw is barred to ordinary people, including the parade ground, while its sprawling layout and lack of a real centre is intentional, designed to deny potential protestors a focal point where they can gather to shut down the city.

Lying in the far south of the dry zone, almost equidistant between Yangon and Mandalay, Naypyidaw is the junta's monument to itself. The generals failed to modernise or improve Burma's cities, or any part of the country, in their almost fifty years in power. But they did leave behind Naypyidaw, a dictator's dream inspired by a necromancer's vision. Five hours' drive north of Yangon, it is a city like no other in Southeast Asia.

Wide, well-maintained avenues are interspersed with landscaped traffic circles sown with colourful flowers, the lawns watered daily and given a weekly short-back-and-sides trim. Newly planted trees and immaculate green verges line proper pavements you can stroll down without risking injury, unlike Yangon's, although Naypyidaw is so spread out that walking anywhere is difficult.

Government offices are stationed around Naypyidaw, miles apart from each other. Parliament, a complex of thirty-one buildings believed to represent the thirty-one different planes of existence that Buddhists can be reborn into, hides behind a high fence that lines a ten-lane road in Naypyidaw's north-west. The road was so deserted when I visited that I stood in the middle of it for five minutes without seeing a car. It was built not to cope with heavy traffic but to allow planes to land and evacuate senior members of the junta in the event of a revolt or invasion.

Apartment blocks housing civil servants – their roofs colour-coded red, green or blue according to their ministries – stand in isolation, separated from each other by wasteland. Villas and mansions, the biggest imitating the new-build houses of Yangon's Golden Valley, their columns and balconies peering over tightly guarded gates and walls, house senior government and *Tatmadaw* figures. Lanes of single-storey houses on hushed, dusty streets act as Naypyidaw's homage to American-style suburbia, with neat backyards and parking for cars out front.

Pedestrians are a rare sight, except in a couple of areas where shopping malls can be found. 'Asia's Greenest City' is Naypyidaw's proud boast. It is certainly the most deserted, a place where you wonder where everyone is. But Naypyidaw is rural, a metropolis that has sprouted out of what was farmland and forest little more than a decade ago. Haystacks teeter by the sides of the roads where animals graze, while Naypyidaw's far fringes blend into fields of rice, sesame and beans that run towards the foothills of the Shan Yoma range, which begin their ascent towards the Shan plateau to the north of the city.

Home to a million-plus people, although it doesn't feel like it, Naypyidaw is now Burma's third-largest city after Yangon and Mandalay. The official residents are almost all government or military employees. But many others have moved here, too, like camp followers trailing behind an eighteenth-century army, toiling as domestic servants or functionaries in

the ministries, manicuring the flowerbeds that line the roads
and staffing the many hotels.

Foreigners are not allowed to rent homes in Naypyidaw.
Nor is there much sign that they want to. Despite the lure of
living in 'Asia's Greenest City', as well as the fastest internet
in the entire country, almost all diplomats have flatly refused
to relocate to the new capital, stubbornly keeping to their
embassies in Yangon's downtown and Golden Valley. Those
foreigners who do have to move to Naypyidaw, mainly
United Nations employees, occupy the hotels that cluster in
two specific zones in the north and south of the city.

Many Burmese are unwilling Naypyidaw residents, required
to live there by virtue of their work for the government, and
their families often stay in their home towns. For foreigners
exiled to Naypyidaw it is an alienating city, one where the
dearth of human contact and entertainment venues, except
for a few restaurants, and the city's sheer size make it an
isolated, lonely posting. But I enjoyed my infrequent visits,
the extreme quiet, lack of traffic and studied neatness a
welcome break from the bedlam of Yangon.

My regular hotel in the north of Naypyidaw was always
a ghost ship. If it hadn't been for the neon sign bearing its
name that was switched on after dark, any of the few passing
motorists might have thought it abandoned, as some hotels
in the city are. There were 130 rooms, with only a handful
ever occupied. But the pool was the best I encountered in
Burma. I could swim every day under a high blue sky, with
just the dragonflies circling above my head for company.

With so much of the city closed to foreigners, and
anyone not in or connected to the *Tatmadaw*, the few casual
visitors to Naypyidaw find it a frustrating, near-meaningless
destination, a place designed principally for the comfort and

security of Burma's military and political elite. It says much about the junta's arrogance and paranoia that it built a shiny new capital only to place large parts of it out of bounds to ordinary people.

There is one place in Naypyidaw where the military is pleased to welcome visitors. The Defence Services Museum occupies 600 acres, including a man-made lake, on the city's far north-eastern outskirts. Like Naypyidaw itself the museum stands as a testament to the ego of the *Tatmadaw*, a preening affirmation of the generals' unshakeable belief in the army's central and indispensable role in Burma since independence.

Despite the museum's size, finding it was a challenge. My motorcycle taxi driver hadn't heard of it and it took forty-five minutes of puttering past a series of barracks, and directions from two military policemen drinking tea at a roadside stall, till we tracked it down. Sitting next door to a colossus of a stadium that was built for the 2013 Southeast Asian Games, an event that marked Burma's return to the regional sporting fold after a long absence, the museum sees few people. Military attachés from Yangon are the most frequent callers, judging by the visitors' book everyone has to sign.

Planes and helicopters dating back to the 1940s were lined up on the vast forecourt leading to the museum proper, their flaps and elevators creaking in the wind. Most were American, British and Chinese models, including a Spitfire from the Second World War. One recent Burma legend is that crates of dismantled Spitfires, now worth millions of pounds each, are buried under the runways of Yangon's airport after being abandoned by the British at the end of the war. But no one has ever found them.

Three pavilions – one each for the army, navy and air force – are grouped around the lake. The army's is by far the biggest, just as it dwarfs the navy and air force in terms of manpower. I was the only visitor and was shown around by a genial sergeant major named Kyaw Soe Hlaing. Short and smart in his pressed green fatigues and polished black shoes – many *Tatmadaw* soldiers wear flip-flops when not on operations – he was a veteran of twenty-six years. The museum was his final posting before retirement.

Like almost everyone living in Naypyidaw, Kyaw Soe Hlaing is from somewhere else, in his case Yangon. 'I go back for a weekend each month because my family are there. They didn't want to move here,' he said in a soft voice. There was no military bluster to Kyaw Soe Hlaing. 'I joined up because I wanted a good job,' he told me, before volunteering the information that he was a fan of Aung San Suu Kyi. 'I think ninety per cent of ordinary soldiers support her,' he said. It is their commanders who are less keen on her being Burma's leader.

Much of the army's pavilion is given over to a comprehensive, but selective, history of Burma's martial endeavours. Kyaw Soe Hlaing maintained a poker face while showing me the gallery devoted to the Anglo-Burmese Wars. He couldn't resist a smile, though, as he pointed out the pictures of the men, including Daw Suu's great-grandfather, who had led the guerrilla resistance to the British after their takeover of all Burma in 1886.

Politics and soldiering have always been intertwined for the *Tatmadaw* and the museum reflects that relationship. Kyaw Soe Hlaing pushed his shoulders back, visibly proud, as we moved through the section on the years leading to independence. It is a treasure trove of exhibits that I thought should rightly have been on display in Naypyidaw's much less impressive National Museum, given their huge significance in Burma's history.

Pamphlets and declarations produced by the student nationalists of the 1930s gave way to rare photos of the Thirty Comrades: Aung San and Ne Win sitting side by side, unsmiling in Japanese uniforms. Many of Aung San's personal items were on display, too, including the H. G. Wells novels he liked to read, as well as books on socialist thought and the writings of China's communist leaders.

Framed side by side at the end of the gallery are the flag of the Union of Burma and the Union Jack that had travelled in opposite directions up and down the flagpole in Yangon on Independence Day. The old Burma banner is very different from the current one with its Rastafarian-style stripes of yellow, green and red. It is mostly red, with a blue canton and a large white star surrounded by five smaller ones, the flag of a more radical country. 'The big star symbolises revolutionary spirit. The other five represent the biggest states in Burma,' Kyaw Soe Hlaing said.

He grew less forthcoming as we toured the final section which details the current conflicts in Burma. Now, there were no more English captions. 'These are the internal wars, the battles against the communist party and the different ethnic groups,' said Kyaw Soe Hlaing. I asked if he had taken part in them. 'Yes. I was in Kayin State for twelve years fighting the Karen.'

Back in 1949 the Karen were the first of the minorities to rise up against the Bamar. The subsequent war against them was cruel, even by the standards of the *Tatmadaw*, until a shaky ceasefire was signed in 2015. That extreme violence was a reaction to the Karen's role in the Second World War, when they were Britain's closest and most effective ally in the fight against the Japanese and the soldiers of Aung San's Burma Independence Army.

Today it is the battles with the various ethnic groups in Shan and Kachin states that are the most violent and seemingly insurmountable of Burma's civil wars. Another conspiracy theory surrounding the establishment of Naypyidaw – one favoured by the minorities – is that the capital was moved closer to Shan State to make it easier for soldiers to travel there if needed. Four armies confront the *Tatmadaw* on the other side of the Shan Hills to the north and east of Naypyidaw, with three others armed and ready to do so. It was time to find out why they were still fighting.

14

The Ta'ang Tea Party

Drowsy in the late afternoon, I sprawled out on the sun-bleached grass. Above me was a cerulean sky while nearby were the stilted huts of the village, corn and chili drying outside, babies crying inside. Women squatted on the wooden porches preparing food and talking, while their children played beneath them, scattering the dogs and chickens poking around the yellow earth of the Shan plateau.

Beyond the homes were crude shelters made of bamboo lashed together and covered in palm and banana fronds, spaced apart from each other and just big enough for two men to lie side by side in them. The equipment of their occupants stayed outside: AK47 rifles and RPG launchers stacked together, machine guns resting on their tripods, newly washed uniforms, boots airing, webbing dangling from tree branches, the pouches stuffed full of magazines and water bottles.

Ponies clip-clopped past, the wooden panniers across their backs loaded with supplies, rousing me from my stupor. Then Major Robert was standing over me. 'We'll be sleeping in the forest tonight,' he said, pointing towards the ridge that was out of sight on the hill behind us. 'You OK with that?' For the soldiers of the Ta'ang National Liberation Army (TNLA), the 'forest' is a euphemism for any place that isn't a village or a town.

Within minutes the pastoral scene had given way to the hustle of a military unit preparing to move. Weapons and kit were gathered and slung across shoulders, backs and waists and then we were off, climbing uphill fast in single file. It was a sweaty twenty-minute march to the ridgeline. 'Sometimes the *Tatmadaw* attack at night. It will be bad for the villagers if we have to fight in the village and this is a better defensive position. But the phone reception is good up here,' said Major Robert.

As if to prove it, he extracted one of his mobile phones from a pocket and called his wife. She was seventy miles away in Mantong, one of the two principal towns in the Palaung Self-Administered Zone, the homeland of the 600,000-odd Palaung people who live in northern Shan State and across the nearby borders with China and Thailand. The TNLA are their army, a force of around 3,500 soldiers who are the current heirs of various Ta'ang militias that began fighting the *Tatmadaw* in 1966. 'We call ourselves Ta'ang,' Major Robert had told me earlier. 'Palaung is the name the Burmese gave us.'

Sinking swiftly beneath the horizon, the sun bequeathed a layer of red light that settled above the green hills that slalomed towards the frontier with Yunnan Province and China, until the encroaching darkness snuffed it out. Some of the soldiers were hacking at bamboo with machetes and gathering leaves, preparing the shelters we would sleep in; others were taking up sentry positions along the ridge. The first mosquitos whined past my ears and I stared suspiciously at the long grass we stood in, wondering about snakes.

Major Robert mistook my frown for a different sort of fear. 'Don't worry about the *Tatmadaw* attacking us tonight,' he said. 'They know we have lots of soldiers here and that we'll fight if they come. And we're at the top here. We can see all around and anyone coming up.' I explained I was more concerned about the prospect of serpents joining our bivouac and Major Robert laughed. 'Yes, there are snakes here. Watch out.'

It grew cold once the sun disappeared, the wind gusting across the ridge, riffling through the trees. I retreated to the shelter that had been prepared for Major Robert and two other officers and which I was sharing for the night. Roofed and walled with banana leaves, piles of grass had been thrown in and covered with groundsheets for our beds. It was comfortable enough once the fire got going, even if there was no chimney, sparks hurtling towards the leafy ceiling, smoke swirling around us.

Lights were allowed and chickens were being roasted outside. Random faces gleamed in the dark, lit up by the phones held close to them, and cigarette tips glowed. The walkie-talkies of the officers hissed intermittently, while Major Robert checked Facebook for the latest updates on the fighting across Shan State. He had already shown me phone footage of the unit in action, RPGs fired at a hillside position held by *Tatmadaw* troops, the grenades rushing towards them in dreadful haste, as well as a clip of a helicopter gunship fluttering above TNLA soldiers and launching rockets.

Some of the chicken found its way to our shelter, the meat crudely hacked up and a lemon drizzled over it, tasting delicious. Chunks of orange and apple came, too, along with a water bottle filled with the local hooch, a clear, rice-based spirit. 'It's like an extra blanket. It keeps out the cold,' joked the second-in-command, who maintained a near-permanent grin on his face that revealed jagged, protruding teeth.

Far below us was Namtu, the nearest town, a ninety-minute drive by motorbike. But we were in a different world on the hilltop, one that was very distant from the Burma I had been in just a few days before, a place where the only hint of the state is the *Tatmadaw* garrison in Namtu. For the minorities who populate Shan the military is often the sole representative of the government they encounter, an imperial garrison force as unwelcome as the British officials and soldiers who occupied inland Burma during the colonial period.

'I became a soldier because the *Tatmadaw* came to our area and they discriminated against us. The military work with the Chinese and other ethnic groups and they close the local economy to us,' said Major Robert. Taller and broader than most Ta'ang men, with dark slashes under heavy, sleep-deprived eyes, he joined up twelve years ago. He has been living and fighting in the 'forest' ever since, seeing his wife and two children during brief periods of leave.

Distinct from the other officers and men in their camouflage, Major Robert wore a dark green uniform, with a peaked forage cap, that indicated his status somewhere between a political commissar and a staff officer. Like the officers who fulfil the same function in China's armed forces, Major Robert was principally responsible for the ideological education of the soldiers. As such, he wields as much power as the technically more senior battalion and brigade commanders and takes part in planning missions. He was looking after me, too, thanks to his fluent English.

For the Ta'ang and the other minorities, their battle with the Burmese state is as much about equality as the desire for self-determination. 'We're fighting for development really, because the government is not fair with us,' explained Major Robert. 'We want the companies who invest here to give jobs to us and not people from outside. We want electricity, clean water, better hospitals and schools and roads. You go to the hospital in my hometown Namhsan and they don't have good medicines and the nurses aren't really trained.'

Fifty-odd miles west of our position, Namhsan is the capital of the Ta'ang region. Like much of Shan State, including the hilltop the TNLA and I were camping on, it is barred to foreigners, as the *Tatmadaw* is anxious to keep westerners from seeing close up the destructive impact of decades of fighting on the communities who live here. The military is also keen to ensure that its role in exploiting Shan State's natural resources, and its involvement in the smuggling of illegal narcotics and other contraband across Shan's shared borders with China, Laos and Thailand, remains as little known as possible.

Tatmadaw soldiers have moved into Namhsan in large numbers in the last couple of years, so I knew I would be unable to visit. But I had been there before, a trip that served to confirm what I was hearing from Major Robert about the lack of development in the Ta'ang homeland. Maurice Collis, the former Rangoon chief magistrate and district commissioner of Myeik in the early 1930s, travelled from the town of Hsipaw to Namhsan in 1937, a journey of fifty miles that took him five hours. Over seventy-five years later I spent six hours following the same route on a road that appeared not to have been upgraded in the interim.

Driving me was a Hsipaw man visiting his girlfriend in Namhsan. We set off soon after dawn, a pinkish sun edging up above the hills atop which our destination sat, wood smoke from the teahouses drifting across the road as their grills and ovens were fired up for the morning rush of customers. The driver's bike was a Chinese-made 125cc model: standard transport in Shan State. Hunched on the back, with my boots perched on footrests that raised my knees up to the level of the seat, I knew it was going to be an uncomfortable ride.

Initially the going was as good as it gets in Shan. We shot off down a sealed two-lane road, passing the barracks and army-owned golf club on the outskirts of Hsipaw. But before two hours had passed the sealed road gave way to a desperately rocky and uneven track that ascended into the hills past isolated villages and fields of maize. I felt every stone, pothole and bump along the way. The steel springs which acted as the bike's suspension weren't designed to absorb the sort of pounding the vehicle was taking with two people aboard.

My knees were wrecked by the time we reached the first Ta'ang village. As we paused for a break a patrol of teenagers casually clutching AK47s appeared, dressed in the green uniforms and bush hats, with brims tightly folded against the crown, worn by *Tatmadaw* soldiers. They were members of the Namhsan Militia, a government-backed force opposed to the TNLA. It was too late to hide, but they carried on moving through the village with only a few curious stares directed my way.

Seemingly endless curves lay ahead, looping so tight I would have felt sick if it hadn't been for the pain in my knees. Finally, we swung around one last bend onto the ridgetop where Namhsan lies. We were now 1,500 metres above sea level and as the view widened dramatically I could see rows of tea trees clinging to the hillsides below. In the distance partially forested hills, scarred with yellow patches where trees had been felled and separated by ravines, soared and dipped towards the border with Yunnan.

Simple wooden homes, tea leaves drying outside them, heralded Namhsan. Ponies with bamboo baskets across their scrawny backs stood tethered, waiting to be loaded with the harvest. Spread out along the narrow road that hugs the ridge, with pagodas at the highest point, Namhsan looked and felt like a frontier settlement that had time travelled from the nineteenth century. When I struggled off the bike, barely able to walk, I wondered if the journey had been worth it.

Little has changed in Shan State in the years since Burma's independence. Dominating the east of the country, Shan accounts for almost a quarter of its landmass, an area bigger than England and Wales combined, but remains overwhelmingly rural, with just a few towns of any significant size. Outside them infrastructure barely exists and the majority of the population are subsistence farmers who live in villages which, motorbikes, televisions and solar panels to provide electricity apart, look much the same as they did a century ago.

Shan State takes its name from the Shan people because they are the majority in the region. There are over five million Shan, making them the most numerous of Burma's 134 official minorities. Large numbers of Shan can also be found across the frontiers in China, Laos and Thailand, where they are known as the Dai or Tai. Their populations have been swelled in recent years by refugees from the poverty and fighting in Shan State. So many Shan have fled to Thailand that they now make up one in six of the people in Chiang Mai, the country's second city.

Living alongside them in Shan State are other minorities: the Akha, Danu, Intha, Kachin, Lisu, Lahu, Pa-O, Ta'ang and Wa. Like the Shan, they spread into China, Laos and Thailand as well, making this patch of Southeast Asia one vast transnational space. People of Indian and Nepali descent, whose ancestors arrived in the colonial era, live here, too, as do an ever-increasing number of Chinese, working as traders and shopowners or running agri-businesses and mining operations.

Bamar migrants from inland Burma are also a presence in the towns. But they are far outnumbered by the 100,000-plus Burmese troops stationed here, around a quarter of the entire strength of the *Tatmadaw*. Opposing them are an estimated 70,000 men and women serving in a variety of different ethnic armies, a figure that doesn't include the former soldiers who act as reservists.

The Second World War precipitated the struggle between the Bamar and the minorities, heightening tensions which had begun to fester after the British made the fateful decision to administer the borderlands and their peoples separately from the rest of the country. Two competing visions of what an independent Burma would look like emerged. The Bamar envisaged a nation controlled by them, with the other ethnic groups suitably subservient. But the main minorities – the Shan, Kachin, Karen, Rakhine, Chin and Mon – wanted a federal state where they would have autonomy over their areas and affairs.

Only after Aung San recognised the right of the minorities to rule their homelands at the 1947 Panglong Conference did they agree to join what would become the Union of Burma after independence. But Aung San's assurances were soon forgotten and in January 1949 the Karen people rose up against the Bamar. By 1961 Shan and Kachin armies had rebelled against the state, too. With the militias of the smaller ethnic groups joining them and communist insurgents roaming inland Burma, the country was gripped by civil war.

THE TA'ANG TEA PARTY

Now, northern and eastern Shan State and the south, west and north of Kachin State are the front lines in the conflict. Four armies battle the *Tatmadaw* in these regions: the TNLA, the Kachin Independence Army (KIA), the Arakan Army and the Myanmar National Democratic Alliance Army (MNDAA). Standing on the sidelines, refusing to sign ceasefires and occasionally clashing with the *Tatmadaw*, are another three armies: the Shan State Army – North, the National Democratic Alliance Army, and the United Wa State Army, the most powerful of all the ethnic minority forces.

Among the four armies involved in full-time fighting, only the TNLA and MNDAA are native to Shan State: the Arakan Army is a unit of Rakhine separatists and the KIA represents the people of Kachin State. But since 2016 the four armies have joined forces in what is known as the Northern Alliance, a rare outbreak of unity between different ethnic groups in Burma.

One of the reasons the conflicts in the borderlands appear deeply confusing to outsiders is the long chain of alliances made and broken over the last seven decades. The many armies and militias formed over the years have fractured into different organisations, often violently opposed to each other. China, whose border with Burma runs partly through areas controlled by the minority armies, plays a disruptive role, too. Beijing maintains an influence with some of the groups that arouses suspicion and fear in the other militias, as well as with the government in Naypyidaw.

This failure of the minority armies to combine effectively under one banner has only aided the *Tatmadaw*, who have enthusiastically adopted the divide and rule tactics once employed by the British in their empire. Some of the ethnic forces have signed truces with Naypyidaw and now act as proxy government units, which allows the *Tatmadaw* to keep more of its troops in the safety of their barracks in the towns.

These new allies are also paid to protect the rubber and banana farms and mines in the frontier areas which are clear of the rebel armies. Owned by Chinese companies in conjunction with local elites and sometimes the *Tatmadaw*, they operate on land taken from the minorities. 'There are gold and tin mines around Mantong and Kyaukme. Those are our resources and they are going to China. We don't think that is right,' Major Robert told me.

While some of the ethnic armies have downed arms because of a genuine desire for peace, the prospect of getting a cut of the huge amount of revenue generated by the border trade in Shan State is perhaps a bigger motivation to agree ceasefires with the government. Apart from the legal commerce, everything from mobile phones, DVDs and motorbikes to endangered wildlife species, precious gems, timber and drugs is smuggled in both directions across the boundaries with China, Laos and Thailand. Around the world, only Iraq and Libya see a greater amount of illegal trade than Burma.

So-called ceasefire capitalism has had a calamitous impact on the Ta'ang people, whose homeland sprawls across the mountainous far north-west of Shan State towards the borders with Kachin State and Yunnan. The symbol of the TNLA, worn by every soldier on the left arm of their uniforms, is three mountains ringed by tea leaves. A twelfth-century CE legend has it that a *nat* spirit bestowed tea seeds on the Ta'ang. Tea cultivation has been their principal occupation ever since then.

Ta'ang tea is highly prized and once found its way all around Burma in the shape of the tea-leaf salads that are a national dish. But in 1991 the Ta'ang signed a ceasefire with the then ruling junta. Soon, pro-government militias were formed, like the one I encountered on my way to Namhsan, while farmland was confiscated for oil and gas pipelines that run from Rakhine State to China via Shan State. Worst of all, the local tea industry was reorganised into a cartel who have kept the price of tea low.

By the time the truce ended in 2005 Ta'ang farmers were also facing fierce competition from tea imported from Yunnan. Just as the East India Company's sales of untaxed Chinese tea to America prompted the Boston Tea Party and the American Revolution, the Ta'ang are driven to fight partly because they see China launching an economic takeover of their homeland. 'Chinese tea has driven the price of our tea down even further. That's why we don't want the Chinese in our areas,' said Major Robert.

Unable to make a living out of growing tea, farmers started cultivating opium instead. 'From 1993 poppy started being grown again because the tea price declined,' said Major Robert. Opium has long been a cash crop here. Shan State is the epicentre of the Golden Triangle, a region that stretches into southern Yunnan, north-west Laos and northern Thailand and which is notorious as an abundant source of heroin and methamphetamines.

Burma is the world's second biggest producer of opium, after Afghanistan, and most of it is grown in Shan State. Along with the illicit traffic in jade from Kachin State, the trade in illegal drugs is by far the country's most profitable industry, worth £20 billion annually, according to the United Nations Office on Drugs and Crime. And those figures are a conservative estimate.

Local farmers can only dream of such riches. They get paid around £160 for a kilo of dry opium. It is the Chinese gangs who buy the opium who make the big profits. Once that same kilo has been refined into heroin and put on sale in China, or exported from there to other parts of Asia, it is worth almost £50,000. For the villagers in Shan State growing opium is simply a means of staying alive for another year.

With drugs present throughout Shan State, and available at lower prices than elsewhere in Burma or abroad, more and more people have fallen victim to them. Every village and town in the Ta'ang region has its addicts. In May 2016 over a thousand people in Namhsan were left homeless when 500 houses and shops burned down in a blaze started by the candle of a local heroin user who had nodded off after injecting himself.

TNLA troops know all about the temptations of narcotics. 'Many of our soldiers are former addicts because it's such a big problem. Up until recently, I'd say the majority of Ta'ang men were taking drugs, heroin especially,' Major Robert told me. I asked if I could talk to some of the soldiers who had been drug users. He took me over to another shelter, inside which four men were hunched over their phones.

Expecting to meet an ordinary soldier, I was introduced instead to the brigade commander and taken aback to discover that he was just thirty-four, the same age as Major Robert. Tar Maw Shan was jovial and informal, arms covered in crude tattoos, combat trousers rolled up to his knees as he relaxed for the night. He joined the TNLA eight years ago and now commands two battalions, the sort of speedy ascent to high rank only possible in guerrilla armies.

The son of a tea farmer from a village outside Namhsan, Tar Maw Shan was introduced to drugs as a teenager. 'I started smoking opium when I was sixteen and carried on taking it for ten years. I had no job, no life really. So I took drugs, like most of the boys in my village,' he said. I asked if the other men in the shelter were ex-users. 'Yes. Heroin and opium. But *yama* is more popular with the youth now.' *Yama* is the local term for the methamphetamine pills produced in their millions in Shan State and exported all across Asia, even reaching North Korea.

A common refrain in the borderlands is that, where the *Tatmadaw* goes, drugs follow. Many of the minorities believe that their homelands are being swamped with cheap narcotics by the military and its cohorts as part of a deliberate campaign to debilitate their communities, so they will no longer be able to resist government rule. Some go further and insist that the easy availability of heroin and methamphetamines is a calculated attempt at genocide, the aim being to wipe out the minorities altogether.

Tar Maw Shan was no different. For him and his brigade of reformed addicts eradicating drugs from the Ta'ang homeland is as crucial as achieving freedom, a goal shared with the rest of the TNLA. The principal targets of their ire are the *Tatmadaw*-backed Panhsay Militia and the Restoration Council of Shan State (RCSS), also known as the Shan State Army – South, one of the largest of the ethnic armies.

After agreeing a ceasefire with the government in 2012, the RCSS moved some of their 8,000 soldiers north from their bases near the Thai border in southern Shan State and now fight the TNLA alongside the Burmese military. The Panhsay Militia operate in the hills between Mantong and the border with China in the far north of the Ta'ang region, an area remote even by Shan State standards and long associated with opium production.

'Our number-one enemy is the RCSS. They kill our people and block the roads so that our people in the hills can't get out to buy or sell anything. The number-two enemy is the Panhsay Militia because they make heroin and *yama*. The *Tatmadaw* is our number-three enemy,' stated Tar Maw Shan. A few days before I arrived there had been intense firefights between his units and the RCSS in the hills west of us. 'We lost two dead and six injured. But we forced the RCSS to retreat back towards Hsipaw,' he said.

Every February, the time of the annual opium harvest in Shan State, the TNLA launches an offensive against the Panhsay Militia. 'We have to stop the Panhsay Militia bringing drugs into our areas. The only way to do that is to go to the hills to burn the poppy and the *yama* labs and to fight them. They are friends with the *Tatmadaw* and the RCSS. They all want the money from drugs,' said Major Robert.

No one doubts that the Panhsay Militia is linked to the Burmese military. Its leader is Kyaw Myint, a local tycoon of Lisu and Yunnan ancestry who is also a member of the Shan State parliament representing the *Tatmadaw*-backed USDP. Alleged to have first made a fortune trafficking timber from Shan State to Thailand, Kyaw Myint was elected to the state parliament in 2010 after promising the people in his future constituency that they would be able to grow opium under his protection.

Many of the government-sponsored militias in Shan State are thought to be involved in the production, sale and smuggling of drugs and, of course, the *Tatmadaw* takes a cut of the profits. Nor is the RCSS the only ethnic army implicated in the narcotics trade. The MNDAA, one of the TNLA's comrades in the Northern Alliance, has a long history of producing heroin and methamphetamines in its enclave in north-east Shan State.

Of all the minority armies, though, it is the United Wa State Army (UWSA) in eastern Shan State who are most infamous for their role in drug production. The United States has cited the UWSA as Southeast Asia's biggest drug-trafficking gang, and its leaders remain on the US Treasury Department's sanctions lists. If any one group can be said to control the Golden Triangle, it is the UWSA who have the best claim.

Money made from heroin and methamphetamines has enabled the UWSA to establish themselves as the largest of the ethnic armies, with 20,000 full-time soldiers and another 30,000 in reserve. The UWSA is also the major supplier of arms in the region, sometimes made in its own factories or passed on from Chinese sources. Despite the TNLA's hatred of drugs, Major Robert admitted that the vast majority of their weapons come from the UWSA. There is an ethnic bond between the TNLA and UWSA, too. The Ta'ang and Wa peoples are distant cousins.

Manufacturing and selling drugs has been the major source of finance for the armed struggle against the Burmese state since the 1960s. But the narcotics-averse TNLA has to find alternative means of income. Major Robert told me that the TNLA garnered financial support from the Ta'ang who live across the border in China. But I knew that the TNLA demanded involuntary contributions from the people in their homeland also, as well as 'taxing' the smuggled goods that move through the areas it controls on their way to and from China.

Compared to the UWSA and RCSS, though, the TNLA is a shoestring operation reliant above all on the extreme loyalty of their soldiers to the Ta'ang cause. Many are still teenagers, joining up at the age of eighteen and sent to the front line after only two months' training. 'There's no more time, we need the fighters,' said Tar Maw Shan. Ordinary soldiers are paid just 10,000 kyat (£5.50) a month, while officers like Major Robert earn 30,000 kyat (£16.50). 'We do this for our people, not for the money,' he stressed.

Having the *Tatmadaw* and its mercenary allies as enemies helps focus the mind of the soldiers as well. Burma's military is an almost exclusively Bamar and Buddhist force, with Muslims banned from joining and the few Christians or members of the minorities who sign up unable to rise above the rank of major. It has never forgotten its Second World War roots as a unit trained by and attached to the Imperial Japanese Army. An unquestioning obedience to orders and a tendency to regard its opponents as less than human are the primary traits of the *Tatmadaw*.

Its recruits are mostly from inland Burma, far from the regions inhabited by the minorities they spend their careers fighting. Many Bamar display a distressing indifference or ignorance towards the other ethnic groups, able to perceive them only through clichés or prejudice. Others have a condescending attitude towards the minorities not dissimilar to the paternalistic view the British held of the peoples of the frontier areas.

Once Burma's soldiers are on the borderland battlefields that casual racism and belief in the innate superiority of the Bamar can quickly turn into a contempt for their enemies that is expressed in the most callous manner. The 700,000 Rohingya pushed across the frontiers into Bangladesh, their villages destroyed and the women raped, can testify to that.

From the 1950s onwards the minorities were vociferous about the unwelcome treatment they received from the *Tatmadaw* units that passed through their areas, citing the way the soldiers were unable, or unwilling, to distinguish between fighters and non-combatant villagers. Worse was to follow in the coming decades, as the military implemented a new strategy to take on the communist insurgents and ethnic minority armies.

First conceived of in the 1960s, the 'Four Cuts' doctrine was designed to separate the rebel armies from the villages that were their bases and sources of support. By doing that the *Tatmadaw* could deprive them of the four things they needed the most: food, money, intelligence and recruits. It was a plan which echoed Britain's response to the guerrillas who roamed upper Burma after the end of the Third Anglo-Burmese War, but was more directly inspired by the tactics employed by the British Army in combating the 1950s communist insurgency in Malaya. Then, half a million villagers were forcibly relocated to deprive the rebels of food and aid.

In Burma the strategy was taken much further. Entire villages in rebel areas were moved and surrounded by government troops, the villagers made to work for the *Tatmadaw* as forced labour. The empty villages left behind became free-fire zones, where anyone seen in them was assumed to be an enemy. People thought to be aiding the insurgents faced summary execution. Further terror tactics included using the locals as human shields, sent through minefields or ahead of advancing *Tatmadaw* units, while the rape of minority women became systematic throughout the borderlands.

Napalm was used, too. The hills I drove through on my way to Namhsan were bombed with it in 1970. Over the years, hundreds of thousands of people have been displaced by the Four Cuts campaigns. Tens of thousands fled across the border with Thailand, where some of them are still confined in refugee camps. Confronted with such brutality it is natural that the minorities remain deeply distrustful of the military and the government.

Aung San Suu Kyi has asserted that bringing peace to Burma is her top priority. So far all she has done to promote that is to maintain the stance of the junta, who insisted that the ethnic armies must disarm and sign ceasefires before any talks about the political future of the borderlands could be held. But those who have agreed truces, as the Ta'ang did between 1991 and 2005, have seen little reward for their good faith. Surrender is now not an option for the TNLA and the other six armies still holding out.

'We want the fighting to stop. We were happy when Aung San Suu Kyi and her government took power. We thought she would work for peace and a ceasefire. Now, we don't think that,' said Major Robert. 'The *Tatmadaw* don't want peace. She needs to talk to them about agreeing a ceasefire, not us. We can't give up our guns. If the whole country is at peace, then maybe.'

Nothing disturbed our night on the hilltop. All that kept me awake was the relentless snoring of the second-in-command. Major Robert's walkie-talkie was crackling while it was still dark, and the entire camp was out of their shelters before dawn. Below us the valleys were obscured by mist, a magic carpet of moisture that floated above them until the emerging sun burned it off.

Gathering around two smouldering logs, Major Robert and the other officers held a morning conference, discussing whether to stay on the ridge or move on. Everyone chipped in with a contribution, including unseen voices on the radios. 'We'll be staying here for a while, maybe a couple of weeks while we wait for fresh orders,' Major Robert told me afterwards. 'There will be more fighting soon. The *Tatmadaw* won't pull back.'

Breakfast was served on a bed of banana leaves: the remains of the chicken, bamboo shoots, a spinach-like vegetable and rice, all eaten with our fingers. After that it was time for me to return to a more familiar Burma. I shook hands with Major Robert and wished him good luck. A young soldier escorted me back down the hill to the village, where a civilian Ta'ang motorbike man was waiting to take me to Namtu.

More of a motocross ride than a taxi, we skidded down further hillsides, past the outlying TNLA pickets, until we reached a stone track that led to a more reasonable road. After I'd put on a helmet to hide my foreign features, we drove back to Namtu passing the golf course, cows grazing on the fairways, sited conveniently close to the *Tatmadaw* base. Most of the soldiers were away chasing the TNLA in the hills and the checkpoint into town was unmanned.

Namtu has a mixed Shan and Kachin population, as well as Ta'ang and Chinese. I hid in the safety of a friendly tea shop, while its owner called around for someone to take me to Hsipaw. A Chinese driver arrived, the son of migrants from Yunnan. We headed back out of town past the barracks, making for a junction where the road forks: one way led to Lashio, the western terminus of the Burma Road during the Second World War and where I had come from, the other route towards Hsipaw.

Before we reached the intersection, the driver slowed and pointed to his right. Motorbikes were parked off the road and beyond them I could see around a dozen people, mostly men but a few women, squatting in the bushes, syringes in their hands. 'Heroin,' said the driver. 'They buy it in Namtu but they come here to take it. Sometimes there are lots of people here.'

15

Sky Lords

Centuries before Shan State was the front line in the battle between the Bamar and the minorities, it was carved into kingdoms governed by hereditary rulers known in Burmese as *sawbwas*, or 'sky lords'. Their principalities ranged from areas no bigger than an English county to regions the size of small countries. The number of kingdoms varied, as warfare and marriages resulted in enforced mergers, but by the time the final vestiges of authority were stripped from the *sawbwas* in 1959 there were thirty-four of them.

Along with everyone else in Burma, the sky lords and their subjects came originally from outside what are now the country's frontiers. The Shan, who divide themselves into a number of different groups, migrated south from China, along with the other minorities who live in Shan State. As the majority, the Shan settled in the valleys of the region as sedentary rice farmers, leaving the less fertile and harsher uplands to the likes of the Ta'ang, Wa, Akha and Lahu.

By the tenth century CE the first Shan kingdom had emerged. Over the following centuries the Shan fought the Bamar for control of upper Burma, which they largely dominated until the warrior king Bayinnaung subjugated Shan State in the mid-sixteenth century. But the *sawbwas* were left to rule their principalities, while intermittently rebelling against the uncertain control of the Burmese state and fighting each other.

Bamar royalty looked to the *sawbwa* families as a source of brides. Thibaw, Burma's last king, was half-Shan, his name a corruption of Hsipaw, where his mother was from. The sky lords provided manpower for Burma's armies, too, joining them in their wars from the seventeenth century onwards. Shan soldiers made up a significant part of the forces the British faced when they invaded for the first time in 1824.

Once Britain completed the full takeover of Burma in 1886, the *sawbwas* were initially allowed to carry on governing much as they always had, after swearing their allegiance to Queen Victoria. But in 1922 the British decided to rule the borderlands separately from the rest of Burma, establishing the Federated Shan States, and the *sawbwas* lost much of their traditional powers. They maintained the right to rule their subjects, oversee law and order and collect taxes, but now half of all the revenue went to the colonial state and the sky lords were overseen by British officials.

Keen to keep the local aristocracy on side, as in India, the colonists continued to treat the *sawbwas* as minor royalty. They were entitled to a nine-gun salute when they visited the governor in Rangoon or Pyin Oo Lwin, a hill town north-east of Mandalay that acted as the administrative capital during the hottest months of the year. Many sky lords attended the durbars of 1903 and 1911, the huge celebrations in India when the maharajahs gathered in Delhi to pay their respects to the latest British king.

Despite this acknowledgement of their exalted position within Shan society, senior British officials did not generally mix with the sky lords socially. And, of course, no *sawbwa* was ever elected to the Pegu Club, which remained restricted solely to Europeans until the very end of the colonial era. The British preferred to refer to the *sawbwas* as 'chiefs', too, rather than lords or princes, a diminution of their status that reflected the racist belief that the Shan and the other minorities of the borderlands were not completely civilised.

Nevertheless, considerable efforts were made to ensure the *sawbwas'* loyalty. This involved granting them access to the institutions of the British elite and tutoring them in their ways. The Shan Chiefs School in Taunggyi, the capital of Shan State, was set up in 1902 as a local version of an English public school for the children of the sky lords and their relatives. A few travelled to the UK to attend the same boarding schools and universities that educated Ritchie Gardiner and the other men who staffed the empire. Some served as officers in the Burma Rifles during the First and Second World Wars.

One sky lord, Sao Shwe Thaike, became the first president of Burma after independence. The *Sawbwa* of Yawnghwe, an area in southern Shan State that includes Inle Lake, Sao Shwe Thaike was picked as a unity candidate for the presidency after the assassination of Aung San. Swiftly sidelined by the then prime minister U Nu, his four-year term as president is most notable for being a rare example of a member of an ethnic minority achieving nationwide political power in Burma.

Hsipaw, my next stop after my stay with the TNLA, was one of the largest and richest of the Shan kingdoms. The then *sawbwa* had been the first of the sky lords to pledge his loyalty to the British, who regarded his principality as especially important thanks to its proximity to China. There was a long-standing plan to use Shan State as a conduit for trade with western China, although little ever came of the idea, and a railway from Mandalay via Hsipaw to Lashio, the closest town of any size to the border with Yunnan, was opened as early as 1900.

Mandalay to Hsipaw is a journey of 130 miles but today it can take as long as twelve hours by train, the locomotives restricted to an average speed of around fifteen miles an hour thanks to the dire state of the track. Burma's rail network has still to recover from decades of neglect under the generals. It is quicker to drive the twisting, two-lane highway that climbs out of Mandalay up to the Shan plateau and which terminates at Muse, the scruffy frontier town with Yunnan.

Off the highway is Hsipaw, snug in a hollow, surrounded by forested hills and divided by the winding Dokhtawaddy River. It is one of the few towns in northern Shan State open to foreigners. I visited it first in 2010, when it was a modest tourist destination drawing backpackers for treks to the minority villages in the area. There were only a couple of guest houses and restaurants, no banks or internet access and the social centre was the cinema, used for screening soccer matches rather than movies. English football was one of the few foreign imports allowed on TV during the junta era.

Over the coming years I watched as Hsipaw experienced a mini-boom, the number of foreign tourists jumping after the generals stepped down. ATMs arrived, unknown in Burma until 2012, along with hotels, mostly financed by Chinese or Bamar migrants. Hsipaw's market began to stock much more than the fresh produce and basic household items previously available, as trade with Yunnan increased. Everyone seemed to have a motorbike and Hsipaw became prosperous by Shan State standards, even if you had only to travel outside town for a few minutes to find the more familiar bamboo shacks and barefoot children.

Now, though, Hsipaw is a Shan State version of Fort Apache. The town is an oasis ringed by hills full of rival armies – TNLA, RCSS and the *Tatmadaw* – the skirmishes coming ever closer and civilians increasingly caught in the crossfire. My closest friends in Hsipaw, a Shan–Chinese family, told of RCSS and Shan State Army – North soldiers, their uniforms swapped for *longyi*, coming to town and demanding annual 'taxes' as high as £7,500 from the most successful businesses, threatening kidnappings if the money wasn't paid.

Cars and trucks were held up at night on the road – closed to foreigners – that runs south to Taunggyi, as Shan highwaymen raised funds for the fight. And the supply and use of narcotics was rising. The first time I saw opium in Burma was in Hsipaw, offered to me by an ethnic Wa man and former soldier in the UWSA. It is heroin that is more widely available now.

My driver took me into Hsipaw by the back road that runs from Namtu, via the junction where the stone track to Namhsan begins its agonising ascent. The road passes close to where the palace of the former *sawbwa* stands. Only six of their palaces remain intact across Shan State. Many have been demolished, after falling into disrepair when their occupants were imprisoned or left Burma for good following the 1962 coup. In a few infamous instances some were pulled down by the *Tatmadaw* as a warning to Shan nationalists across the region.

Hsipaw's *sawbwas* were regarded as the most cosmopolitan of Shan's aristocrats. Maurice Collis returned to Burma just once after he left Myeik and retired from the Indian Civil Service, touring Shan State in 1937 and stopping at Hsipaw for lunch at the palace. He and the *sawbwa* were old chums, first encountering each other on the boat out to Burma from England in 1919. Collis was immediately impressed by his charm and sophistication. But then the *sawbwa* had gone to the same school and university, Rugby and Oxford, as Collis.

On my first visit to Hsipaw the palace was closed, its gates chained, by order of the *Tatmadaw*. Its guardians, Mr Donald, the nephew of the last *sawbwa*, and his wife Mrs Fern were under effective house arrest. Donald had already been imprisoned between 2005 and 2009 for supposedly advising a proscribed Shan political party, but mainly because he was a relative of a sky lord. They were allowed to receive foreign visitors again only after the military gave up power. I had met Mrs Fern on a number of occasions since, introduced by a Hsipaw friend whose grandmother had been a family retainer to the *sawbwas*.

She was waiting for me at the gate when I went to the palace the day after my arrival. Short, with spectacles, her black hair in a bun, Mrs Fern was in her customary flowery *htamein* and a traditional Shan blouse buttoned to the neck. She is a princess herself, officially known as Sao Sarm Hpong, one of eight daughters of the last *Sawbwa* of Mongyai, a kingdom south-east of Hsipaw that had covered an area about the size of Devon. Now seventy-four, Mrs Fern's life has been quietly dramatic, but no trace of that shows on her tranquil face, her dark eyes expressionless unless she is smiling, which she does a lot.

Trailed by her pack of half-feral dogs, we walked down the rocky path that leads to the palace, past the disused tennis court with grass and weeds sprouting from its cracked concrete. 'We didn't restore it because, while Donald likes to play, we knew the soldiers would want to play too and we didn't want them to enjoy themselves at our expense,' said Mrs Fern, who speaks English with the precise pronunciation of a 1950s BBC presenter. The palace has been the unwilling host of *Tatmadaw* troops at various times.

A water buffalo was grazing in the tangled, overgrown garden enclosed by a brick wall and overlooked by tall tamarind trees. An ancient tractor was parked in front of the steps to the main entrance of the palace, while a flagpole leaned at an angle. 'It is very hard to find local people to work here now,' Mrs Fern said regretfully. 'So many young people have gone to Thailand to work and we can't afford to pay very much.'

The palace once stood on five acres of land, now reduced to what I could see around me. Built in 1924, it is not a palace in the traditional sense of the word. Instead, it is a dilapidated, but still imposing, white stone mansion, part supported by pillars, with a red-tiled roof and wood-framed windows. A mournful air infuses it, as if the house itself could remember the times when it was staffed and played host to glamorous parties, its walls freshly painted and the lawns around it tended. Alone out of the six surviving *sawbwa* palaces, it is the only one still occupied by a sky lord's family.

Inside there are parquet floors, high ceilings and solid wooden furniture that looks as old as the house. Photos of Donald and Mrs Fern's relatives and ancestors sat on bookcases and tables in the drawing room. A large Shan flag, a white circle representing the desire for peace imposed on horizontal yellow, green and red stripes, hung on one wall. Mrs Fern's grandson, a junior officer in the Shan State Army – North, back on leave from his base north-east of Lashio, popped his head into the room to say hello. As usual, Donald was away at their other home in Taunggyi.

These days, the family income comes mostly from Mrs Fern hosting visitors – both locals and foreigners – drawn by the chance to hear first-hand the romantic story of the doomed last *Sawbwa* of Hsipaw, Sao Kya Seng. Inheriting the title from his uncle, Maurice Collis's friend, he went to university in Denver, where he met and married his Austrian wife Inge Eberhard, who was studying on a Fulbright Scholarship. Only after they returned to Shan State in 1954 did she realise that her husband was a sky lord. He hadn't mentioned it.

Coming home to Hsipaw with ambitious plans to modernise farming techniques in his kingdom, Sao Kya Seng handed over the rice fields owned by his family to the people who worked them. He was a member of the upper house of Burma's parliament, a supporter of a federal state and a critic of the military's cruelty towards the Shan and other minorities. That was enough for Ne Win to mark his card. Last seen being taken into custody at an army checkpoint soon after the 1962 coup, Sao Kya Seng died in unknown circumstances at a *Tatmadaw* base in southern Shan State.

His wife tried vainly to find out what happened to her husband, before departing for Austria and then the United States in 1964 with their two daughters. Mrs Fern saw them off at Yangon Airport and photos of the now middle-aged daughters, resident in Colorado, are prominent in her drawing room. Inge wrote a book, *Twilight over Burma*, about her marriage and its tragic end, which was made into a movie in 2015. It was banned in Burma, the government insisting also that it not be shown in Thailand.

From the 1930s on the *sawbwas* were allied to the Shan nationalist cause, disgruntled by the reduction of their rank under the British. Later, some became advocates of the federal state which had been agreed in theory at the 1947 Panglong

Conference but was never put into practice. By the 1950s, though, the sky lords were also coming under pressure from both their own subjects and the government to renounce their rights to rule their kingdoms. Not all the *sawbwas* were as progressive as Sao Kya Seng, and resentment of the feudal-like power they wielded in the independent Burma was acute.

In April 1959 the *sawbwas* bowed to the march of time and gave up their authority in a ceremony at Taunggyi overseen by Ne Win. A millennium of tradition came to an end with each of the thirty-four sky lords accepting a state pension, withdrawn after the 1962 coup, in return for no longer being able to levy taxes on their subjects. Since then there have been no *sawbwas*, although their descendants are still identified by their prestigious ancestry.

For Mrs Fern it has been a steep fall from grace. 'The contrast between now and then is big. We were royalty,' she said simply. 'I went away as a boarder to convent school in Namtu, but I remember playing in the palace in Mongyai as a child and celebrating the festivals. But the palace became a barracks after 1962 and the army left it in a bad way. My father went to prison after the coup and when he was released in 1968 and saw the state of it he ordered it to be demolished.'

Did she ever yearn for the old days? 'Well, it was much more peaceful in the British era. It was the British who created Burma and they kept the ethnics ruling, under them of course. The Shan didn't want to take independence at the same time as the Burmese, but Aung San persuaded them by offering the chance to secede from the country after ten years. Politics is a dirty business. The Bamar wouldn't agree, of course. The Burmese were never happy after the royal family was exiled.'

Many of her siblings and relatives are now in the US or UK. 'Most of the educated people in Shan left after the coup, to Yangon or abroad,' said Mrs Fern. She is related to numerous sky lord families. In the old Shan State there was no middle class. You were either royalty or a farmer. The female children of the *sawbwas* married other sky lords or their junior relations, or stayed single. It was one of the reasons why the *sawbwas* often had a number of wives at the same time.

Mrs Fern believes one positive development in recent years is a revival across the regional borders of the sense of what it is to be Shan. 'I think there has been a renewal of Shan culture and identity. You see on Facebook that Shan people are celebrating the festivals and Shan National Day in Assam [there are Shan in India, too], Thailand, Laos, even in Yunnan they wave the Shan flag. I think that's why the Burmese are afraid of us, because there are so many of us. We could overpower them numerically,' she stated.

'But of course the Shan fight among themselves. Shan State is very big and once the military took over the different parts were isolated. I think they didn't repair the roads deliberately. So there was a lack of communication and that created problems. Facebook has helped improve that, although you can't believe everything you see on it. I am half optimistic and half pessimistic about the future. The army is still strong and they have a lot of money. Peace depends on them.'

Shan disunity isn't just a result of poor infrastructure or the ideological and political splits that have prompted the formation of so many rival armies. There are also stark issues of trust between the different branches of the Shan people that not even the presence of a foreign army, the *Tatmadaw*, in their territory has enabled them to reconcile. Speaking distinct languages, the rivalry between the Tai Yai, who make up the majority of the Shan, and the Tai Khun, Tai Leng, Tai Lü and Tai Nua groups is very real, if often unspoken.

Kengtung, sometimes known as Kyaingtong, in the south-east of Shan State is the heartland of the Tai Khun. Just fifty-five miles west of the border with Yunnan and less than a hundred miles from the frontier with Thailand, its remoteness means it is little visited by foreigners, who are barred from travelling there overland from the rest of Shan State. The sole road open to foreigners in this part of the region is the one that meanders towards Kengtung from Tachileik, the border town with Thailand.

Five years had passed since I last travelled the road to Kengtung from Tachileik, a place best known for black-market trading, and little appeared to have changed along the way. Beyond the town, past an army checkpoint, the road starts to rise to the Shan plateau, leaving the farms of the lowlands behind for tiny villages that are home to the Akha people. Out of sight to the east was the Mekong River, which marks Burma's boundary with Laos. After four hours of puffing uphill, the bus began the descent to the plain where Kengtung stands amidst rice paddies glowing emerald green.

During the colonial period Kengtung was the biggest of the Shan kingdoms, larger in size than Belgium. Its namesake town is one of the most striking in all Burma, the steep streets home to pagodas and forty monasteries that draw Buddhist scholars from across the nearby borders. The Tai Khun are the majority, with a smaller number of Tai Lü people. Outside Kengtung, inhabiting the increasingly deforested hills that encircle it, are communities of Akha, Lahu and Wa, who come to town to sell their produce at the large market, many still wearing their traditional dress.

Dominating the heart of Kengtung is Nyaung Toung Lake, on whose banks the palace of the *sawbwa* stood until 1991. A few colonial-era mansions overlook the lake still, although they are far outnumbered now by newer, gaudy homes built in the Chinese nouveau riche style – all pillars and pastel colours. Some are owned by those who have prospered in the drug trade, long the biggest business in the area.

Apart from being a Tai Khun centre, Kengtung is the unofficial capital of the Golden Triangle, thanks to its proximity to the Mekong and the borders with Yunnan, Laos and Thailand, as well as the territory controlled by the Wa people and their army. Until relatively recently the hills north of town were one of the prime places for opium cultivation in Shan State. Kengtung was a marketplace for the poppy grown nearby, the *sawbwas* overseeing a flourishing concern that saw the opium sold on to buyers in Thailand.

'People used to grow poppy here just to make an income, but not anymore, although some do in the Wa areas,' said Sai Hong Kham, the former private secretary to the last *Sawbwa* of Kengtung, as we sat stationary in the late-morning traffic. I was surprised by the gridlock. But Sai Hong Kham, still spry at eighty-eight, was adept at threading his SUV through the cars, trucks and motorbikes that clogged the narrow roads as we made our way to his home.

Few octogenarians are active in politics, let alone set up their own party in order to run for public office. But Sai Hong Kham did just that before the 2015 election that swept Aung San Suu Kyi and the NLD to power, establishing the Eastern Shan State Development Democratic Party (ESSDDP) and standing for one of Kengtung's seats in the parliament in Naypyidaw.

Over an early lunch he told me why. 'We are Tai Khun people here and we get no support from the central government, while the other Shan political parties are for the Tai Yai, Tai Leng and Tai Lü,' he said, between mouthfuls of pork and rice. 'This is a party for locals, for everyone in the nine townships in eastern Shan State. If I can get elected, then I can do something for them.'

He and his party failed to win any seats at the 2015 election. Six of the townships in eastern Shan State voted for the USDP, the other three for the NLD. 'The USDP have money and they gave a lot to the villages, so they voted for them,' said Sai Hong Kham. 'Without money, you can't do anything in politics in Burma. The local people like the idea of a party that represents them, but they want pocket money too.'

Most of the eighteen political parties allied to the different ethnic groups in Shan State did poorly in the 2015 election. People voted mainly for the NLD because they saw the poll as an unprecedented opportunity, for all but the oldest of them, to eject the army from power. Others took the USDP's cash. That sparked recriminations among the parties, with Sai Hong Kham's ESSDDP accused of both splitting the vote and being a front for the USDP. 'I wanted to cooperate with the other parties, but they rejected that,' he insisted. 'It's just rumours that we are a proxy for the USDP. Who would give me money to set up a party?'

Sai Hong Kham has also been frustrated in his plans to form links with the National Democratic Alliance Army (NDAA), who control the town of Mong La on the border with Yunnan. Flush with cash from various illicit activities – drugs, gambling and smuggling – and with close ties to Chinese businessmen and politicians across the frontier, the

NDAA has turned Mong La into something of a beacon for development in this backwater of Shan State.

'We need more cooperation with the people who run Mong La, but Naypyidaw doesn't like that because they want the NDAA to lay down their arms first. For example, we have an electricity problem in Kengtung: not enough of it. But in Mong La they have hydropower, a dam built by technicians from Shanghai. They'd sell us electricity, but we have to get permission from the government. I have asked, but they haven't replied,' said Sai Hong Kham.

'It's the same with doing more trade with China. We're only a two-hour drive from the border here, but we haven't received permission from the Shan State parliament in Taunggyi to increase trade. Sometimes they won't even let us sell our rice surplus to Yunnan because they don't want the Chinese to have it. The problem is that the Shan don't trust the Chinese. They are very cunning people and the Shan fear that.'

I was enjoying Sai Hong Kham's company. In an expansive mood and refreshingly unguarded throughout our conversation, he was clearly still as a sharp as a knife. He is a witness to much of Burma's tumultuous recent history, from the 1930s onwards, and a figure of respect, as well as controversy, in Kengtung. I noticed how people addressed him with a *wai*, the prayer-like greeting and slight bow used in Thailand, but seen less frequently in Shan State.

Part of that is down to the years he spent as the private secretary to Sao Sai Long, the last *Sawbwa* of Kengtung. He was one of the youngest of nineteen children fathered by the previous *sawbwa* and his six wives. The Shan kingdoms did not operate a strict hereditary line, with eldest sons sometimes passed over in favour of younger ones, or even cousins. Sao

Sai Long became the *sawbwa* after the original choice was murdered in front of fifty of his bodyguards. No one was ever convicted of the crime, but Maurice Collis claimed the victim was shot by another of his brothers, angry at not getting the position.

Assuming his role as *sawbwa* after the Second World War, Sao Sai Long recruited Sai Hong Kham as his right-hand man. They were distant relatives; Sao Sai Long married Sai Hong Kham's cousin, and both men attended the Shan Chiefs School in Taunggyi. 'He went to Adelaide to finish his education. When he came back from Australia, he asked me to be his secretary. I was his best friend and he trusted me. I was twenty and he was twenty-one. It was just as well we were good characters, because we had to look after all the money,' smiled Sai Hong Kham.

With the British about to depart, responsibility for running the kingdom and managing the accounts fell on the youthful sky lord and Sai Hong Kham. 'On an average day, I'd go to the office in the morning and for five or six hours without a break people would come and see us with their problems,' he remembered. 'A farmer might come and say, "I've got an issue with water supply" and then we would solve it.'

Even at the height of the colonial period Britain barely concerned itself with Kengtung, one of the most isolated outposts of the Federated Shan States, as long as the tax revenue was handed over. 'There were only three British based here: the resident official, an engineer and an army officer who commanded a company of Shan levies. So the administration was mostly done by the *sawbwa*,' said Sai Hong Kham. Nor had the British lived in Kengtung, preferring to stay in Loi Mwe, a small hill station twenty miles south-east. 'The air in

Kengtung wasn't good for them, especially in the monsoon season.'

Today, Sai Hong Kham wishes that the government still stayed out of Kengtung's affairs. 'We want federal rule obviously, like in the British times,' he said. 'Eastern Shan State is calm now. The people here don't want any more fighting. It's a waste of their lives. But Kengtung is still the headquarters of the Golden Triangle Command, run by a major general, although the army doesn't interfere in civilian life, not like in the junta days.' Kengtung remains full of *Tatmadaw* soldiers, their base close to the Golden Triangle Golf Club, and most locals would like to see them gone.

There is little nostalgia among younger Shan for the rule of the sky lords, though. 'The new generation don't like the *sawbwas*. They say the *sawbwas* sold Shan State to the Burmese. But a lot of the *sawbwas* didn't want to be close to the Burmese,' said Sai Hong Kham. Like Mrs Fern, Sai Hong Kham claims the Shan didn't desire independence alongside the Bamar. He blames Sao Shwe Thaike, the sky lord who became Burma's first president, for the deal made at Panglong which tied Shan State to becoming part of the Union of Burma.

'Yawnghwe was close to the Burmese and he was influenced by Aung San,' he said, referring to Sao Shwe Thaike by the name of his kingdom. 'We would have been better off as part of the British Commonwealth, but Aung San didn't want that. He persuaded Yawnghwe to accept Panglong and then Yawnghwe persuaded the other *sawbwas*. They were younger and felt bound to follow him. I met Yawnghwe. He was pleasant, but he didn't have the mind of a politician. He wasn't a clever man. He didn't do much for the Shan while he was president. He was too busy with his four wives and having an easy life.'

Whether Aung San would have given the Shan and the other ethnic groups autonomy over their regions if he hadn't been assassinated is a question much debated in the borderlands. Sai Hong Kham thinks not. 'Aung San was a politician. He wouldn't have kept to the terms of Panglong.' Nor does he have much faith in his daughter. 'I organised a place for Aung San Suu Kyi to speak when she came to Kengtung before the 2015 election,' he told me. 'We had a long talk. She is a very intelligent person. But I believe maybe half of what she says about giving more power to the minorities.'

Sao Shwe Thaike tried to make amends for being outmanoeuvred at Panglong, as Sai Hong Kham and many other Shan see it. He became a vocal advocate for the minorities after his term as president was over, standing up for the Rohingya. Sao Shwe Thaike declared that if they weren't considered one of Burma's indigenous races, then neither could the Shan be. In 1960 he formed the Federal Movement, a coalition of the Shan and other ethnic groups who debated the need for constitutional reform.

Ne Win seized on the Federal Movement as the excuse to launch his coup on 02 March 1962. In a final twist of the *sawbwas'* long history, Sao Shwe Thaike and the other sky lords became the scapegoats for Burma's escalating civil wars, accused of encouraging separatism and tarred as 'vampires' who wanted their kingdoms back so they could live off the blood of their subjects. The reality is that Ne Win had probably already decided that a military takeover was the only way to counter the minorities' demands for self-rule, to say nothing of the need to satisfy his own lust for power.

Like the *Sawbwa* of Hsipaw, Sao Shwe Thaike disappeared into army custody never to be seen again. His middle son was killed during his arrest, the only fatality on the day of the coup. Almost all the other *sawbwas*, including Mrs Fern's father, were jailed. Sao Sai Long was detained while in his hospital bed in Yangon. 'He had piles,' recalled Sai Hong Kham. 'He was taken to Insein Prison four days after the coup and imprisoned for six years. A condition of his release was that he had to live in Rangoon. He had to ask permission when he wanted to visit Kengtung.'

After Ne Win snatched power Sai Hong Kham was offered the chance to carry on in the Kengtung government. 'I said, "No." I was a loyal subject of the *sawbwa*. So I became a merchant. I opened a pharmacy and a garage. I didn't enjoy it much.' Sao Sai Long's children left for the United States. 'I stayed in touch with the *sawbwa* until he died in Yangon in 1997. I helped look after him in his final days,' said Sai Hong Kham.

Before he passed away the generals inflicted one final indignity on Sao Sai Long. In November 1991 the *Tatmadaw* demolished his palace. It was the most impressive of all the sky lord residences, a domed fairy tale of a royal home with arched gateways and windows. 'His grandfather had attended the 1903 durbar in Delhi,' said Sai Hong Kham. 'He saw the palaces in India and decided he wanted one like them, so he brought an Indian architect back with him and built one. It was a beautiful place.'

Away visiting his daughter in Australia, Sai Hong Kham received a call from the *sawbwa* telling him that the palace had been flattened. 'I didn't believe him,' he remembered. 'Then I came back and saw that it was gone. It took the army three days to pull it down. While they were doing it, the soldiers surrounded the area to prevent people getting close. They were frightened that the locals would be angry. They were right. The people were upset.'

Why does he think the junta took such a drastic decision? 'The Burmese are superstitious. They believe in astrology and spirits and numbers. They destroyed the palace because the *Tatmadaw* officers thought that, by doing so, they would inherit the power of the *sawbwa*. They destroyed the palaces in Lashio and Hsenwi at the same time. It was deliberate timing. They wanted the spirits of the *sawbwas* to pass to them with their power,' said Sai Hong Kham. 'It's the story of the country, really.'

16

A Tale of Two Border Towns

A chorus of Chinese ringtones – drifting classical flutes and Cantonese pop – broke the silence and the motorbike men reached for their phones as one. 'The road is clear. Let's go,' said my driver. I gripped the metal bar behind the seat as we roared out in convoy along a concrete path, before turning onto a forest track. It was wet and muddy, the legacy of recent rain, the dirt spraying off the wheels of the bike as we swerved through tightly packed trees.

Then it was a sudden stop at a concrete shell of a building. A middle-aged Chinese woman in jeans and a shapeless sweater emerged, her children behind her. They went from bike to bike collecting ten yuan (£1.10) from every passenger. I asked the woman what the fee was for. 'It's my road,' she replied. Toll paid, we accelerated away, the driver and I leaning forward as he gunned the throttle and we crested a steep slope, leaving Yunnan Province and China for Shan State.

Descending down the other side of the hill, we turned a corner and there beneath us was Mong La. This was no scrappy border outpost like Rihkhawdar in Chin State, where the stilted houses and wood-built shops appear temporary, as if they could be blown away in a fierce storm. Hotels as tall as twenty storeys and pink and white apartment blocks looked down on the smaller blue-roofed commercial buildings lining the wide main road that curls through town.

Flowing slowly to the west, a mud-brown river acts as a natural barrier between Mong La and the thickly forested, bumpy hills that close in on the slender valley the town occupies. Their untamed presence added to the incongruity of seeing such substantial structures in this isolated part of Shan State. I knew that beyond the town there would be the usual villages of wood and bamboo shacks. The only real road in the area was the one I could see below me, running on from Mong La to Kengtung.

Teenage soldiers in jungle-green uniforms manned a checkpoint at the bottom of the hill. They were from the NDAA, the 4,000-strong militia of Shan and Akha troops that controls Mong La and the surrounding area. None showed any surprise at the presence of a foreigner. 'Where are you from?' one asked in thick, Yunnan-accented Mandarin when I handed him my passport. I told him. 'Fifty-three yuan [£6.10],' he said, the charge to enter Mong La from China, giving me a receipt after I paid.

Construction sites and cranes were busy as we drove into the centre of town, more high-rises being readied. The driver told me that a new road was being built south to Tachileik, on the border with Thailand, and the streets were hectic with cars. Many had Yunnan licence plates, but others bore identification that was a roll call of Shan State's disputed border regions: SR-4 for Mong La, KK for Kokang, WA for the Wa territory and WD for Panghsang, the Wa capital. Some vehicles had no number plates at all.

Dropping me at the market the driver passed on his phone number, so I could call him to pick me up when I was ready to leave, and raced off back to his own country. I found a room in a Chinese-owned hotel. The staff – Shan and Wa – spoke bad Mandarin rather than Burmese, the clocks were set to Beijing time and I paid my bill in Chinese yuan. Geographically I was in Shan State, but Mong La has its own status within the Sino-Burmese borderlands. It is a town built on the back of crime that has become a playground for the Chinese and a refuge for the minorities escaping the fighting in the hills beyond.

To the authorities in Naypyidaw, Mong La and the countryside around it is Special Region 4. There are seven special regions across the most contested parts of Shan State – the Ta'ang homeland is Special Region 7. They were established under the junta as a sop to the minorities, places where the army would supposedly step back and allow them to be self-administered by the majority ethnic group inhabiting them. In practice, as I saw during my time with the TNLA, the majority are special in name only with the *Tatmadaw* maintaining a presence in many of the zones.

But Special Region 4 is autonomous and *Tatmadaw*-free, as is Special Region 2, the homeland of the Wa people, and Special Region 1 in the north-east of Shan State, an area known as Kokang that is populated by the descendants of Chinese migrants who arrived in the eighteenth century. Aung San offered self-rule to the minorities at Panglong in 1947, only for successive governments to deny them that. But the peoples in Mong La, Kokang and the Wa territory have established their own version of independence anyway.

Enabled by the staggering profits from the drug trade, as well as gambling operations and the smuggling of all manner of contraband, rich and powerful ethnic armies control these three zones. All have close links to China, which sits just across the frontier from their regions, further boosting their ability to function as mini-countries complete with their own governments, tax systems and police forces. There is no hint of the Burmese state in these areas at all. Unique in Southeast Asia, they are self-governing territories run by minority peoples.

Foreigners are, of course, strictly barred from entering the special regions. Mong La was once open to westerners visiting with a guide, but today it is firmly off-limits. It is just a two-hour drive from Kengtung, but the army checkpoints along the road turn back foreigners. The *Tatmadaw* does not step inside Special Region 4, but it is based all around it.

China's border with Burma is impossible to guard, though. Straggling south from the Burmese Himalayas in Kachin State to the south-east of Shan State for 1,370 miles, running through mountains and remote rainforest, it has always been a loosely enforced boundary. In part that is a tacit recognition by Beijing of the transnational status of Yunnan and Kachin and Shan States, where the same ethnic groups live on both sides of the border and have never cared much for formal frontiers.

These days the Chinese side is more closely regulated than it was when I made my first illicit crossing to Panghsang and the Wa region in 2010. There are now police checks on buses travelling near the frontier and occasional roadblocks, but they are searching for dissidents or restless minorities seeking to escape China. For everyone else, moving between Yunnan and Shan State without legally exiting or entering China and Burma remains easy enough if you know where and how to cross.

Dalou in the deep south of Yunnan's Xishuangbanna region is where the backroads route to Mong La begins. After arriving by bus I found one of the motorbike taxis that make the run to Mong La. My driver was Akha, numerous in Xishuangbanna as well as the hills of Shan State. He sang as he steered the bike. But we came to an abrupt halt on the outskirts of the last village before the border, after he received a call warning that there were police up ahead.

We waited two hours for the officers to depart, more drivers arriving all the time with their Chinese passengers. To them our destination was Xiaomengla, or small Mong La, to distinguish it from Mengla County in Xishuangbanna. There are other routes to Mong La too, including one that is big enough for cars and small trucks to navigate, a vital conduit for the smugglers who move between Xishuangbanna and Shan.

Mong La has a reputation as a sin city in Yunnan. The big draw is gambling, which is illegal in China except in Macau, the Las Vegas of the Orient. As we waited to cross curious locals engaged me in conversation. They all asked if I was going to Mong La 'to play'. In Mandarin, 'play' can have different meanings. There is the innocent literal translation, having fun, as well as a more ribald definition. Admitting you're going to Mong La to play is code for a night of betting, drinking, karaoke and women.

When I made my way in the early afternoon to the huge market that sits in the centre of Mong La, some Chinese were already playing, sitting in front of computer screens and gambling online. Interspersed with the clothes stalls and food stands are betting shops. Card games were going on, too, while the sharp clack of mahjong tiles being slammed on tables rose up above the babble of accents, mainly Yunnan but others from farther afield in China. I encountered people from Shandong Province on the east coast, as well as from Hunan and Sichuan.

Away on the other side of the market, in the north-east corner, the animal traders were waiting for customers. Their wares were laid out on mats and in baskets in front of them: bear claws, a variety of horns and bones, including elephant tusks, animal skins, fur and dried internal organs. But there were also baby monkeys and bears in cages, fat snakes and lots of turtles. Occasionally, even a clouded leopard or tiger can be found here.

Often described as the wildlife trafficking capital of the world, Mong La is just one of a number of places in Shan State where endangered species can be found for sale. The trade thrives in Tachileik and Panghsang, too, as well as in parts of Kachin State. Even in Yangon it's possible to obtain items made from ivory and elephant bones. Buying and selling such animal parts is now illegal in Burma and China, but the hunters in the Shan Hills who source the beasts are beyond the law, as are the vendors – mostly Chinese but some Shan – at Mong La's market.

Despite repeated calls to shut down this unsavoury sector of the local economy, the traders will continue to operate as long as there are animals left to capture and people from China eager to buy them. They are required for the aphrodisiacs, tonics and remedies that many traditional Chinese medicine healers peddle, or just as good-luck charms. Some Chinese come to Mong La solely to dine on exotic species; bears, pangolins, civet cats, barking deer and snakes can be ordered off the menu at restaurants, too.

Wildlife is not all that is trafficked. Mong La is also a people smuggling hub. North Korean defectors have passed through on their way to Bangkok and then Seoul. Economic migrants leaving China for the rest of Southeast Asia sometimes depart from Mong La. Most recently, Uighurs – the Muslim ethnic minority native to China's far western province of Xinjiang – have started fleeing abroad via the town. The rise in the number of Uighurs absconding is the reason why there are now more bus and vehicle checks in Yunnan's borderlands.

Deceptive during the day, Mong La can appear innocent, a Shan State imitation of a Yunnan country town. Vendors sit outside their shops waiting for customers. Locals visit the market for food purchases, or wander the shopping mall. In the late afternoon, as the heat of the day subsides, barbecue stalls – grilled meat or fish, corn on the cob, tofu and vege-tables – are set up for the evening rush. Families take the air, babies pushed ahead of them in buggies. A small park has swings for children, or they can jump up and down on the bouncy castle operating in the market area.

Yet the top floor of the shopping mall is given over to bars with working girls. Pickup trucks with armed NDAA soldiers in the back travel the streets. Close-up, Mong La is as dusty and dirty as any Shan town, too, the river that flows through the west of town polluted and stinking in the sun. And everywhere is the opportunity to bet. Streets are lined with gambling parlours and arcades with slot and pachinko-like machines, or the Mong La version of craps: giant dice thrown by the pull of a rope, the players tossing down one hundred yuan (£11.70) notes without a care.

Along with the betting shops in the market, these places are for the low rollers. The big money is at the casinos that are a twenty-five-minute drive west of the town. Mong La exists for the Chinese, and it is they who make up almost all of the casino customers. But gambling has become so pervasive that the Shan, Akha and Wa who live in Mong La, or commute to work from their villages, have adopted the gaming habit, too, whether they can afford it or not. Some people in the street joints were placing wagers as low as ten yuan.

Night fell like everywhere in Southeast Asia, a slow descent from bright sun to red sunset and then the sudden switch to darkness. Now Mong La is in its element. The neon signs on the big hotels flick on, flashing out their names in characters and Burmese script, powered by the Chinese-built dam that Sai Hong Kham in Kengtung is jealous of. Suddenly the streets are busier, the families present earlier in the day back in their homes, replaced by a small army of Chinese punters out to play.

Around the market the karaoke bars and shopfront brothels open for business. Outside them the girls – often just teenagers – sit in their tube tops, micro-skirts or denim shorts, feet in high heels or platform flip-flops. They while away the wait for customers with their phones, WeChatting with boys, friends and family in far-off villages and towns. In Mong La, as well as the other areas along the frontier, everyone uses Chinese social media.

Many of the girls are temporary migrants from across the border, mainly Yunnanese but some from Sichuan, working for a few months at a time. Staffing the hotels, shops and gambling dens are the Shan, joined by an increasing number of Wa people. 'There are more visitors to Mong La than to Panghsang now, so we come here to work,' one woman told me.

Panghsang, the capital of the Wa region, is a three-hour drive north of Mong La and also right on the border with Yunnan. But it is a rough-edged, less comfortable town for visitors. The Wa have a reputation in both Burma and China for being both ferocious and unwelcoming to outsiders, a consequence of their history as headhunters, a habit they only gave up in the 1970s in the most remote hills. With just one casino, Panghsang isn't much of a place to play unless you have Wa friends.

Not only does Mong La offer the prospect of better-paid employment than elsewhere in eastern Shan State, it provides sanctuary also. For some people Mong La is a place to escape the *Tatmadaw*, to get as far away from the Burmese state as is possible. When the Four Cuts campaign was extended to Shan State, the locals started fleeing ahead of the *Tatmadaw* into the zones controlled by the ethnic armies. They function as places to hide, as well as playgrounds.

While Mong La was still slumbering the next morning, in recovery from the excesses of the night before, I took a trip to the town's museum, possibly the strangest exhibition hall in Burma, a land of peculiar museums. Its official English title is 'Museum in Commemoration of Opium-Free in Special Region 4', but it really stands as a symbol of how the NDAA and its allies in Wa and Kokang have managed to carve out their mini-states on the back of the manufacture and sale of heroin and methamphetamines.

As usual the museum was free of staff and visitors, a musty smell pervading throughout, the glass enclosing the exhibits thick with dust. Senior junta figures and agents from the US's Drug Enforcement Administration (DEA) witnessed the destruction of poppy fields in faded photos from the 1980s. A six-step guide revealing how to refine heroin from opium is on display, just in case the farmers in this part of Shan State don't know how to do it. Best of all is the diorama with life-sized dolls of a heroin user's journey to redemption, from long-haired reprobate in jeans and t-shirt to clean-cut chap in a white shirt and *longyi*.

Contrary to its current neglected status, the museum was opened to some fanfare. It was all part of a campaign by Lin Mingxian, the seventy-something man who runs Special Region 4, to convince the outside world that his 1,900-square-mile fiefdom was now drug-free. Also known as Sai Lin, or Sai Leun, Lin is of Yunnan and Shan ancestry and was a Red Guard in China's Cultural Revolution of the 1960s. For the next twenty years, he rose through the ranks of the Communist Party of Burma, which had retreated to the borderlands and recruited the local ethnic groups in its battle with the junta.

In 1989, though, the minorities rebelled, splitting from the communists and swiftly establishing the three armies – NDAA, UWSA and MNDAA – which control Mong La, the Wa region and Kokang. Lin emerged as the head of the NDAA. He and the other leaders of the armies agreed uneasy ceasefires with the generals in return for being left in control of their regions. Lin and his friends in Kokang and Wa were already involved in the Golden Triangle drug trade, but over the next few years they oversaw a rapid expansion of poppy cultivation in their territories, setting up refineries to produce heroin as well.

Soon the US State Department was taking an interest. In 1995 they cited Lin and his cohorts in Wa and Kokang as some of the world's leading heroin traffickers. Lin's masterly reaction was to open his drug eradication museum two years later as proof that he had given up the narcotics business. His friends in the junta backed his claim and Washington decided to believe him. In 2000 the State Department declared Special Region 4 to be free of opium fields.

By then Mong La was already being transformed into Shan State's gambling capital. The town had started its rise to infamy in the late 1970s as a marketplace for Chinese goods. With the Cultural Revolution over, China was opening up again and cross-border commerce, both legal and illicit, took off. Mong La became a key junction in the trade between Shan State and Yunnan.

That wasn't enough for Lin Mingxian. Using his contacts from his Red Guard days among Yunnan politicians and businessmen to generate support and investment, Lin started opening casinos. And despite occasional crackdowns on the flow of Chinese crossing to gamble, Mong La is prospering today as never before. The new hotels and apartment blocks going up are proof of that, along with the road being constructed that will link the town to Tachileik and Thailand.

Lin Mingxian's biggest test came in 2005, when Chinese soldiers moved briefly into Mong La to close the casinos, following a succession of scandals involving Chinese officials and their relatives gambling away government money. Lin responded by building a new casino zone in the village of Wang Hsieo, ten miles from Mong La. He expanded into online gaming, too. Today, people bet remotely from as far away as Shanghai.

Casino vans shuttle punters to and from Wang Hsieo along the road that slides through the valley Mong La occupies on its way to Kengtung. Additional buses stop at the villages on the way to pick up the blue and red vested croupiers and the other staff who work in the casinos. The gambling industry is the major employer in the area now, along with the Chinese-owned rubber and banana plantations that have replaced the opium fields.

For the NDAA and the Wa and Kokang armies drugs are said to be less of a money-maker than they once were. Agri-businesses, mining and smuggling, all done in conjunction with Chinese concerns, draw far less attention from the outside world. Like Lin Mingxian the Wa leaders insist their region is now free of poppy farms. But heroin and methamphetamines destined for China and Thailand continue to move through the areas run by the NDAA, UWSA and MNDAA, while they control meth labs and opium fields located in other parts of Shan State.

All three armies remain closely linked, with the Wa dominant thanks to the sheer size of their force. UWSA soldiers are based in Special Region 4 to make sure Lin Mingxian isn't tempted to cut a deal with the government. Naypyidaw, though, shows no sign of wanting to disturb the status quo in this part of the borderlands. China views the special regions along its frontiers as a way of maintaining leverage with Burma. Shutting them down would be damaging to Sino-Burmese relations, as well as costly for the *Tatmadaw*, who would have to fight their way in.

Some of Wang Hsieo's casinos sport famous names like Casino Lisboa, a homage to Macau's oldest gaming house. But Wang Hsieo is no Macau. There is a glaring absence of glitzy big-name shows, global poker tournaments or wide-eyed tourists. Wang Hsieo is barely even a village; no more than a few shops and restaurants around the mostly low-rise casinos that sit side by side, their names displayed in neon, all dwarfed by the jungle-covered hills that fence in the settlement.

Inside the casinos are uninviting rooms with low ceilings. Little thought has been given to the decor. Alcohol is banned, but many of the customers smoke furiously, wreathing the tables in a thick haze. Computer screens livestream the action for the remote gamblers. Roulette apart, the games – Fan Tan, Dragon Tiger – are a mystery to most foreigners, played only by the Chinese. Westerners are not welcome in any case. My arrival was immediately noticed by the plain-clothes NDAA soldiers who act as security and I was warned against taking photos. I returned to Mong La, called my Akha driver and prepared to leave.

Back in Yunnan, I moved north, tracking the frontier with Shan, out of Xishuangbanna into Dehong Prefecture, the heartland of the Tai Nua people in China. My destination was Ruili, the capital of the region. Xishuangbanna is associated with drug trafficking, but jade is the king in Ruili. The town sits opposite the point where Shan State meets Kachin State to the north, and Kachin is where the world's largest deposits of jadeite – green jade – are found.

Jade has a mystical resonance to the Chinese and is the most popular and desirable item of jewellery for most women in the country. They have been buying Burma's green gold for a thousand years. Ruili is the place where much of it enters China, whether legally or smuggled, via the Shan border town of Muse. The city's centre is the ever-expanding jade market. It is staffed by Chinese and a growing contingent of Rohingya refugees, easily identifiable by their taqiyah caps, beards and *longyi*.

I was in Ruili waiting for a ride into Kachin State. North of Ruili, on the other side of the border, is an enclave controlled by the Kachin Independence Army. It is a thin shard of land in the far south-eastern corner of Kachin, bounded to the west by hills where the KIA is involved in frequent and fierce fighting with the *Tatmadaw*, and running parallel to the frontier with China in the east. Two towns – Mai Ja Yang and Laiza – lie at either end of the KIA's territory.

My destination was Mai Ja Yang. It was two days before I got the call, telling me to be at the corner of one of Ruili's main streets in the early afternoon. The border here is more tightly guarded than farther south in Yunnan and I had been expecting to cross at night. But today was a Sunday. 'The border police don't work on Sundays, so you can go any time,' said the man at the end of the phone. He arranged my transport, but we never met.

Standing at the junction for almost an hour, I thought the driver wasn't going to show up. Then a small minivan stopped and a short, dark-skinned man motioned me in. I got my first hint of the many differences between Mai Ja Yang and Mong La when he explained that he wasn't late, but that Mai Ja Yang runs on Burmese time rather than following China's clocks like Mong La does. The driver was a Chinese citizen, born near Ruili, but he was ethnically Kachin. There are around 150,000 Kachin in Yunnan, where they are known as the Jingpo, not including refugees and temporary economic migrants.

Another million Kachin live in Burma, where they divide themselves into six principal sub-groups. They reside predominantly in Kachin State, the country's northernmost region, which they refer to as 'Kachin Land', as well as in northern Shan. The driver told me he now lived in Mai Ja Yang. 'I can make more money driving between Kachin and Ruili than I can working in Ruili,' he said.

Heading north for forty minutes, we swung left on the outskirts of a small town and navigated a succession of streets until we joined a brick road. It was flanked on both sides by rice fields, over which women were bent double, their faces shielded from the sun by wide-brimmed floppy hats. We wound through the farmland, rice giving way to corn, the driver pointing to the hills in the distance: 'Kachin.' The road narrowed and got progressively worse, deteriorating from brick to a rocky track and finally a pitted dirt trail, and I knew I was back in Burma.

Downtown Mai Ja Yang appeared, low-rise grey and white buildings topped with metal roofs lining a now-paved road. Immediately west are the hills that are the front line between the KIA and the *Tatmadaw*, rising steeply as they roll towards the rest of Kachin State. There were hardly any other cars and few pedestrians. A deserted traffic circle marked the centre of town. The driver told me 8,000 people live in Mai Ja Yang and I wondered where they were, because there was little sign of life around us. It was the same at the hotel, where the staff outnumbered the guests.

From my room window I could see across the fields to the Chinese villages we had passed through. Mai Ja Yang is semi-rural itself, sugarcane growing on the outskirts, and hushed to the point where I could hear the birds twittering in the trees outside and the hotel workers two floors beneath me. Only the odd growl from a passing motorbike disturbed the peace. The near-silence was a shock after much louder Ruili.

Waiting in the lobby was Htoi Pan, a Kachin teacher whose name I had been given. As we walked back towards the town centre along the main road, past mostly shuttered shops, phone numbers daubed on them for prospective buyers to call, she explained what I was seeing. 'Mai Ja Yang was doing well when I first came in 2005. The casinos were open and that's when all this was built,' she said, waving an arm at the buildings on either side of us.

Those were Mai Ja Yang's boom years. In 2002 the Kachin Independence Organisation (KIO), the KIA's political wing, started granting casino licences to Chinese businessmen to raise cash for their battle with the Burmese. Soon a sleepy border village was transformed into a tawdry haven of flashing neon, raucous karaoke bars, brothels, arcades and gambling halls, a baby Mong La that drew gamblers and partygoers from Yunnan in their thousands on the weekends. Then it all went wrong. 'The casinos started closing in 2009, after the son of a senior Ruili official was killed here,' said Htoi Pan.

'Since then everything has slowed down. The biggest casino has reopened a few times, but when it does the Chinese put pressure on for it to close again. A lot of people come here from other parts of Kachin and Shan State, but they don't stay because business is bad. One day you walk past their shop or restaurant and it's gone. Then someone else arrives and it starts again.' The only places I saw open were general stores, a couple of beauty salons and clothes shops, the odd basic pharmacy and motorbike repair places.

At the end of the main road where it disappears into the hills towards Shan State and another front line between the KIA and the Burmese army, Mai Ja Yang stops abruptly. The last building is the covered market. A few stalls were still functioning, alongside a couple of noodle stands. Opposite the market is what had been the town's largest casino. Pink and blue paint peels off the concrete walls, the windows are broken and deserted guard posts, where the gamblers were screened for weapons, stand at the entrances.

Behind the casino is a forlorn square of chained gambling joints, one domed in imitation of a Mongolian yurt, and karaoke bars, their names written in both Chinese characters and the Latin alphabet introduced to the Kachin by American Baptist missionaries. Electronic gaming gadgets were abandoned outside some of them. We walked into one arcade whose doors were still open to find three lads playing pool, furniture stacked up around them, the walls lined with slot machines, dusty and destined never to light up again.

Wooden boards covered the entrance of the optimistically named Sheraton Hotel, while chickens and dogs roamed where punters had once thronged. The only sign of human life was on a lane off the square, where there was a wildlife emporium I could smell twenty metres away. Its Chinese owner was inside amidst the stench, while outside two black bears were confined in a cage far too small for them, tossing their heads from side to side, going mad in their prison.

Mai Ja Yang stands as an example, or warning, of what happens when the Chinese turn off the money tap. All the special regions along the Sino-Burmese frontier are dependent on both China's cash and goodwill to survive. But the KIO and KIA don't have the same warm relationship with the Chinese authorities that the rulers of Special Region 4 and the Wa and Kokang areas enjoy. The murder of a senior official's son was the cue for China to withdraw their support for Mai Ja Yang's casinos.

Chinese companies are present across Kachin State, operating everything from agri-businesses to hydropower projects, as well as being heavily involved in the jade trade. The KIA is no fan of China's economic presence in their homeland. And unlike the militias in Shan State the KIA dabbled only briefly with Burma's communist insurgents, sometimes fighting against them. Its leaders aren't former Red Guards and Marxists with connections to the Yunnan government.

Adding to the wariness between the KIA and China is the fact that the Kachin people are predominantly Christian, mainly Baptist but some Catholic. The Chinese Communist

Party has an extreme suspicion of organised religion, viewing it as a potential vehicle for dissent. Beijing dislikes Christianity the most out of all the faiths because it regards it as a western religion. Christians are closely monitored in China and those who worship in underground churches face persecution.

Htoi Pan and her friend and fellow teacher Htoi Paw were both devout Baptists. 'Do you believe in Jesus? You look like someone who does,' asked Htoi Paw, who joined us for dinner at the only restaurant I saw open in Mai Ja Yang. I wasn't sure how to react to that. Maybe it was because I'd shaved that morning. Tall, slim and pretty, Htoi Paw was younger than the more rotund Htoi Pan. She had grown up in Mandalay, while Htoi Pan was from Myitkyina, the Kachin capital. I thought they must find Mai Ja Yang extremely quiet. 'It's OK as long as we have internet,' replied Htoi Pan. 'And we go home at Christmas.'

Both women teach at the Institute of Education, a college for students who live in the conflict areas of Kachin State. Mong La has no university, for all its riches, but tiny Mai Ja Yang is an unlikely higher education centre with two colleges, one based in a former casino. Kachin students are banned from attending university if the authorities discover they grew up in areas controlled by the KIA. Many others are unable to afford the cost of living in the cities where Burma's universities are located.

'Here they pay £500 a year for food, board and education. After six months studying with us, they can easily pass the exams at the universities in Burma,' Zau Seng, the Institute's head, told me when I visited the next morning. Funded by international NGOs, with some support from the KIO, the college is on the western outskirts of town, where the hills start the climb towards the battle zone. The students were smiley and keen, most speaking reasonable English. 'The quality of high schools in Kachin is lower than in Burma,' said Zau Seng. 'But here they do six hours of classes a day and three hours of homework.'

Named in honour of one of the KIA's founders, Zau Seng referred to Burma as if it is a separate country from Kachin. And for many who live in Kachin Land, Burma is a foreign state. 'In my heart I think of Kachin as an independent country. But I know it is not a tangible thing, that it is not realistic. But autonomy within a federal union is a realistic aim,' Htoi Pan told me over lunch. But she isn't expecting self-rule soon. 'I am not optimistic about the future. As long as the Burmese army is around us, we don't feel safe and there can be no peace. We don't want conflict, but we believe we have no choice.'

Like the TNLA the KIA has tried a ceasefire, downing arms between 1994 and 2011. They got little in return, except for an influx of businesses into Kachin territory controlled by the now-familiar nexus of local elites, Chinese money and the *Tatmadaw*. Htoi Pan and her colleagues were scornful of Daw Suu's attempt to regenerate the peace process by naming the latest round of talks the 21st Century Panglong Conference, after the 1947 meeting where the minorities were persuaded to join the Union of Burma by Aung San. 'The second Panglong trap,' said one teacher with unconcealed contempt.

Invoking the ghost of her father is an unwise move by Daw Suu. None of the minorities have happy memories of the original Panglong Conference. 'It's not us who have changed. The KIO has been very faithful to the idea of a genuine federal union. It is Burma and the army who gave up on that,' stressed Htoi Pan, a forceful and articulate advocate of the Kachin cause. 'I don't like Aung San Suu Kyi, even if she is the best option. I don't believe she cares about the grievances of the ethnic peoples. I don't think she is sincere about wanting to address them or resolving the conflicts. I don't think she realises the history.'

Penned in their refuge by the *Tatmadaw*, while also defending positions in the north and west of Kachin State, as well as northern Shan, the 10,000-odd soldiers of the KIA are stuck in a grim stalemate. 'We know the conflict is unwinnable for us in a military sense, and the Burmese army cannot win without it getting very ugly,' said Htoi Pan. 'But it is not about winning or losing for us. It's about being on the right side of history and we are on the right side.'

Unlike Shan State, with its myriad militias and rival political parties, the Kachin have in their favour the fact that they are broadly bonded together. There are dissenting voices and splits have occurred within the KIO and KIA. But compared to the Shan the Kachin are far less factional. 'It is our tradition that no matter where you are from, who you are, whether you are Baptist or Catholic, we are all Kachin. We are all united,' Zau Seng told me.

Later, as dusk fell, Htoi Paw drove me on her motorbike to the headquarters of the KIA's Third Brigade, north of Mai Ja Yang on the road that leads to Laiza, the KIA's capital. Outside town the road is only paved for a mile or so, giving way to a stone and dirt track. We passed one of the camps for the internally displaced that are scattered throughout the KIA's territory. Around 100,000 Kachin have fled their homes because of the fighting, the *Tatmadaw* employing heavy artillery and air strikes in its battles with the KIA. Htoi Paw told me some of her students had been raised in the camps.

Waved through the base's guard post, we drove uphill past the long wooden huts where new recruits live. The sound of lusty singing emerged out of a hall. We looked in and saw an NCO leading teenage boys in the tune. 'It's a patriotic song. Learning it is part of their training,' said Htoi Paw. At the summit of the slope were bungalows that are the homes of the senior officers. I was struck by the unpretentious nature of their housing. Even the largest place I saw in Mai Ja Yang, the home of a former senior KIA commander, was modest in comparison to the mansions in Mong La and Panghsang occupied by their top militia men.

Money is in short supply for the KIA, though. There are no profits from the heroin and methamphetamine trade to be spent on luxury items, villas or infrastructure. The KIA is an organisation as vehemently anti-drugs as the TNLA and posters warning against taking them are plastered across Mai Ja Yang. Most Kachin believe they are targeted with narcotics in an attempt to reduce their numbers.

'Flooding our communities with drugs is being done deliberately by the Burmese government. They don't take any action against the drug dealers, only we do,' said Salang Kaba, the general secretary of the KIA's Third Brigade. 'There are Chinese people living in Burma who are selling drugs and they are being protected by the Burmese army, who are making money from it. The Bamar regions aren't so affected by drugs. Why is that?'

Salang Kaba was sixty-six, short and powerfully built with a dark brown, lined face. Informal in a white vest and purple trousers, he sat with me in his office drinking green tea. He oversees his unit's ideological education and its interactions with civilians, while occasionally negotiating with both the Burmese authorities and China. 'We have no political relationship with the Chinese, but we sometimes cooperate with them on anti-drug projects,' he told me.

Lacking narcotics money to fund their cause, and with the casinos of Mai Ja Yang closed down, I was curious how the KIA supports itself. I knew, too, that the KIA had largely lost control of the jade mining area of Hpakant in western Kachin State, once a prized income source, during the 1994–2011 ceasefire. 'We raise funds from logging and trading, although the logging has mostly been closed down now. But we mine as well, gold, amber and limestone,' said Salang Kaba.

They are being squeezed on the battlefield as well, the front line now closer to Mai Ja Yang than before, just two hours' march away in the hills. 'There have been many clashes in the last few days,' admitted Salang Kaba, deliberately interspersing his sentences with sips of tea, a way of keeping control of the conversation. 'No KIA have died but two villagers delivering rations to the soldiers stepped on landmines and were killed. I have heard that the brigades farther south are fighting hard because their positions are next to the TNLA. The *Tatmadaw* has entered our areas to try and fight the TNLA.'

Unsurprisingly, Salang Kaba was not optimistic about the prospects for peace. 'In my opinion it will be very difficult for any talks to succeed,' he stated. 'The *Tatmadaw* were led by Aung San in the past and the generals will tell Aung San Suu Kyi that they are following his ideals and plans. I think she will do the same as her father. She won't do anything to betray him. In the long term I think the situation will stay the same.'

Returning to the hotel, the road was deserted. There were only the stars above us and the fireflies frolicking in the bike's headlight for company, until we passed the refugee camp. Its inmates will surely be here for years yet, stranded in this nominally independent but beleaguered strip of territory. As we regained the paved road, the lights from Yunnan were glowing on the horizon, a different world from Kachin Land.

17

Enter the Dragon

I was briefed on the journey ahead outside the 7-Eleven in Soppong. 'When you get stopped at the checkpoints, just say you're going to visit the hospital and school,' said my contact, before introducing me to Ket, who was going to drive me to Loi Tai Leng in the deep south of Shan State. Both men were wrapped up in jackets against the nip in the air. Winter mornings in the far northern hills of Thailand are always colder than you expect.

The drive from Chiang Mai to Soppong had been one long curve, more than 800 bends, some of the passengers in my minivan vomiting along the way. But it was a spectacular ride. We careened down hillsides covered in brilliant green ferns, sun-dappled forest glades in the distance, then corkscrewed back up towards the skyline, past fields of rice and maize, banana and mango trees and cosy hamlets of wooden houses.

Soppong was hardly a town, its major buildings – post office, petrol station, shops – spread out on either side of the highway, a lazy river running to the east and houses scattered down the lanes that branched off the main road. With Shan State just twenty-five miles to the north, their residents are mainly Shan. But Karen, Lahu and Lisu live here, too, alongside a small community of Chinese, the descendants of Muslim immigrants from Yunnan. Thais make up just 20 per cent of the population.

There are only two roads north from Soppong. The main one, which I had travelled from Chiang Mai, loops south-west to Mae Hong Son, close to the border with Kayah, Burma's smallest state, a stub of land descending from the far southern reaches of Shan. Around Mae Hong Son are villages with largely ethnic Chinese populations. Their oldest residents are veterans of the remnants of the Kuomintang (KMT), or nationalist, armies that retreated to Shan State after the communist takeover of China in 1949.

Over the next twenty-odd years they launched ineffectual raids into Yunnan, backed by the CIA and Taiwan, while finding more lucrative work as foot soldiers for Shan State's drug syndicates. They escorted the opium caravans south to Chiang Mai, before the Thai government recruited them to fight its own communist insurgency in the hills that border Shan. Their reward was citizenship and homes in the most remote stretches of northern Thailand.

Our route was the other road from Soppong. Ushering me to his pickup truck, Ket barrelled off at an alarming rate, the road winding uphill almost immediately after leaving town. He didn't slow down for the turns, rushing through blind corners at sixty miles an hour. Lahu villages went by like a speeded-up film, their occupants manning stalls of food, drinks and souvenirs for the Shan who would be passing through on their way to celebrate their national day in Loi Tai Leng.

Four Thai army checkpoints lie along the road to the border. The Thais are much more rigorous about guarding their frontier with Burma than the Chinese, unless you travel off the few roads that run to Shan State, and the crossing to Loi Tai Leng is normally closed. But no one asked the reason for my journey, the soldiers just noting my name in a book. Shan State was already visible in the shape of the highest hills ahead, clumps of trees atop them, looking rugged and wilder than Thailand's more manicured mountains.

As Shan grew closer, the road degenerated into a deeply rutted dust track which we lurched along at no more than walking pace. In the rainy season it serves to cut the link to Loi Tai Leng. 'No four-wheel drive, no come,' Ket said in his broken English. The border sat on a ridge, overlooked by a small stockade manned by the Thai army. A red and white pole draped in barbed wire separated Thailand from Burma. The pole lifted, Ket drove on and I was back in Shan State.

Loi Tai Leng lies along the twisted spine of the ridge, which dips and rises as it traverses the top of the mountain, over 1,550 metres high. The road through town is compacted earth overlaid with yellow dust, which coats everything and everybody. Bamboo poles flying the Shan flag stood every ten metres or so. All available space at the sides of the road was taken up by temporary stalls covered by blue awnings. They far outnumbered the permanent buildings built of wood and topped with metal roofs.

Tracks have been carved out of the green hillsides, running downhill from the ridge in all directions and leading to more substantial structures and homes, bounded by trees and sun-blanched shrubs. Loi Tai Leng is laid out like a snakes and ladders board, an unplanned sprawl of a mountaintop town. 'Almost everything here was built in the last few years. There was no water or electricity until five years ago,' explained Yawd Maung, when we met at the house that was to be my home for the next couple of days. 'Water had to be hauled up from the river in jerrycans and buckets.'

A lieutenant colonel in the Restoration Council of Shan State, also known as the Shan State Army – South, Yawd Maung oversees the RCSS's department of foreign affairs, a fancy title that essentially means dealing with foreign journalists and diplomats. From Mong Kung in central Shan State, he was forty-two, a former monk with bristling hair, a wide face and an expanding paunch. 'I learned my English at the temple in Bangkok,' he said. 'Then I decided to be with the people. I've been in the RCSS for twenty years, eight years in the jungle.'

Spread between Tachileik in the east of Shan State and Loi Moong Merng, farther west of us near Mae Hong Son, the RCSS occupies five bases along the Shan–Thai border including Loi Tai Leng. A force of 8,000 soldiers, the RCSS maintain positions in the north of Shan, too, where they have joined the *Tatmadaw* in its fight against the TNLA, after signing a ceasefire agreement with the government in 2011.

For most of the year Loi Tai Leng is quiet, the town a mere adjunct to the camp where the RCSS's recruits come for nine months' training, far longer than the two months the TNLA's soldiers receive. But on 7 February Loi Tai Leng plays host to the biggest commemoration of Shan National Day in this part of Shan State, drawing some of the hundreds of thousands of Shan people resident in Thailand for a three-day party.

'This is a special year,' said Yawd Maung. 'We're celebrating three anniversaries: twenty years of the RCSS, seventy years of Shan National Day and on the 8th it is the chairman's sixtieth birthday.' The chairman is Yawd Serk. He founded the Shan State Army – South in 1996 after splitting from another Shan army led by the late Khun Sa, the most infamous of all the

Golden Triangle's drug lords. Technically the RCSS is the political wing of the Shan State Army – South, but both its soldiers and rivals refer to the army simply as the RCSS.

Shan National Day was first celebrated in 1947 in honour of the Panglong agreement, which appeared to guarantee the Shan self-rule over their region. I had arrived the day before the main event. Yawd Maung asked if this was my first visit to a Shan State conflict zone. I told him I had spent time with the TNLA, a tactical mistake given that the RCSS and the TNLA are sworn enemies. 'Be careful of them,' he said, fixing me with a stare, his mood darkening instantly. 'We know they will try and attack us tomorrow on our big day, but we are ready for them.'

He showed me to a room where I would be sleeping on the floor with as many people as could be crammed in. 'We are a revolution. We don't have the money to pay for the media's comfort,' said Yawd Maung. I decided it wasn't the right time to ask about the allegations that the RCSS profits from the drugs that move through the areas it controls. There was a Buddha shrine at one end of the room. 'I'd like to see you meditate,' scoffed Yawd Maung. I thought that you can take the boy out of the monastery, but you can't take the monk out of the man.

Out on the main street the atmosphere was friendlier and increasingly festive, the Shan diaspora arriving in ever greater numbers. They came in pickup trucks laden with whole families, on motorbikes and some on foot. Women paraded in brightly striped *htamein* and close-fitting blouses, and many men wore t-shirts advocating Shan independence. Food stalls had been set up, ice boxes full of beer to the side, and the RCSS Women's Association stand was serving fine Shan coffee.

Soldiers were everywhere. Some were off-duty teenage trainees strutting around in their camouflage, forage caps and the green plimsolls worn by farmers and militia alike in Shan State. But others wore boots, helmets and flak jackets and clasped American-made M-16 rifles. With far more money than the TNLA and KIA, the RCSS doesn't have to rely on weapons bought from the Wa region. The soldiers patrolled up and down the road in a meaningless show of force for the visitors. I knew that the closest *Tatmadaw* positions were a three-day march away.

By the early evening the main street was a press of people, despite the wind that blew chilly across the ridge. Gaggles of girls walked arm in arm, giggling at the soldiers and teenage boys ogling them. The clothes shops were busy, offering t-shirts and hoodies alongside traditional Shan dress. Elderly women were selling trinkets and mementos, their wares laid out on blankets by the road, illuminated by candles and torches gripped in the mouths of the vendors.

Clouds of smoke rose above the crowd, spiralling towards the stars, as skewers of pork, sweet potatoes, chicken feet and thick trails of intestines were grilled. Thai beer and whisky and local rice wine sold in recycled water bottles was available everywhere. Some of the stalls were makeshift karaoke bars, housing mobile music machines and microphones for customers to croon Shan ballads and pop songs. There were fairground stands, too: lucky dips and darts, air guns fired at small balloons, the prizes alcohol or soft drinks for children.

Later, I attended the dinner held on the parade ground, a big expanse of land at the town's highest point. Flagpoles lined three sides of the square, their banners beating back and forth in the stiff wind. A roofed stage garlanded with flowers took up the remaining side. Tables were set up in front of it, each adorned with food and two bottles of whisky. Men in Shan costume appeared on stage beating giant drums, before the sound system took over, blaring out an incongruous medley of easy-listening classics, and we started to eat.

Almost immediately, though, everyone was standing up as a white pickup truck arrived at the side of the stage. A group of black-clad men jumped down from the back and stood around the vehicle as Yawd Serk emerged from the cab. We regained our seats, watching as the chairman went first to the top table reserved for dignitaries and greeted them. After that he made his way around all the tables, his bodyguards following, shaking hands with every guest.

My table was one of the last to be visited. Up close, Yawd Serk was a head shorter than me, and I am not tall, bulky in an overcoat buttoned to the neck, a maroon beret with the RCSS badge on his head. We shook hands and, stupidly, I said, 'How do you do?' Yawd Serk looked confused for a second, before replying, 'Thank you' and moving on. 'He doesn't speak English,' Yawd Maung told me. 'Try Thai or Shan next time.'

After dinner there was a performance of traditional Shan dancing from the RCSS's dance troupe. As people rushed the front of the stage to film it on their phones, Yawd Maung sat down next to me. He was genial again, a couple of whiskies inside him, poking me in the ribs, one eye on the dancing girls. I learned that his grandfather had been killed when the *Tatmadaw* razed his home village, part of the Four Cuts campaign in central Shan State. It was the reason why he had left the monastery to join the RCSS.

His revelation made me better disposed to him. But the alcohol couldn't heat up his cold eyes and soon he started quizzing me about the TNLA, asking for details of their defences and equipment. I offered up what he knew already.

'AK47s, RPGs, heavy machine guns.' Yawd Maung nodded grimly. 'The TNLA say they are protecting the Palaung people, but the Palaung and the Shan have been brothers for hundreds of years,' he said. 'Some Palaung ask us for protection. Just because people wear a TNLA uniform that doesn't mean they are TNLA.'

It was an attempted smear, typing the TNLA as mere gangsters living off the people they were supposed to defend, and brazen, too, given that I knew that the RCSS imposes heavy taxes on the locals in the areas it controls. I asked why the RCSS couldn't strike a deal with the TNLA. 'We have offered to negotiate with them, but they say they will only talk if we withdraw from our positions in the north. That is an impossible demand. We have to protect our people – the Shan – and they want us to do that,' insisted Yawd Maung.

Notwithstanding its home bases in the deep south of Shan, the RCSS recruits from across Shan State. Many of its soldiers come from the areas where the TNLA fights. But there is also the rival Shan State Army – North stationed in northern Shan, and I wondered why they couldn't be left to guard the Shan there. Yawd Maung didn't like the question. 'I leave it to the chairman to talk for us,' he said finally.

National day dawned early for everyone in the house, a consequence of sleeping on the floor. Nursing his hangover, Yawd Maung seemed to bear no grudge about our exchange of the previous night. I asked about the RCSS's relationship with the UWSA, the Wa army, and he started reminiscing about the time in 2005 when the UWSA had besieged Loi Tai Leng for forty-five days, supported by *Tatmadaw* mortar teams. 'We fought them off. But many people died. It was a long time ago. Forget it.' I said, 'Of course' and wrote it down promptly, just in case I didn't remember.

At 8.45 a.m. the soldiers marched from their barracks to the parade ground, the stamping of their feet sending puffs of dust up around their shins. They were preceded by a band of teenagers in white uniforms who played 'YMCA', the Village People song, repeatedly. Following behind, I found a crush of people ten deep around the square. Monks clad in both the orange robes of Thailand and the crimson ones of Burma had found a vantage point standing on the flatbeds of pickup trucks parked to the side.

From the edge of the stage, I could see the chairman in his beret and blue dress uniform sitting with other senior RCSS men around him. The special guests were behind them. They included prominent Shan figures, representatives from the Karen and Chin peoples, as well as western diplomats who had travelled up from their embassies in Bangkok. Having signed a ceasefire with Naypyidaw, the RCSS is now respectable to the outside world.

We watched a series of displays. Members of the RCSS's elite commando unit, including two young women, paired off and demonstrated how to disarm someone with a knife or gun. They were followed by students clad in white with red headbands, who stood in long lines across the parade ground and showed off a series of martial arts moves. Then there was a dramatisation of the RCSS rescuing farmers from an unnamed band of masked men, complete with sound effects of shots and explosions.

Yawd Serk sat impassive throughout, his eyes behind thick-lensed glasses. I was reminded of the Bruce Lee film *Enter the Dragon*, in which the super-villain on his island fortress off Hong Kong is protected by a private army of fanatical bodyguards who flaunt their skills at his whim. The parade ground had become a theatre and what we were witnessing was a spectacle fetishising the RCSS, turning the conflict in Burma's borderlands into a movie to be broadcast by the TV crews present, with the chairman as the undisputed star.

Yet there was no doubting the crowd's enjoyment of the show. Nor was there any question about their desire for self-rule. People living in the conflict areas may complain of the violence that follows the ethnic armies, as well as the enforced taxes, but the ordinary Shan gathered in Loi Tai Leng all wanted autonomy. This was their national day, an occasion when the Shan forget their long and continuing history of fighting among themselves and instead imagine an ideal: their homeland and its resources under Shan control. The audience cheered the soldiers and appeared proud of them.

Finally, we reached the last act. Troops clad in combat uniforms brightened up with yellow neckerchiefs started marching onto the square in formation. They lined up until the entire parade ground was occupied, the flags of their units flying above them. An honour guard approached the chairman and he took their salute, before giving a surprisingly succinct speech calling on the government to honour the 1947 Panglong agreement.

While the other dignitaries followed Yawd Serk with far longer addresses, I pondered the fact that the chairman was merely an exaggerated and corrupted version of the *sawbwas* who had once sliced Shan State into their own personal kingdoms. And sitting behind Yawd Serk on the stage was the youngest son of Sao Shwe Thaike, the sky lord who became Burma's first president. Stripping the *sawbwas* of their powers ended feudalism in Shan State, but not dominion by local chieftains. The men who control the ethnic armies oversee their regions with a power as absolute as the hold the *sawbwas* once exerted.

Conflict and opium have made Yawd Serk, elevating him to a position where he meets now with Aung San Suu Kyi and holds court with foreign ambassadors. He started his career by rising through the ranks of the Mong Tai Army, a merger of Shan militias led by Khun Sa, the one-time king of the Golden Triangle and the most notorious opium warlord of them all. In 1948, the year of independence, Burma produced just thirty tons of opium annually. By 1996, when Khun Sa surrendered to the junta, over 1,700 tons of opium was coming out of Shan State each year.

That astonishing rise in poppy production was largely down to the efforts of Khun Sa, as well as of Lo Hsing Han, a warlord from the Kokang region of Shan State. Both men, though, were simply providing the raw material to the ethnic Chinese who ran the heroin refineries in northern Thailand, backed by criminal gangs in Bangkok, Hong Kong and Taiwan. The Chinese have always been the financiers of the Golden Triangle, and migrants from Yunnan introduced local farmers to opium cultivation in the nineteenth century.

Most of Shan State's poppy now heads to refineries in Yunnan. But from the 1950s to the 1990s Thailand was the primary destination and point of export to elsewhere. Like the Chinese, the Thais had been forcibly supplied opium by the British. The ships of the East India Company carrying the black tar from India to China would stop off in Bangkok along the way. Until 1959 it was legal to buy opium from state-licensed outlets in Thailand. Once the drug was outlawed, and American soldiers serving in Vietnam were introduced to heroin, a space was created that allowed Khun Sa to flourish.

Khun Sa's real name was Zhang Qifu. He was born in 1934 in an area of northern Shan State that was part of the Mongyai kingdom ruled by the father of Mrs Fern in Hsipaw. After Khun Sa's ethnic Chinese father died when he was a child, his Shan mother remarried a man who was a tax collector for the *Sawbwa*. The teenage Khun Sa joined one of the KMT units that had fled to Shan State from China, but soon split off and formed his own armed group.

In 1963 his force was recruited by the junta as a local militia. Like the border units sponsored by the government today, such as the Panhsay militia the TNLA fights, groups like Khun Sa's were allowed to profit from opium in return for battling insurgents on the generals' behalf. But Khun Sa's men didn't do much fighting. They concentrated on selling poppy. By the late 1960s he and Lo Hsing Han had established a grip on the Shan State drug trade that wouldn't be seriously challenged for another twenty years. And when Lo Hsing Han was arrested in 1973, it was all Khun Sa's.

Similar to the pirate Samuel White, who made Myeik his personal fiefdom in the late seventeenth century, Khun Sa was equal parts charm and ruthlessness. 'He was very charismatic. He'd greet you as a friend with a joke,' I was told in Loi Tai Leng by an elderly Frenchman who had interviewed him on a number of occasions. 'He communicated in Yunnanese mainly. He used to say he was part of the Shan family because his mother was Shan, but Yunnanese was his first language, then Shan and a little Thai.'

Despite his Shan heritage, Khun Sa was essentially apolitical. Making money was always his principal objective. He adopted his Shan moniker – Khun Sa means 'prosperous prince' – only in the mid-1970s, when he renamed his force the Shan United Army and started claiming that he was fighting for self-rule in Shan State. 'It was a marriage of convenience between the Shan nationalists and Khun Sa,' said the Frenchman. 'He needed an army to guard his drug convoys and the nationalists needed money for the struggle.'

Cloaking his criminality with the Shan flag didn't prevent Khun Sa from being pursued by the law enforcement agencies of different countries, the United States in particular. As heroin-addicted soldiers returned from Vietnam and narcotics from Southeast Asia poured into American cities, the then president Richard Nixon declared a war on drugs in 1971. The DEA made Khun Sa its number one target. It was easier to go after the Shan drug lords than their ethnic Chinese backers.

Holed up first in an isolated pocket of northern Thailand and later back in Shan State at a base now used by the RCSS, Khun Sa responded by suggesting that the United States government take his opium off the market by buying it all directly. Washington declined the offer. By now his Shan United Army had mutated into the Mong Tai Army, a force of 20,000 soldiers at its peak, including the young Yawd Serk as one of its junior officers.

Although he was indicted by a New York court on heroin-trafficking charges in 1989, the Americans never did catch Khun Sa. It was competition from fellow Shan State drug dealers which forced him out of business. From 1989 a coalition of the armies of the Wa and Kokang people and Lin Mingxian's militia in Mong La moved aggressively into the opium trade. With his army under attack and his power declining, Khun Sa decided it was time to make a deal with the junta, with whom he had retained contacts throughout his career.

Surrendering to the authorities in January 1996, Khun Sa moved to a compound near Yangon's airport overseen by military intelligence. Accompanied by four teenage mistresses from Kengtung, he remained there until he died in 2007. Like the *sawbwas* of old, and dubbing himself the 'prosperous prince' was surely a nod to their status, he was a prolific father: he had around thirty children. At his death Khun Sa was believed to own a significant property portfolio in Yangon, Mandalay and the Shan capital Taunggyi, as well as a ruby mine and cash in bank accounts across Asia.

Much of the Mong Tai Army disarmed along with Khun Sa. But Yawd Serk led a breakaway unit of 800 soldiers who refused to surrender. They would become the Shan State Army – South/RCSS. The RCSS has repudiated its heroin heritage in recent years. Just like the Wa and Lin Mingxian in Special Region 4, Yawd Serk insists that they are no longer in the drug business. Loi Tai Leng has its own miniature version of Mong La's Drug Eradication Museum, a one-room hall with the usual photos of burning poppy fields.

Renouncing their past has been a spectacular success for the RCSS. Just over twenty years ago Khun Sa was one of the most wanted men on the planet, described by the then US ambassador to Thailand as 'the worst enemy the world has'. Now, diplomats from the American embassy in Bangkok join Yawd Serk for dinner in Loi Tai Leng. What can't be forgotten, though, is the way that Khun Sa and those who followed him have irretrievably reorientated Shan State's economy towards the production of illicit drugs, and the disastrous effect that it continues to have on communities across the region.

Before leaving, I joined a group of mostly Thai and Shan journalists for an audience with Yawd Serk. We were loaded into pickup trucks and driven down a dust track to a modern two-storey house painted in camouflage colours, Shan flags flying from its terrace. It is one of the two residences in Loi Tai Leng used by Yawd Serk. Beyond the house, green hills staggered away to the interior of Shan State. A chair was set up in the shade for the chairman, a translator by his side, while his overbearing bodyguards were stationed nearby.

Faced with a series of parochial and gentle questions Yawd Serk batted them away with ease. I asked about the current clashes with the TNLA. 'It's a misunderstanding,' said the chairman in his not very martial voice. 'The TNLA doesn't want to talk to us. We're like a boy who wants to talk to a girl, but the girl doesn't want to talk.' It was a homespun analogy for the conflict between the two groups, but the chairman qualified it with a more forceful assertion. 'We will go anywhere in Shan State where the people want us.'

More surprising was his admission of burgeoning ties with the Chinese government. Traditionally, the RCSS has always been closer to Thailand. Now, though, the RCSS is eager to claim a portion of the lucrative cross-border trade with China. 'Shan people and the Chinese are like brother and sister. We share a border, our people go there all the time and most of the goods sold here are Chinese. We have to maintain a good, close relationship,' said Yawd Serk.

Again, though, he sounded a warning. 'China doesn't interfere with our internal policies,' stated the chairman. 'No one influences the RCSS. We stand and fight alone.' It was a unilateral declaration of his army's independence and a reminder of how partisan the warlords of the region are. National day was almost over and the usual rivalries would soon surface again. Shan solidarity could be forgotten until it was time for next year's performance.

18

The Triangle

Dropping altitude, propellers droning and our ears popping, the plane began the descent into Putao. I gazed down on forests so dense they disguised the contours of the hills they smothered, forming what looked from above to be one giant tree blooming in an explosion of dark green foliage. Rough squares cut out of the valleys, glimmering lime in the sunlight, indicated rice fields. Carving through the land were two rivers, the N'Maihka and the Malihka, racing each other to a confluence point just north of Myitkyina where they form the Ayeyarwady River.

Myitkyina, the capital of Kachin State, was 220 miles south. No buses or trains run north of there. Only private vehicles and *Tatmadaw* trucks travel the dire road that connects Myitkyina to Putao. It is a journey that takes twenty-four to thirty-six hours, longer in the rainy season, depending on how fast you drive and the level of discomfort you are willing to endure. But foreigners are banned from the road. Plane was the only way for me to reach Putao, Burma's most northerly town and the last settlement of any size before the country collides with the Himalayas along the borders with India, Tibet and China.

Waiting at Putao's tiny airport was Ngwalisa, recommended to me both for his local knowledge and excellent English. Sturdy, with a brown face and thinning black hair, he was in the hiking gear that was his only apparel during our acquaintance. Ngwalisa had learned his English in bible school, before polishing it further by studying in Bangalore, across the nearby border with India. He was thirty-three, married with three kids and Lisu, the ethnic minority who make up around half of Putao's population.

From the back of Ngwalisa's motorbike, a perch I got to know well, Putao appeared as a leafy town set on the flat plain of a large valley irrigated by a tributary of the Malihka. Two paved roads divide Putao, rocky lanes and dirt tracks branching off them. There are a number of churches, principally Baptist, and a large market in the centre of town where alongside the snow trout I was surprised to see an abundance of grapefruits, blood oranges and tangerines, all grown locally.

'American missionaries introduced them to Putao,' explained Ngwalisa. 'The Morse family. They came here in the 1950s and saw that the people were vitamin-deficient. So they started growing citrus fruits.' The Morses converted most of the Lisu to Christianity, along with the Rawang, the second most numerous minority in Putao, before being expelled from Burma in 1965. Buddhists are represented by the Tai Khamti people, a branch of the Shan family found in northern Burma and India, and the Bamar, almost all of whom are government officials or soldiers.

Beyond the town are the Burmese Himalayas, marking the frontiers with India and Tibet. Putao can be foggy in the early morning, the mist settling above the valley from the late afternoon and staying throughout the night. As the sun rises, though, the snow-capped summits emerge. To the west and the border with Arunachal Pradesh in India, the mountains seem close and not that high. But they are all over 4,000 metres and it is a five-day trek to the frontier.

Farther away to the north is the boundary with Tibet and more forbidding peaks. Just inside Burma are Hkakabo Razi and Gamlang Razi, the two highest mountains in Southeast Asia at almost 6,000 metres. It is a three-week march to their base camps from Putao. South-east of those peaks, the frontier with Tibet bleeds into the border with the far north-west of Yunnan Province. Putao's proximity to India, Tibet and China means the region is sometimes known as 'The Triangle', the borders with Arunachal Pradesh to the west and Tibet and Yunnan in the east making up the legs of the trilateral.

During the colonial period Putao was considered part of the North East Frontier, the far eastern edge of India. Herbert Robinson, the miscreant army officer and friend of George Orwell who inspired the character of Flory in *Burmese Days*, was based here with the military police in the early 1920s. Setting out on horseback from Myitkyina, it took Robinson over three weeks to reach Putao. The town was newly built at that point, having been laid out in 1914 by the then deputy commissioner William Hertz, who gave his name to the local army base.

Ritchie Gardiner came close to Putao, too, escaping over the Chaukkan Pass, just south-west of town, to India in July 1942. He had returned to Burma soon after fleeing Rangoon on a futile mission to join the fight against the Japanese. But by the time Gardiner arrived the battle was over and the British were in full retreat. With the rest of the country under Japanese control, Gardiner was forced to head north to Kachin State. It took his small party two months to reach India, struggling through leech-infested mountains in the monsoon season and fording endless rivers, men dropping dead along the way.

So remote was Putao at that time that the Japanese didn't bother occupying the town. A small garrison of mostly Indian soldiers stayed at Fort Hertz throughout the war, manning an emergency airstrip used by the American and British supply planes flying over the eastern Himalayas from India to China. Putao feels like a lost world even today, cut off from the rest of the country, the few roads north of the town soon petering out so that access to the frontier areas is by foot only.

Nothing remains of Fort Hertz now, except for some stone steps on the gentle rise of land in Putao's northern outskirts that it once occupied, much of it now home to the police station. Walking there the day after my arrival, I thought that Putao, no matter how isolated, is still more pleasant and developed than many other places in rural Burma. It is a tidy town of substantial wooden houses separated from each other by gardens of banana, tea and citrus trees, as well as palms with fan-shaped leaves and spiky stems, a species unique to northern Burma.

As usual in the borderlands, I was faced with *Tatmadaw*-imposed constraints on where I could go. Putao and the far north was mostly barred to foreigners in the junta era. Opened up afterwards for the odd mountaineering expedition and parties of high-end tourists, the region was shutting down again by the time I arrived. Foreigners were no longer allowed to spend nights outside Putao, and various villages in the surrounding area were closed. Ngwalisa assured me that we could still go where I wanted during the day. But I would not be able to visit the Chaukkan Pass or trek to the border with Tibet.

These restrictions are a consequence of the conflict farther south in Kachin State. Putao itself is home to few Kachin people, and the KIA does not operate in the town. Nor do the Lisu fight. Having supported the KIA in the 1960s, with some joining as soldiers, the Lisu sit out the ethnic conflicts these days. Alone of the minorities of their size in Burma – around 350,000 people spread across Kachin, the neighbouring Sagaing Region and Shan State – the Lisu do not have their own army.

But the 70,000-odd Rawang people are represented by the Rebellion Resistance Force, a snappy title for a very modest militia that devotes most of its time to trafficking timber into Yunnan with the tacit assistance of the Burmese military. And the KIA is active in areas south of Putao. There is bitter fighting around the town of Tanai, home to gold and amber mines that the KIA relies on for funds, as well as being the contraband capital of northern Kachin State with smuggling routes leading west across Sagaing into India.

Unable to get close to Tibet, Ngwalisa consoled me by introducing me to some of his Tibetan friends. I was barely aware that there are Tibetans living in Burma. Tashi was the proof, a slight eighteen-year-old with a perpetual smile on his face. It was obvious straightaway that he was Tibetan, despite his jeans and baseball cap, his features much closer to central Asia than those of Burma's other peoples. And he declined the offer of some of Putao's delicious fruit. I have never known a Tibetan eat anything except meat, noodles, dumplings and tsampa, the barley flour they mix with butter tea.

Tashi is one of eight children of a ninety-year-old father, five of whom died in childhood. 'We couldn't get them medicine,' said Tashi. When he told me where he lived, I realised that finding a doctor nearby was not an option. His village sits at 2,000 metres, 1,600 metres above Putao but low by the standards of Tibet. It is a five-day trek from Hkakabo Razi's base camp and two days to the frontier with Tibet. On his phone he showed me a photo of a stone standing in utter isolation with the characters for China carved into it. 'That's the border,' laughed Tashi.

Taking photos is all Tashi's phone is good for in his village and the area around it. 'The nearest place with phone reception is Nogmung. That's a week's walk from my village,' said Tashi. 'You can't drive past Nogmung, not even a motorbike. You have to walk.' Nogmung is a Rawang outpost, little more than a village itself, a day's drive north-east of Putao. Tashi's family and the other villagers visit it once a year to stock up on supplies, before hauling them back home.

'Each Tibetan can carry thirty *vis*,' said Tashi, using the traditional Burmese measure of weight. One *vis* is equivalent to just over one and half kilos, so Tashi would have close to two thirds of my bodyweight on his back. 'We walk twenty hours a day. We take a break for a few hours at midnight.' I knew he wasn't exaggerating. Tibetans travel fast at altitude, something I had witnessed while trekking around Mount Kailash in western Tibet. Most westerners complete the hike in three days. Tibetans do it in eighteen hours. It would probably take me over two weeks to walk from Nogmung to Tashi's village.

The Triangle is home to four Tibetan settlements, each with around one hundred residents. In a land of remote places and peoples, Burma's Tibetans might be the most distant of them all. They are in the country because of the idiosyncratic border between Burma and China and past conflicts in Tibet, most notably the 1959 Tibetan uprising. It was a rebellion against Chinese rule that lasted three years, cost over 85,000 Tibetans their lives and resulted in the Dalai Lama fleeing into exile in India.

'We always lived on the Burmese side of the frontier, but there was no real border so we considered ourselves to be living in Tibet. We paid tribute to the monks in Tibet,' Tashi told me. 'But then the war with the Chinese happened and the border was demarcated in 1960. My father thought it would be safer to stay in Burma.' Soon after came Ne Win's coup of 1962. The Tibetans in Kachin State found out quickly that it isn't just the Chinese Communist Party who have an unreconstructed attitude towards minority ethnic groups.

'Tibetans were treated badly here when my father was young. We weren't even allowed to come to Putao. That's changed in the last ten years and we got given our identity cards. Now, I think the Burmese regard us like they do the Rawang or Lisu. We're just ethnic people to them,' Tashi stated. Three Tibetan families are now resident in Putao. 'More Tibetans will come in the future. It's a less hard life here.'

Out in their villages, though, the Tibetans continue to live as their counterparts do on the other side of the border in the far south-east of Tibet. Few speak Burmese, something that will change as more move to Putao, and they marry other Tibetans, although Tashi said people occasionally take Rawang partners. Crucially, they practise Tibetan Buddhism, a newer version of the religion than the Theravada Buddhism that dominates Burma. 'We follow the Dalai Lama,' said Tashi, showing me a picture of him on his phone. 'When my father was young, the lamas would come to our villages from Tibet.'

Barely touched by the trappings of modernity, Burma's Tibetans lead an uncomplicated life. I asked Tashi to describe a typical day in the village. 'We wake up at daybreak, we cook dumplings – wheat ones with beef – then we feed the chickens and pigs and release the mithun to go off and graze for the day,' he said. Mithun are a breed of cow found across the Himalayan region.

'After that we work in the fields, we grow barley and wheat, or in the summer we go looking for mushrooms and herbs. We sell them to Tibetans across the border and they sell them to the Chinese. They're good for health. Sometimes we hunt for barking deer and serow. My father hunted a lot when he was younger. We come back home at five in the afternoon, feed the animals again, fetch water from the stream and start cooking tsampa. We listen to the radio – we get Burmese radio stations – and we are in bed by nine. We don't feel bored. There are always things to do.'

Like the Wa and Kokang peoples in their enclaves in Shan State the Tibetans in Kachin live in a space that is outside Burma proper. But they don't have to fight or manufacture and sell drugs to establish an existence beyond the state. Geography does the job for them. 'We never see anyone. No army, no police, no government officials. Where we live is too far for the Burmese to walk to,' said Tashi, his eyes twinkling.

They have become even more isolated in recent years as China tightens its grip on Tibet. Unlike Yunnan, Tibet's frontiers are now guarded zealously by both drones and soldiers. The villages along the borders are closely watched, and army patrols will open fire on any Tibetans discovered trying to leave the country. For Tashi and the other villagers that means no more visits from lamas or relatives across the frontier.

'People used to come from Tibet, but not in the past few years. The Chinese government won't let them,' Tashi said. Nor do the Chinese cross the border anymore. 'Occasionally they would come to buy animal parts. But it's too hard to find rare animals now, so that doesn't happen anymore.' Ngwalisa nodded in agreement. His father had once traded in endangered species – tigers, clouded leopards, pangolins, Himalayan black bears and the antelope-like takins – selling them to Chinese dealers from Yunnan.

'When I was young there were still tigers around here, maybe fifteen years ago, and my father would buy the skins and bones from the hunters and sell them on. But there are no tigers now,' said Ngwalisa. 'It is very difficult to find even pangolins now. It's easier to find bears. But I think they are mostly bears who come from India. They are wandering bears, and they regret it. They end up in China. The Chinese don't care about getting stopped at the border with animals or their parts. They say, "We'll just give the army money", and they do.'

Perhaps in acknowledgement of their separation from the rest of Kachin State, Burma's Tibetans are allowed to cross into Tibet without having to pass through official border posts. 'We can go to the villages just over the frontier. It's illegal to go further. But sometimes we do, travelling by motorbike. I've been as far as Cawarong, which is the nearest town. I'd like to go to Lhasa one day,' said Tashi.

Despite Beijing's continuing assault on traditional Tibetan culture, with monasteries monitored by the government and children made to study in Mandarin rather than Tibetan, Tashi said he wished his village was on the other side of the frontier. 'I think most of the Tibetans in Burma would rather live in Tibet. It's much more developed. They have roads and television. But the Chinese won't let us. They say we are Burmese now.'

Unlike his father, though, he won't grow old in his village. Ngwalisa has already identified Tashi as a future guide, someone who can lead the groups of rich Bamar who come to the Triangle for an adventure in the foothills of the Himalayas. With his mountain upbringing and equable personality, I thought Tashi would do very well. He will join the Tibetans already living in Putao, and many others will follow him to the town or beyond in the future. I wondered if the four Tibetan villages would still be inhabited in twenty or thirty years.

Just as the Tibetans suffered under the generals, so did the Lisu and Rawang. Some Lisu reacted by choosing to live in India. Around six thousand walked across the mountains in the 1960s, on the advice of the Morse family, in an effort to find a better life. They and their descendants are still in Arunachal Pradesh, also home to large numbers of Tibetans, and the Lisu continue to move between India and Burma. Ngwalisa told me that one of his friends residing across the frontier was back visiting relatives in his home village and we set off to meet him.

Travelling south from Putao on the road to Myitkyina, we ran through mostly Rawang villages. In Putao the minorities live side by side, but out in the country the villages are not mixed and there is little intermarriage between the different ethnic groups. Some of the women wore *htamein* with horizontal red, white and blue stripes, the traditional Rawang colours. While I could sometimes recognise whether people were Lisu or Rawang from their faces – the Rawang have wider ones – it was much easier to identify them by their different patterned and coloured clothing.

Cows and goats grazed along the verges of the road, released from the backyards of houses for the day, while women walked home bent almost double under baskets loaded with firewood. Electricity has yet to arrive in the settlements outside Putao, the villagers still waiting for hydroelectric plants to start generating power. Away to our right were forested hills and towering beyond them in the far distance were the mountains, the highest peaks dusted with snow, and the frontier with India.

Turning off the main road onto a more primitive track, Mulashidi Village appeared at the bottom of a hill which was thickly wooded with bamboo and oaks. 'The only reason they haven't been chopped down is that the roads are so bad around here. It's too hard to transport the timber,' said Ngwalisa. The village is divided by a tributary of the Malihka, which we crossed via an uncertain bridge, its planks creaking under the weight of the motorbike. Beneath us the water was a translucent turquoise in the sun, and I could see every rock on the riverbed.

Ngwalisa's friend Siliw was hacking away at a stack of bamboo outside the front of his family home with a group of men. They were building a temporary extension to the house for a wedding, the reason Siliw had returned from India. Out back, in a garden that was a riot of papaya and palm trees, the women were preparing a huge pile of vegetables for the party. Ngwalisa told me that it was rare to see so many men in the village at this time of year. 'Once the rice is harvested, they go to Tanai to work in the gold or amber mines, or farther south to Hpakant for the jade. Women raise the children around here,' he said.

Siliw offered us juicy grapefruit and green tea served in bamboo cups, while we searched for shade from the midday heat. He was thirty-eight, slender with the trace of a moustache, and had first ventured across the mountains to India for work in 2003. 'People told me walking was the cheapest way to get to India. It's a nine-day walk from Putao to where the Lisu villages are. You have to carry everything you need: rice, a plastic sheet to cover yourself at night. But we are used to hill-walking,' said Siliw.

He told me there are four different routes into Arunachal Pradesh from Putao, and that there was little scrutiny of the frontier by the authorities on either side. 'The Indian army checks the border once a year. The Burmese army are too lazy to check. But the smuggling goes on farther south near Tanai.' Siliw studied at bible school in India, where he learned both English and Hindi, and then decided to stay in Arunachal Pradesh as a pastor and teacher.

'I prefer it there. It feels more free than here,' he said. 'It's a simple life, more simple even than here. The villages aren't the same. It's mostly bamboo houses, and it is higher and colder there. We're a four-day walk from Miao, the nearest town. But everyone has land for rice and people grow enough to live on.' After a protracted tussle with the Indian government the Lisu were granted citizenship in 1994. Some now join the Indian army as an alternative to farming.

Mulashidi is also known for being the site of the first church built by the Morse family, replaced now by a far more prominent structure. The large wooden house the missionaries lived in until they were forced out of Burma by the military still stands on the outskirts of the village, windows open to the elements and increasingly decrepit. Beyond Mulashidi we bounced along trails that weaved through grassland, as

Ngwalisa cut across country to reach Machanbaw, our next destination. Away from the rivers, the yellow soil of the Triangle is far less fertile and the land here was untilled.

Machanbaw lay on the other side of the Malihka, east of Putao. The Kachin are the majority ethnic group here and the KIA keep soldiers in the surrounding area. Consequently the town is home to a large *Tatmadaw* base, whose soldiers eyed me suspiciously, as well as a couple of government-built pagodas, a rare sight in this Christian-dominated region. Machanbaw was barely awake in the afternoon sun, the modest market already shut for the day with just a sole food stand open to serve us a late lunch of noodles and fatty pork, followed by dried persimmons.

Returning to Putao, we went through a succession of Lisu villages. Sugarcane and banana and papaya trees encroached on the bamboo and wooden houses with thatched roofs – firewood stacked to the side and rice drying on plastic sheets out front – a natural bounty for their residents. Ngwalisa waved at some of them as we drove past. They were his people and he admitted he was less comfortable with the Rawang or Shan. 'There is some tension between the Lisu and Rawang,' he said. 'It goes back to the old days, before the British came, when the Rawang had to pay tribute to the Lisu.'

In the late afternoon the Triangle grows cold, the sun's rays diminished by an unwelcome wind that rushes through the valleys. It grew rawer by the minute as we drove through mile after mile of grassland stretching away to the hills in the distance. The mist was gathering above us, curls of condensation linking together, ready to render Putao wet and freezing overnight. Poking above the vapour, bathed in soft light, were the mountains, sculpted by the same icy air currents that had me hunkered low on the back of the bike.

While the different minorities distrust each other, they do unite to combat what all of them see as the most pressing problem in the region: the ever-increasing levels of drug abuse among the young. Ngwalisa had pointed out some of the local addicts soon after my arrival, teenagers and young men driving three to a motorbike past my guest house and the complex next door that is home to the Putao Baptist Association, on their way to meet their dealers around the market.

A meeting with the leaders of the All Religions and All Tribes Combined Group revealed the sheer scale of the heroin epidemic in the Triangle. It is one of a number of community anti-drug organisations formed in Kachin State in recent years. The biggest and best known is Pat Ja San – the Kachin for 'Fighting against drugs' – with 100,000 activists backed by the Baptist and Catholic churches. They run their own rehabilitation programmes, but act also as vigilantes: beating up dealers and burning poppy fields, as well as occasionally flogging recalcitrant users.

None of the men sitting opposite me seemed the type to be wielding whips. They were middle-aged or older, some balding, in woolly hats, fleeces, tracksuit tops and *longyi*, a mix of Lisu, Rawang, Shan and Kachin ethnicities. We met in a village south-west of Putao, green tea and an array of snacks on the table in front of us, our conversation punctuated by the sound of sunflower seeds being cracked between teeth.

U Aung Aung was their unofficial spokesperson, an intense Shan man with glasses. 'We started in 2004, before Pat Ja San. Even then there were a lot of addicts. People were overdosing and dying and the police numbers were too small to do anything. We couldn't look on and do nothing, so we persuaded the heads of the different peoples to be patrons of our organisation.' He spoke in Burmese, the common language between the different minorities. 'We started out just trying to raise awareness, to inform people about why doing drugs is so bad.'

Now the group has become much more proactive, while not being as aggressive as Pat Ja San, who clash often with the militias who oversee drug production. 'Since 2010 we have concentrated on getting the dealers arrested. We have informers in all the villages who tell us what is going on. Families here all live together, so people don't do drugs at home. It's too easy to spot. So they tend to go to one house in the village, or a place outside, to take drugs. When we identify the house and the dealer, we tell the police,' U Aung Aung said.

'Women are often the dealers. They're less suspicious to the police, especially when they are stopped at the checkpoints on the road from Myitkyina. So now we have women to help us search them in the villages. Most of the dealers are Lisu. We tell the addicts the consequences of what they are doing, and that they need to stop or we'll have them arrested. The dealers we get arrested straightaway. But it's very hard to get the ones above local level. They won't say where they get the drugs from. They just say they got them in Myitkyina.'

Some dealers are able to pay their way out of trouble. 'We got one man arrested and his wife tried to bribe us first,' recalled U Aung Aung, waving his hands in disbelief at her audacity. 'But then she paid the judge and he was released quickly. He runs a restaurant near the airport now. And we've had cases of army officers and police supplying drugs to the local dealers. We can't do much about that.'

Opium and heroin are the narcotics of choice, although U Aung Aung said *yama*, methamphetamine pills, is becoming more popular. In part that is because the minorities have always used opium as a medicine. 'Young ethnic people think it is not a big deal to use opium or heroin, but they don't realise that taking heroin is not the same as using opium to alleviate pain,' said U Aung Aung.

'One injection of heroin costs 5,000 kyat [£2.80] – the price is dropping because the supply of drugs is increasing. Addicts normally inject twice a day, so they need 10,000 kyat [£5.60]. That's a lot of money for people around here,' said U Aung Aung, speaking ever faster as he grew more passionate, the men to his side nodding their silent assent. 'The addicts don't even realise they are victims until they haven't got any money left and start stealing from their families and neighbours. Then it gets worse and worse. Some even use guns to rob people at night on the roads.'

Easy access apart, why did they think drug use is so prevalent among young minority people? 'Each individual will give a different reason. Some say because their friends are doing it. Some will say they use it to relieve pain. But there is a lack of job opportunities here, especially for the young people whose families can't afford to send them to school, or who drop out,' noted U Aung Aung.

Their organisation is entirely funded by local people, with donations solicited from villages and businesses. 'We've asked the local government for help, we've written to our MP and to the Minister for Ethnic Affairs, but they never reply,' U Aung Aung said. 'We've never seen anyone get arrested because of the central government's policies to eradicate drugs. But I don't think the government is too worried about ethnic people dying from drugs. They know what's going on.'

Ngwalisa told me that a Baptist church, the Assembly of God, ran its own rehabilitation centre outside Putao. After a few phone calls he found out where it was, isolated out in the grasslands on the way to Machanbaw. It was just visible from the main road, a bamboo longhouse on stilts with a thatched roof, set in a dip of the plain, the tall grass all around it swaying in the stiff breeze.

Two smaller huts stood behind the main building, washing slung on lines suspended from bamboo poles between them. Sitting under an awning at a long table that acted as the dining area was Tang Raw, the head of the centre, a 43-year-old Kachin man from Myitkyina and former heroin addict. He ticked me off for lighting a cigarette, asking me to put it out. Rehab centres in the West are full of people who smoke like chimneys. Tang Raw, though, regarded tobacco as the start of a slippery slope that leads ultimately to shooting smack.

Rehab facilities run by the churches in Kachin State are far more rigorous than the ones in Europe or the States. I had heard stories of people being locked in cells to detox, or even being chained up. A glance inside the longhouse, a line of sleeping mats on a raised wooden platform, made it clear that this was a basic operation. 'We've been here two years,' Tang Raw told me. 'The students have been through a year's rehab. They're Kachin and Lisu, mostly from Myitkyina. Heroin addicts mainly, but some who took *yama* and a few alcoholics.'

Ranging in age from nineteen to fifty, all undergo the same initial process. 'We don't give them other drugs when they're coming off heroin. For the first few days they go under the shower or in a water tank ten to fifty times a day. Anytime they crave drugs we put them in the cold water. When they are aching we massage them,' said Tang Raw. 'After we've taken care of the physical side we look to their spiritual care. We introduce them to the gospels and they study the Bible. Some are Buddhists when they come here but they convert.'

Tang Raw claims a 70 per cent success rate for his rustic rehab. 'We don't lock anyone up and some run away. We don't bring them back by force but we encourage them to return. I think our way is better than the government rehab centres. I went to them a few times, but the moment I got out I bought drugs. The government method cures you physically but doesn't remove the desire to take drugs.'

Joshu, the Lisu version of Joshua, is one of his success stories, a twenty-year-old from Tanai, thin in a replica Barcelona football shirt with bad teeth and a cheeky expression that hinted at his bad-boy past. 'I took opium, heroin and *yama*. I started at fourteen because all my friends were doing it. I smoked heroin at first, then I started injecting when I was sixteen.' Joshu recounted his drug-taking history in a matter-of-fact tone, as if he was reciting one of the biblical texts he had learned while in rehab.

'My parents realised I was addicted when I was fifteen. They're rice farmers, although my dad used to grow a bit of opium, too. My father beat me and said he'd throw me out if I carried on. But they didn't. Finally, they sent me here. By that time I was stealing motorbikes and animals to get the money for drugs,' said Joshu. 'I was craving a lot at first. I wanted to run away. But I couldn't face my parents again if I did that. So I stuck it out. But I still wanted heroin. It took a long time not to want drugs.'

Hard as the regime is the students seemed happy, joking with the volunteers who come for a few weeks at a time to care for them and teach the Bible. Tang Raw warmed up, too, revealing an empathy with his charges as he recalled his fifteen years as an addict. He showed me his forearms, badly scarred from injecting for so long. 'My teeth are all damaged, too,' he said. He has been clean for thirteen years now, and has a wife and four kids in Myitkyina.

Before then, he worked for years in the jade mines of Hpakant in the west of Kachin State. The hills around Hpakant contain the largest and highest quality jadeite deposits anywhere in the world, and it is just 120 miles from Hpakant to the border with China, where the lust for jade is unrivalled. That seemingly auspicious proximity of mines to marketplace has made the trade in green jade the most profitable industry in Burma, along with drugs, worth over £20 billion annually.

Hpakant's mines are mostly owned by Chinese interests, cronies, families of former senior junta figures, the *Tatmadaw* and the warlords of Shan State. Around 80 per cent of the jade mined is thought to be sold illegally, smuggled into China through areas controlled by the military or the KIA. Hardly any of the revenue goes to Kachin State. Just as narcotics trafficking benefits only Chinese gangs, the ethnic armies and militias and the *Tatmadaw*, so the profits from Burma's other major industry disappear into the pockets of the elite and Chinese companies. All the peoples of Kachin get in return is a nightmare.

Located in a conflict zone where the KIA battles the *Tatmadaw*, Hpakant is Burma's heart of darkness. It is an environmental disaster, with entire hills blasted away in the hunt for green gold and rivers polluted with the waste, and is notorious as the heroin and HIV capital of the country. So toxic is Hpakant that the government makes strenuous efforts to hide the area from foreign eyes. It is the most restricted place in all Burma, far harder for a westerner to reach than Shan State's special regions. The closest I came was

Indawgyi Lake, about forty miles south, beyond which lie army checkpoints, minefields and guerrilla war.

Only the Chinese get to travel the abysmal road from Myitkyina to Hpakant, which is near-impassable in the rainy season. Any other foreigners found there are instantly deported. But people from across Burma flock to Hpakant. They do so for the same reason that wagon trains crossed America to reach the gold rush towns of California in the mid-nineteenth century: the opportunity to make a swift fortune.

An army of freelance miners scrambles across the moon-like terrain of collapsed hills and giant craters. There are said to be more bulldozers in Hpakant than anywhere else in the world, digging out hillsides and shovelling away the debris. Swarming over the slag heaps are the so-called 'hand-pickers', sifting the rocks and earth for jade that has been overlooked by the industrial mining concerns.

'Find one medium-sized lump of jade and you can return to your village, build a house and live comfortably for years,' said Tang Raw. That is if you don't die in the frequent landslides or get seduced by Hpakant's most popular recreational activity, heroin. 'People take it because it is such a hard life being a jade miner. A few companies pay their workers in heroin,' noted Tang Raw. Hpakant is a place where methamphetamines provide the energy to dig all day and opiates soothe the pain in the evening.

Not everyone who moves to Hpakant ends up an addict. The man who drove me to Namhsan, the Ta'ang capital, had worked as a freelance miner there for seven years without taking drugs. But neither did he become rich. Even if you find a decent-sized piece of jade, getting a fair deal from the Chinese buyers is a challenge. 'I never found good jade,' Tang Raw remembered. 'But the traders won't pay a good price to an addict. They know that they just have to offer a low one and you'll take it because you need to score.'

These days, Tang Raw visits Hpakant to try and save people from heroin. The town sits in a bowl surrounded by devastated hills of red earth. In their lee are the shanties where an estimated 200,000 migrant workers live and Tang Raw preaches the gospels. He showed me phone footage he had shot on his most recent trip. There were no hidden away shooting galleries, like the one I saw outside Namtu in Shan State. People wandered openly with syringes tucked behind their ears, or crouched outside their lean-to shelters, the needles still in the veins of their arms.

Overdose victims lay where they had died, covered in plastic sheets, waiting to be collected by local NGOs. A woman was breastfeeding while also injecting herself in the hand. 'She's twenty-four, or was. A Karen from Mawlamyine,' said Tang Raw. Another woman in a dirty red *htamein* sold heroin outside her shack. I was surprised by the number of female users, but prostitution is rampant in Hpakant, too. With both the women and their customers shooting heroin, it is little surprise that HIV is rife in the town. Watching the film, I thought that some of Burma's barred areas are worth avoiding.

There was one last task to complete before I departed Putao. Three roads run northwards of the town, heading north-east, north-west and north, tapering out before the forests and hills that lead to the Himalayas. I wanted to travel as far as I could on one of them. Ngwalisa recommended the road that leads due north. I would be in an area technically out of bounds to foreigners, but we would be able to get to the end of the road and back to Putao in a day.

Our route took us through Shan villages for the first time, the centres of some of them featuring expanses of open land, the local version of a village green. There were small pagodas and monasteries, too, as well as fields of coriander, mustard, garlic and beans. Pink roses flowered in the gardens, along with citrus fruit trees. Stone and dirt tracks connect the villages, logs lashed together acting as bridges over the many streams that cleave through the earth here. 'We won't see any police,' said Ngwalisa. 'Only motorbikes and ox carts can get across the bridges.'

Diverting to the west, we visited a timber camp in a forest. Two elephants nudged the fallen trees towards an electric saw with their foreheads and trunks, having dragged them down from the logging area a four-hour ride away using chains that trailed behind them. Piles of sawdust and elephant dung littered the camp. The pachyderms were from near Indawgyi Lake, as were their Shan mahouts. One had previously mined in Hpakant. 'I went when I was fifteen,' he told me. 'I didn't find any jade. I prefer being with the elephants.'

Still widely used as working animals in the borderlands, with the KIA employing them as transport, elephants remain as valuable in Burma today as they were in 1926, when George Orwell made the mistake of shooting one in Mawlamyine. They can cover twenty miles a day and a trained elephant costs as much as £30,000. 'We don't think it is cruel to use elephants for work. It is normal for us,' the mahout said. 'We raise them in captivity now as there aren't really any wild elephants left around Indawgyi. When they are too old to work, we let them go to the forest and they die there.'

Moving on, we reached Setilaw Village, a small Lisu settlement that is the final outpost of civilisation due north of Putao. It was one of the poorest villages I'd seen in the Triangle, humble patches of land given over to rice and sugarcane, wells providing water and bamboo houses on stilts lining both sides of a dust track that ran straight towards the hills. In the far distance was the 4,700-metre peak of Madaw Razi, with only a few wispy clouds above the snow-clad summit to disturb the dazzling blue sky.

To my eyes the hills appeared much closer here. But Ngwalisa knew better. I was being deceived by a mountain mirage. 'It's a six-day walk from here to the main hills. The first two days are easy, after that it is very up and down,' he said. Beyond the last house in the village the track veered abruptly west. There was only prairie to the north now, the thick grass reaching above my knees. 'This is where you start walking for the mountains,' said Ngwalisa. I nodded and returned to the bike. There was nowhere else to go.

List of Abbreviations

AFPFL	Anti-Fascist People's Freedom League
ARSA	Arakan Rohingya Salvation Army
DEA	Drug Enforcement Administration
ESSDDP	Eastern Shan State Development Democratic Party
KIA	Kachin Independence Army
KIO	Kachin Independence Organisation
KMT	Kuomintang
MNDAA	Myanmar National Democratic Alliance Army
NDAA	National Democratic Alliance Army
NLD	National League for Democracy
RCSS	Restoration Council of Shan State
TNLA	Ta'ang National Liberation Army
USDP	Union Solidarity and Development Party
UWSA	United Wa State Army

Acknowledgements

I owe a huge debt to everyone who spoke to me for this book. Some names have been changed at the request of those interviewed or where I felt it necessary. I am especially grateful to Robin Gardiner for sharing his memories of his father and for granting me access to his personal papers.

Michael Fishwick, Sarah Ruddick and Marigold Atkey at Bloomsbury were ever-supportive and patient. Richard Collins did a sterling job as editor. Thanks also to Patrick Walsh.

The following people provided assistance and advice during my time in Burma – my gratitude to you all: Mr Anthony, Aye Chan Bo, Eaint Thiri Thu, Japha, Kaung Myat Min, Mya Wutyee Hlaing, Nang Htwe Lin Yu, Saw Closay, Shunn Lei, Su Mon Pyae, Swe Zin Htaik, Thaiddi, Tin Maung Maung Aye, Wae Win Khaing, Win Naing, Win Sandar Soe, John Buchanan, Colin Hinshelwood, David Scott Mathieson, Jochen Meissner, Bruno Philip and Samara Yawnghwe.

Select Bibliography

Charney, Michael W., *A History of Modern Burma*, Cambridge: Cambridge University Press, 2009.

Cockett, Richard, *Blood, Dreams and Gold: The Changing Face of Burma*, London: Yale University Press, 2015.

Collis, Maurice, *Siamese White*, London: Faber & Faber, 1936.

— *Trials in Burma*, London: Faber & Faber, 1938.

— *Lords of the Sunset: A Tour in the Shan States*, London: Faber & Faber, 1938.

— *Into Hidden Burma: An Autobiography*, London: Faber & Faber, 1953.

Colquhoun, Archibald Ross, *Amongst the Shans*, London: Field & Tuer, 1885.

Crick, Bernard, *George Orwell: A Life*, London: Secker & Warburg, 1980.

Croker, B. M., *The Road to Mandalay: A Tale of Burma*, London: Cassell, 1917.

Enriquez, C. M., *A Burmese Enchantment*, London: Thacker, Spink & Co., 1916.

Fielding-Hall, H., *The Soul of a People*, London: Richard Bentley and Son, 1898.

Fraser, George MacDonald, *Quartered Safe Out Here: A Recollection of the War in Burma*, London: Harvill, 1992.

Furnivall, J. S., *Colonial Policy and Practice: A Comparative Study of Burma and Netherlands India*, Cambridge: Cambridge University Press, 1948.

Gibson, Richard Michael and Chen, Wenhua, *The Secret Army: Chiang Kai-shek and the Drug Warlords of the Golden Triangle*, Singapore: John Wiley & Sons, 2011.

Hall, D. G. E., *Burma*, London: Hutchinson University Library, 1950.

Ibrahim, Azeem, *The Rohingyas: Inside Myanmar's Hidden Genocide*, London: C. Hurst & Co., 2016.

Larkin, Emma, *Secret Histories: Finding George Orwell in a Burmese Teashop*, London: John Murray, 2004.

— *Everything Is Broken: The Untold Story of Disaster Under Burma's Military Regime*, London: Granta, 2010.

Law-Yone, Wendy, *Golden Parasol: A Daughter's Memoir of Burma*, London: Chatto & Windus, 2013.

Lewis, Norman, *Golden Earth: Travels in Burma*, London: Jonathan Cape, 1952.

Lintner, Bertil, *Burma in Revolt: Opium and Insurgency Since 1948*, London: Routledge, 1994.

Ludu U Hla, *The Caged Ones*, Bangkok: Orchid Press, 1998.

MacLean, Rory, *Under the Dragon: Travels in a Betrayed Land*, London: HarperCollins, 1998.

Marshall, Andrew, *The Trouser People: A Story of Burma in the Shadow of Empire*, Berkeley, CA: Counterpoint Press, 2002.

Maung Aung Myoe, *Building the Tatmadaw: Myanmar's Armed Forces Since 1948*, Singapore: ISEAS Publishing, 2009.

Oh, Su-Ann (Editor): *Myanmar's Mountain & Maritime Borderscapes: Local Practises, Boundary-Making and Figured Worlds*, Singapore: ISEAS Publishing, 2016.

Pearn, B. R., *A History of Rangoon*, American Baptist Mission Press, 1939.

Popham, Peter, *The Lady and the Peacock: The Life of Aung San Suu Kyi of Burma*, London: Rider, 2011.

— *The Lady and the Generals: Aung San Suu Kyi and Burma's Struggle for Freedom*, London: Rider, 2016.

Robinson, H. R., *A Modern De Quincey: Autobiography of an Opium Addict*, London: Harrap, 1942.

Sadan, Mandy (Editor): *War & Peace in the Myanmar Borderlands: The Kachin Ceasefire 1994–2011*, Copenhagen: NIAS Press, 2016.

Scott, James C. *The Art of Not Being Governed: An Anarchist History of Upland Southeast Asia*, Yale University Press, 2009.

Scott, James George, *The Burman: His Life and Notions*, London: Macmillan & Co., 1882.

Singer, Noel F., *Old Rangoon*, Gartmore Kiscadale Publications, 1995.

Smith, Martin, *Burma: Insurgency and the Politics of Ethnicity*, London: Zed Books, 1991.

Somerset Maugham, W., *The Gentleman in the Parlour*, London: William Heinemann, 1930.

Taylor, Robert, *The State in Myanmar*, London: C. Hurst & Co., 2008.

Thant Myint-U, *The River of Lost Footsteps: Histories of Burma*, London: Faber & Faber, 2007.

Wade, Francis, *Myanmar's Enemy Within: Buddhist Violence and the Making of a Muslim 'Other'*, London: Zed Books, 2017.

Yawnghwe, Chao Tzang, *The Shan of Burma: Memoirs of a Shan Exile*, Singapore: ISEAS Publishing, 1987

Yawnghwe, Samara, *Maintaining the Union of Burma 1946–1962: The Role of the Ethnic Nationalities in a Shan Perspective*, Bangkok: Institute of Asian Studies, Chulalongkorn University, 2013.

Yi Li, *Chinese in Colonial Burma: A Migrant Community in a Multiethnic State*, London: Palgrave Macmillan, 2017.

Index

Insein Prison 90–1
Inya Lake 65
Irrawaddy, river *see* Ayeyarwady
   River
Islam *see* Muslims

jade: industry and trade 51, 307, 316,
   343, 351–2
Jama Mosque, Sittwe 209–10, 215
Japan: defeated in Burma 112, 229;
   invades Burma (1942) 105, 112,
   355–6; victory against Russia
   (1904–5) 218
Jar Lann (island) 190–1, 193
John ('the Baptist'; Chin Christian)
   115, 118, 121, 123
John ('the Catholic'; Chin Christian)
   114–16, 119
Johns, Captain W.E. 188
Johnson, Boris 163
Joshu (Lisu drug addict) 350
Journey to Pyay (film) 234
Junaid (Mawlamyine Muslim) 172
junta: belief in occult guidance
   241; corruption 50–1; refuses
   international help after Cyclone
   Nargis 74; reports little bad news
   99; revises constitution 75–6;
   suppresses student activism 63, 65–6

Kachin Independence Army (KIA)
   263, 307, 309–11, 313–16, 337, 345
Kachin Independence Organisation
   (KIO) 62, 309, 311–12
Kachin people 214, 308
Kachin State: anti-drug policy 315–
   16, 346–7; autonomy movement
   62, 263, 313–14; border with China
   298; Chinese money and support
   in 311; Christianity in 101, 311; civil
   war in 254; higher education in

312–13; jade mining and trade 265,
   307, 316; population 308; sense of
   unity 314; Tibetans in 340; wildlife
   trafficking 300
Kadan Island 186
Kalaymyo (Kalay) 103–5, 107, 137
Kam Suan Mang 124–7
Karen people 110, 162; rebel 232, 253,
   262
Katha (town) 39–40
Kaung Myat Min 148–9
Kawthoung 175, 185, 187
Kayah 318
Kayin State 162
Kengtung, Shan State 285–6, 288–90
Kennedy Peak, Chin State 112
Ket 317–19
Khen Thang, Felix Lian, Bishop
   120–1, 123
Khin Kyi (Aung San Suu Kyi's
   mother) 58–9
Khin Nyunt 149
Khin Zaw Lwin 88
Khine Hmin Wai 82
Khun Sa (Zhang Qifu) 320, 327–30
Kipling, Rudyard 162–4, 166;
   'Mandalay' (poem) 163–4
Ko Min Min 205–6
Ko Min Nyo 153–4
Ko Myint 218, 233
Kokang (Special Region 1, Shan
   State) 297, 305
Kublai Khan 145
Kyaikthanlan Pagoda, Mawlamyine
   161–3
Kyaingtong, Shan State 285
Kyaukme 264
Kyaw Mint 268
Kyaw Soe Hlaing, Sergeant Major
   252–3
Kyunsu, Kadan Island 186

201; flee to Bangladesh 204, 212; language 200; numbers 153; origins and status 195–8; persecuted and discrimated against 198–203; in Rakhine State 80, 195–6, 200, 203, 210–11, 213–15; Sao Shwe Thaike defends 291; support British in World War II 203, 209; in Yangon 201
Rohmer, Sax 92
Rowe & Co. (department store) 50
Ruili, Yunnan Province 201, 307
Russo-Japanese War (1904–5) 218

Saffron Revolution (2007): and Cyclone Nargis 75; filmed 221; monks in 142; opposes army rule 1, 138–44
Sai Hong Kham 286–8, 289–92
Salang Kaba 315–16
Salone people 182, 186, 189–94
Sangermano, Vincentius 89
Sao Kya Seng 282
Sao Sai Long 288–9, 292
Sao Shwe Thaike (Yawnghwe) 277, 290–2, 326
sawbwas ('sky lords') 275–7, 279–80, 282–4, 288–90, 292–3, 326
Saya San 157
Scott, James George 44, 225
Sea Gypsy (boat) 187, 189, 193
Setilaw village 354
786 (Muslim Basmala) 169
Seven Stars group 62
sexual harassment and violence 225
Shah Bandar mosque, Mawlamyine 172
Shahida (Rohingya woman) 201–3
Shan National Day 320–6
Shan people 214, 261, 275, 354

Shan State: border with China 298; civil war in 254, 256–9, 263, 264; conditions 259–61, 284, 319; disunity 284–5, 314; in election (2015) 287; ethnographic and demographic composition 261–2, 284–7; history as state 275–8; jungle 176; opium growing and consumption 265–6, 327, 330; political-economic situation 286–92; Special Regions 297–8; as threat to Burmese rulers 284
Shan State Army - North 324
Shan State Army - South *see* Restoration Council of Shan State
Shan United Army 328
Shunn Lei 224–6
Shwebontha Pagoda, Pyay 149
Shwedagon Pagoda, Yangon: ATMs installed 18; character 3–4, 19–20
Shwesandaw Pagoda, Pyay 147
Siangsawn Village, Chin State 123–8
Sichuan Province (China): earthquake 76–7
Siliw 343–4
Sittwe (*earlier* Akyab), Rakhine State: conditions 207–12, 215; Rohingya Muslims in 198, 201–2, 210–11, 214; University 200
sky lords *see sawbwas*
smoking (tobacco) 349
socialism 237–9
soothsayers 241–4
Soppong 317–18
Southeast Asian Games (2013) 251
Special Regions 297–8
Sri Ksetra 147
Steel Brothers (company) 42
Sucittasara (monk) 169–70, 172
Sule Pagoda, Yangon 25

British occupy 37; British town
planning 22, 25; buildings and
conditions 5–7, 10, 22–6, 32,
48; Chinese community and
crime 92; cinemas 218, 228–9;
cosmopolitanism 43–4; crime and
police in 86–9, 97–8; damaged
in war 229; dogs in 6, 28, 31;
East India Company invades
(1824) 37; effect of Cyclone
Nargis on 221; émigrés return
17; evacuated and devastated in
war (1942) 105–6; extent 8; food
32; Japanese abandon (1945) 112,
229; Japanese occupy (1942) 35;
Legislative Council 46; life in
27–9; limited entertainment
97; low life cleaned up by junta
96; modern traffic 12–13; name
4; neighbourhoods 23–5, 47–8,
69–71; origins and growth 4;
population 24, 43, 73; port 3,
29–30; poverty 97; rents 79;
reputation as sin city 91–2;

Rohingya numbers in 201; shanty
settlements 79–80; shanty-
dwellers relocated 197; social life
47–8; supposed cache of Spitfire
aircraft 251; unemployment 89;
wildlife 26–7; *see also* Golden
Valley; Hlaing Tharyar
Yangon river 4
Yangon University (*earlier* Rangoon
Arts and Science University;
RASU): campus dispersed by
junta 63, 66; student nationalism
and protests 56–7, 61–6
Yawd Maung 319–21, 323–4
Yawd Serk 320, 323, 325–7, 329–31
Yunnan (China): border with
Burma 298–9, 307; Kachin in 308;
Soppong Chinese attack 318

Zau Seng 312–14
Zay Yar San (fortune-teller) 245–7
Zokhawthar, Mizoram (India) 130–1
Zomi Congress for Democracy
(Chin State) 134

Note on the Author

David Eimer is the author of the critically acclaimed *The Emperor Far Away: Travels at the Edge of China*. A former China correspondent for the *Sunday Telegraph*, Eimer was the Southeast Asia correspondent for the *Daily Telegraph* between 2012 and 2014. He is currently based in Bangkok.

Note on the Type

The text of this book is set Adobe Garamond. It is one of several versions of Garamond based on the designs of Claude Garamond. It is thought that Garamond based his font on Bembo, cut in 1495 by Francesco Griffo in collaboration with the Italian printer Aldus Manutius. Garamond types were first used in books printed in Paris around 1532. Many of the present-day versions of this type are based on the *Typi Academiae* of Jean Jannon cut in Sedan in 1615.

Claude Garamond was born in Paris in 1480. He learned how to cut type from his father and by the age of fifteen he was able to fashion steel punches the size of a pica with great precision. At the age of sixty he was commissioned by King Francis I to design a Greek alphabet, and for this he was given the honourable title of royal type founder. He died in 1561.